PASSION AND POLITICS

'This original volume offers insights and learning for all academic writers, whether experienced academics or apprentice students.... [It] is novel in drawing upon experienced writers and their reflections, looking at writing from the basis of a lifetime's engagement. The writers open themselves up to the personal and emotional, social and professional dimensions and not just the technical skills.'

Brian V. Street, Professor of Language in Education,
King's College London

'Passion and Politics: Academics reflect on writing for publication is an engaging enquiry into the place of writing in the careers of 18 well-known writers in education. It is a work that adds to our knowledge of the craft and processes of (academic) writing, providing insights through interview of what goes into the making of published texts. As well as discussion of approaches to writing, an interesting strand that emerges is discussion of craft instruments and technologies and of the affective, as well as intellectual, relationship of these writers to the creative practices in which they engage. This is a useful and stimulating addition to the literature on academic and professional writing.'

Fiona J. Doloughan, Lecturer in English,
University of Surrey

'By interviewing a number of scholars across disciplines, Passion and Politics reveals to students and fellow academic staff alike the very real joys and pains of writing. As the authors state, this is about "the lived experience of writing but it is also about the hazards and blessings encountered on the journey to becoming a voice that is heard ... to becoming published". Even so, the lessons in this book have broader

ramifications as they speak to how research is undertaken and how even the questions they ask are shaped by the very real contexts and restrictions of the spaces in which they occur.

Students will delight in learning that scholars whose work they read undergo the same stress, anxiety and writing processes (including procrastination) that they do. Thus this book is an excellent learning tool for educators who work with students who write in any field. Aspiring and present academics will find comfort in reading how well-known scholars, like them, have had to work at their writing and yet still take pleasure in it. They, like students will gain strategies for and confidence in developing their own writing styles. Managerial staff will learn how they can set up support systems, communities of writers and a network that foster the very real conditions within which academics can productively succeed as researchers.

Demonstrating that writing is disciplinary and contextually situated, this collection encourages other higher education institutions to map their own local spaces – and provides a way for them to do so. Underscoring the creative, recursive, exploratory nature of writing, these scholars speak personally about how making sense of the world through their words impacts the world around them, and how students also can engage in reshaping their worlds through the very real work that language affords us.'

Joan Mullin, Chair of English Studies,
Illinois State University, USA

'[T]he book is exploring a vital and exciting topic that the academy needs to address. Academic identity, writing, the RAE, and staff and personal development in higher education are all issues that need to be addressed on a national scale and this book is certainly taking the right steps towards that end. I would recommend it to any academic or researcher who struggles with the writing process and seeks insight into how to get it write/right.

Jess Moriarty, Senior Lecturer, School of Language,
Literature and Communication, University of Brighton

Passion and Politics

Academics reflect on writing
for publication

Eileen Carnell,
Jacqui MacDonald,
Bet McCallum and
Mary Scott

First published in 2008 by the Institute of Education,
University of London, 20 Bedford Way, London WC1H 0AL

© Institute of Education, University of London 2008

ISBN 978 0 85473 802 1

The opinions expressed in this publication are those of individual
contributors and do not necessarily reflect the views of the Institute of
Education.

Contents

Acknowledgements   vii
Introduction   ix

PART 1 THE STUDY

1 **The history of the study**   3
  Origin, grounds and purpose   3
  Collecting the writers' stories – our task, method and stance   4

2 **The participants and their experiences**   6
  Their concerns as educationists   7
  Writing and a personal sense of identity   9

3 **Their journeys**   11
  Becoming a writer   11
  Learning the craft   15

4 **Going about writing**   25
  Finding and managing time   25
  Planning and playing   26

5 **Producing a text**   29
  Considering and imagining the reader   29
  Language and style   31
  Smoothing the way   33

6 **Engaging in the process of writing**   35
  Academic writing and the creative arts   35
  Feeling the process   36
  The love of writing tools   39

7 **The politics of writing for publication**   42

The 'power' of publishers   42

Writing and publishing in English   43

Gender issues and power   44

Writing in higher education   45

The Research Assessment Exercise   46

8 **Writing, thinking and learning**   48

9 **Learning from the writers**   51

Building on the findings   54

Reflections on the analysis   56

Future research   58

References   62

PART 2 TRANSCRIPTS OF THE INTERVIEWS

Stephen Ball   67

Ron Barnett   75

Jan Blommaert   85

Shirley Dex   95

David Gillborn   103

Lucy Green   113

Judy Ireson   123

Gunther Kress   129

Diana Leonard   137

Barbara MacGilchrist   145

Pam Meecham   151

Heidi Safia Mirza   159

Peter Moss   171

Ann Oakley   177

Michael Reiss   187

Jeni Riley   197

Chris Watkins   205

Geoff Whitty   213

Appendix 1 Conduct of the research   219

Appendix 2 Areas of inquiry   220

Acknowledgements

We would like to thank the 18 interviewees for their fascinating contributions to this publication. We were struck by the writers' willingness in responding to the invitation and their desire to support this project. During the interviews we were impressed by their integrity and readiness to explore and analyse their writing.

We would also like to thank Robert Taylor, the photographer, for his work, flexibility and good humour throughout this project.

We are grateful to the Staff Devclopment unit who funded this project; to Mark Tester and Pratistha Khadka for all their support; to Jim Collins, Brigid Hamilton-Jones and Sally Sigmund in the Publications team for all their work in bringing the book out; to Michele Greenbank for copy-editing the manuscript and to Marcia Beer for proofreading; to all who commented on early drafts, including Susan Askew, Anne Gold, Theresa Lillis, Caroline Lodge, Fiona Rodger and Liz Wright and to Helen Green and David Budge for brilliant and detailed feedback.

Introduction

This is a book about academic writing that focuses on writing for publication. It is based on interviews we carried out with 18 prominent academic writers on education or the social sciences from the Institute of Education, University of London. The writers surveyed their careers as published academic writers and provided close-up 'readings' of their own histories and experiences. Their memories, speculations and insights represent quite vividly the pain and pleasure, the challenges and the passion (Thaiss and Zawacki, 2006) in writing for publication.

And so the title *Passion and Politics: Academics reflect on writing for publication* encapsulates two of the strongest themes emerging from the interviews. 'Passion' was included because of the enthusiasm for and delight in writing that comes across in the writers' accounts; and also because of the loving way in which they describe the process and their poignant descriptions of the feelings and sensations associated with writing. We included 'Politics' in the title because of the academics' emphasis on their concern to use their writing to address social injustice, and because they illuminated the power of different groups, bodies and agendas to affect writing for publication. For example, they talk about the effects of the Research Assessment Exercise (see note, p. 47), the power of publishers, their readers and how gender can limit possibilities.

Academics reflect on writing for publication was added to the title to clarify that this is a book about *academic* writing. It is about the lived experience of writing, but it is also about the hazards and blessings encountered on the journey to becoming a voice that is heard … to becoming published.

Our reasons for collecting and examining such stories are first, to produce an analysis that will be interesting, useful and inspiring to staff both experienced and new to higher education and new to writing for publication. Second, we hope that the book will stir readers to think about their own writing – that they will constantly hold up these experiences against their own, learn from the comparison and be extended by the process. A further aim is to provide insight into becoming a published academic writer and so to help the Institute of Education and other universities and departments (and the individuals who work in them) to imagine a productive future and to develop initiatives that will be most effective in supporting academic writing. Finally, we hope that our theoretical perspectives and suggestions for future research will be of benefit to teachers, researchers and students at the Institute of Education and elsewhere.

Our study's difference from other work in the field rests primarily on the kind of material that we gathered: interview transcripts in which the respondents took their cues from questions that allowed them to range widely. We quote extensively from the interview transcripts because we hope both to capture the felt experience, differences, personalities and insights of the writers and to do justice to their conscientious self-searching. We also publish the full transcripts to afford the reader a greater sense of the different writers, their backgrounds, interests and approaches.

The extracts and transcripts should raise a smile of warm recognition from writers and teachers in higher education, but the book aims to appeal to a wide-ranging audience, including researchers, academics who are novice writers, students at Masters and PhD level, senior managers in higher education as well as staff development departments in higher education. The extracts (and more so the full transcripts) allow the novice writer to empathise and understand that the hardships, experiences, feelings and frustrations described are faced by even the most eminent and prolific writers. Novice writers will be able to draw on the wealth of approaches, ways of thinking and advice in the transcripts, while students and researchers may take an added interest in the theory and references to current work in the field. Managers may well be attracted to the whole initiative, which could easily be replicated in other settings.

We summarise here what we consider to be the merits of the book and how it might benefit the reader. The book:

- provides a rare opportunity in the UK – and internationally – to hear about aspects of the experience of writing not evident in the final published product
- utilises theoretical concepts not previously used in studies of writing for publication and shows their illuminative potential
- focuses on the social aspect of writing without neglecting individual perspectives
- indicates the complexity and multifaceted nature of the writing process
- suggests ways in which the study can inform organisational initiatives to promote writing for publication
- suggests possibilities for further research.

To conclude this Introduction, we explain how we have organised our text. Part 1 is arranged in nine sections. In section 1 we tell the story of the research and describe its origins. We specify the methods of interview and analysis (with further details in the appendices). This is followed by section 2, in which we name the participants and their location within our organisation and, moving to a more abstract level, their location within a particular disciplinary space: education.

Our analyses follow in sections 3 to 8 and we rely as much as possible on the participants' words, weaving in concepts from a social practice view of writing where it is illuminative.

Section 3 is central to the emphasis contained in our interview schedule on the participants' stories about learning to write. The section is arranged in a narrative sequence with the participants' metaphor of a never-ending journey as a unifying thread.

The fourth section outlines the ways in which the writers go about writing: finding and managing their time and their general approach, whether planning or playing.

There is another kind of journey to which the participants refer and which is the focus of the fifth section: the journey towards a finished product, a publishable text in a particular genre. This led the participants to discuss the importance of considering the reader and also matters of language and style, always in relation to making meaning. They talk about ways of smoothing the progress of a piece of writing.

Engaging in the process of writing is described in section 6, not only the ways of thinking about writing that are productive – imagining similarities to writing a play, carving out a sculpture – but also the felt experience of struggling with half-formed ideas and being attached to different tools and materials.

The politics of writing is a theme we discerned in several forms: gender differences, the status of English as a world language, the power of publishers and, coming close to home, the effect of the Research Assessment Exercise (RAE). This comprises the seventh section.

In section 8 we consider the fact that writing is many things to the participants but that it is primarily – a dominant theme – a means of thinking and learning.

We end part 1 with a section in which we discuss how we might build on our research and in which we construct statements informed by our analysis of the writers' stories. These statements are intended to create dialogue to challenge assumptions and routine practices, while suggesting real possibilities for change. Finally, reflecting on our analyses, we augment our theoretical perspective and include possibilities for further research.

Part 2 of the book contains the transcripts of the interviews, which we felt strongly should be included in full.

Part 1
The study

The history of the study

In this section we locate the publication in time and place and explain its origins and purpose.

1.1 Origin, grounds and purpose

The idea for this publication developed from discussions we have had as writing mentors in the Institute of Education's writing mentor scheme. Because colleagues frequently asked for a text that would help them to understand the writing process better and encourage them in their writing efforts, we imagined that a series of interviews with successful Institute writers would help them towards those purposes.

Furthermore, we wanted to give colleagues the opportunity to talk about this aspect of their work. Research has shown that this is something rarely offered 'in the everyday silo-like culture of departments within universities, [where] these groups often do not mix, certainly not to share experiences as researchers and writers' (Grant, 2006: 486).

We were interested in what experienced, prominent writers would have to tell about their development as writers, their engagement with writing and their understanding of the process. What had they learned about writing? What had they learned about getting published?

We wanted to hear their stories, explore them and produce an analysis that would be interesting, useful and inspiring to staff both experienced and new to higher education and to writing for publication. We were sure that we did not wish to produce a handbook, a how-to-write manual or list of tips as these often suggest that there is only one way of going about writing. Rather, we hypothesised that the interviews would bring out individual perspectives and explanations of the nature of academic writing as an activity. We were hopeful that the accounts (and our understanding of them) would cause readers to think about their own writing.

1.2 Collecting the writers' stories – our task, method and stance

We are aware of a difference between our task as co-authors and that of the participants who so generously responded to our request for interviews. They surveyed their careers as published academic writers, searching inside themselves for words and phrases that might give precision and resonance at the moment of utterance to memories, speculations and insights. Our task is to construct a more distanced perspective. We can perhaps sum up the challenge we face by borrowing, and adapting to our own different purpose, an image that de Certeau (1984) uses in a metaphorical focus on writing and reading. He contrasts the view of Manhattan from the top of a tall building with the experience of walking in the streets below. From high above, the city is an abstraction, an over-generalised representation. It transforms the complexity of the city into a transparent readability (Ahearne, 1995: 176). This bird's-eye view is at variance with the activity and perspectives of the walkers in the streets, with the walkers making use of spaces that cannot be seen from on high.

De Certeau does not, however, set up irreconcilable perspectives: the bird's-eye view and the experience of walking in the street need to be seen as mutually illuminating. Extending de Certeau's metaphor to our situation, we see our task as finding a language of description, i.e. a conceptual framework in which to nest analyses that can add visibility and significance to the writers' close-up personal readings of their experience in writing for publication.

And so to explain how we collected the writers' stories. Over the spring and summer of 2006, we interviewed the 18 writers, using a semi-structured schedule (Appendix 1). We enquired about writing they were pleased with and why, about writing they felt less happy about. We invited them to talk about influences and events in their writing careers and about what they had learned about getting work published. We wondered to what extent they saw themselves as 'writers' in comparison to, say, teachers, sociologists, philosophers, etc. Would they go on writing if they left academia? We queried how they liked to go about writing and what they got out of it.

Generally, the interviews lasted around an hour and were tape-recorded. The taped interviews were then transcribed verbatim and a full transcript was sent to each author to ensure accuracy. Very little editing occurred. With the writers' agreement, we took out the 'ums' and 'ers' before publishing the interviews here.

The transcripts were read several times by all four of us individually and we made tentative notes on emerging themes. Then, using the constant comparative method (Glaser and Strauss, 1967), we came together and began to develop a theoretical coding (Strauss and Corbin, 1997). We maintained a regular and frequent exchange of ideas through email and telephone conversations both alongside and within the text of our drafts. We met several times as a group to discuss the transcripts and the drafts. Meetings, both arranged and by chance, created a forum for dialogue.

Standing back from the whole endeavour, we considered the transcripts, our conduct of the interviews and the assumptions behind our schedule as inter-related. A consequence of this stance is that writing as a social practice (Gee, 1996; Kress, 1989; Street, 1985, 2003) – and not as simply a set of linguistic skills – emerged as an overarching conceptual framework. In this view, language use and writing is seen as situated, i.e. the emphasis is on writing as an activity-in-context (and on the values and meanings there). From this perspective 'place' and 'space', which can be variously delineated, can represent both the actual and the symbolic, i.e. as the carrier of meanings and values. The themes we identified derive from this focus on the situatedness of writing.

Our method of working was for one of us to draw up a data display of themes and illustrative quotes, then for another to compose a first draft based around those themes. From there we took the lead to develop themes that particularly interested us individually, delved into research and theory, and circulated, commented and queried draft upon draft until we felt sufficiently satisfied to send this to our writers and readers.

In the period before publication, the edited transcripts were re-sent to the writers for permission to publish. We enclosed our twelfth, penultimate draft of the book to ensure that the selected quotations reflected their views and that our analysis and argument were based on an accurate understanding of their meanings. At the same time, we sent the draft out to readers. Finally, changes were incorporated to reflect our new understandings drawn from the feedback of our writers and readers.

The participants and their experiences

Eighteen Institute of Education writers gave interviews for this publication. The most difficult task was to select them. First, we wanted the writers to have strong publication records and be well known. Our criteria then were that they should represent:

- all the schools and research units that make up the organisation
- an equal balance of women and men
- a range of career experiences, specialisms and disciplines
- a balance of people who are predominantly teachers or researchers
- a range of time working in this organisation.

While we know we could have included many others who would have made equally important contributions, we feel that our selection can be seen to reflect those criteria. These are the voices that are heard:

Stephen Ball
Ron Barnett
Jan Blommaert
Shirley Dex
David Gillborn
Lucy Green
Judy Ireson
Gunther Kress
Diana Leonard
Barbara MacGilchrist
Pam Meecham
Heidi Safia Mirza
Peter Moss

Ann Oakley
Michael Reiss
Jeni Riley
Chris Watkins
Geoff Whitty

The 18 writers have held senior positions in the organisation, although the time they have spent at the Institute varies widely (from 36 years to less than a year). Since the interviews were recorded some have taken on new roles, at the Institute or elsewhere, including retirement. The writers have produced an extensive amount and range of work, including reports of empirical studies, journal articles, books, reviews, syntheses of literature, materials for teachers and students, press releases, reports for politicians and fiction. A small number have been involved in translating; the majority have edited the work of others and have participated in different forms of collaborative writing.

2.1 Their concerns as educationists/social scientists

All the participants in this study are involved in education, in social research and theory-making. In talking about their writing they expressed a general wish to employ ideas in ways that can make a difference.

All are concerned with the creation of a more equitable society in which the humanity of all individuals is respected. Michael Reiss refers to this as a genuine commitment across the Institute of Education, and it is the aim of the Director of the Institute of Education, Geoff Whitty, that his writing should reflect this aspect of the Institute's mission. Gunther Kress offers a similar goal, namely, to be 'a human being in relation to others'.

In some cases these values are given particular modulations by the participants' disciplinary allegiances or pedagogic roles. For example, the wish to be an agent of change as a writer is strongly elaborated in the following response in which a sociologist focuses on current social actualities:

Responding to the problems of the world, things you see to be unfair and unjust, and wanting to address them, to understand and explain them, and use that as a basis for achieving some sort of change. What almost always drives me to write, to fill in gaps or to engage with things that people are not attending to properly. I want to say, 'Hey! look at this, this is happening, we need to attend to this, we need to think about this, these are important things. This stuff is going on, and it's having effects, and we should be paying attention to it' (Stephen Ball).

The comment below, from an academic with a strong background in philosophy, is similar in its goal but looks beyond present actualities to imagined possibilities that would be obtained in the 'best of all possible worlds':

> *I'm trying in my writing to imagine a new kind of future, but not a future that is totally imaginary. I'm trying to imagine a future that is a feasible future. I'm trying to put into the world ideas that could, in the best of all possible worlds, have a realistic chance of being achievable (Ron Barnett).*

Within the general concern with social justice and the wish to make a difference, there are examples of specific social issues that the participants address in their writing. One such issue is race and racism. A new member of staff speaks of the opportunity that being in education offers her to make a difference in this area:

> *At the Institute I'm hoping to take what I have learnt and focus more on educational issues as a way to challenge racism, whether it's in the classroom or in the workplace. So this … is a great opportunity for me to do important research that makes a difference (Heidi Safia Mirza).*

This theme is echoed below in a comment in which the speaker traces his concern with racial inequality back to his own observations as a school student:

> *I knew school was a performance, I knew there were people who were getting the wrong end of the stick about what other people could do. It was at secondary school when I started to recognise that all the black kids in the school were basically being treated like second-class citizens. They were all in the bottom streams, they were all in the bottom class, black kids dominated the sports teams, none of them were in any of the academic groups. And that was just wrong … I look into other inequalities, but race is the thing that really drives me (David Gillborn).*

Within the accounts there are also examples of strong advocacy for the advancement of different subject areas. For example, in the following extract, the speaker describes her desire to theorise the under-theorised area of art education and raise the profile of this aspect of teaching and learning:

> *I became increasingly interested in art history and theory and I also felt I had something to say. That was the first thing. Art education, particularly at school level, also needed advocacy. There were very few people coming out of art education who were writing. There also were very few journals that published art education articles. I felt that art education needed people to talk about it and write about it, but there weren't very many people to work with (Pam Meecham).*

Those who are heavily involved in initial teacher education speak about a wish to transform what happens in schools:

I want to make a difference out there. That's what motivates me to write, wanting to make a difference for children and teachers (Barbara MacGilchrist).

In the quotation below, in a comment on the writer's self-selected 'best' piece, this wish is linked to the relation between theory and practice:

I had a very deep sense that I wanted to get some of my ideas about that research to early years teachers because I felt it could really transform their practice. I just wish it was something I'd known when I was working in the classroom. So I think that kind of intimate knowledge of the theory and what it might mean for practice is what helps to make it a good piece of writing (Jeni Riley).

2.2 Writing and a personal sense of identity

In their accounts some of the writers also refer to writing as central to the identities that they willingly inhabit: writing is part of the core that makes them who they are and they regard themselves as 'writers' over and above, or alongside, their roles as managers, researchers, teachers, sociologists, psychologists or scientists. Others see writing as one task among many and fit writing in around other commitments.

The emphasis expressed by some on writing as being central to a personal sense of identity is strongly affirmed in the following comments:

I'm in the first place, before anything else, before being an academic or a scholar, I think, I'm a writer. Writing has become crucial to my own identity (Ron Barnett).

I've always considered myself to be a writer, so that's a core part of my identity (Ann Oakley).

Another of those interviewed emphasises the social aspect of a writer's identity: writing is both about representing who you are and about situating that self in the world:

Writing is about a means of saying who you are, and locating yourself in the world, and representing yourself in the world. So my way of representing myself in the world has been through writing. So that it's been an essential part of me (Gunther Kress).

Writing is also strongly linked to psychological effects. Some of the writers can feel lost at times when they are not writing ... low, sad, bereft. Writing lifts their spirits and has become an inextricable part of their lives:

> *... for me, it has always been the case that unless I'm engaged in some sort of writing project, I tend to feel quite kind of depressed and I need to have something on the go, even though it is difficult to fit it in (Ann Oakley).*

In many of the interviews, it is a professional self that comes across. The participants relate their writing to their areas of research and scholarship:

> *Writing for me is about research because I research in archives, museums, galleries, in visual culture generally. That means travel and looking and spending time with other people who also write and talk about the visual arts and I can't imagine that disappearing. That is part of who I am or who I've become over the past 50 or so years. So, no, I wouldn't give up writing because that would mean giving up visual culture (Pam Meecham).*

The following account similarly refers to a professional allegiance that the interviewee regards as shaping the identity that informs his texts:

> *Perhaps the way I write tells people something about at least me as a sociologist. That is an openness and tentativeness, leaving space for the possibility of other interpretations, and recognising the role of interpretation itself. That might tell people something. But I don't know if it reveals anything deep about my psyche (Stephen Ball).*

However, another writer comments on the tensions between two spaces – that of her discipline and education. This places her on the boundary between each of them, which, she concludes, is a good place to be:

> *In a way I'm working at boundaries. I suppose I work at the boundary of psychology and education, and that, if you've read Engstrom's work on activity theory, is 'a challenging place to be'. It's difficult, it's sometimes dangerous, you can be attacked from both sides. But I think it's worth being there and it's a space for me to understand better (Judy Ireson).*

3

Their journeys

The semi-structured interviews asked participants to range across time in recounting their experiences as academics writing for publication. We were interested in their rite of passage narratives, i.e. in how they – to adapt Turner's (1974) anthropological perspective – crossed the threshold and 'arrived' as voices that are heard (Hymes, 1996).

We derived our first set of analytical themes from this invitation to the writers to tell an autobiographical story. We focused on their accounts of what they have learned over time, what contributed to their learning and we examined how they appropriate and give their own nuances to certain conventional metaphors such as the journey, space and boundaries.

3.1 Becoming a writer

Starting out

In analysing the data we are able to detect a developmental process the writers described, not least through their reference to 'the journey'. One participant talked about starting out as a tutor, not knowing where his career was heading:

> *I started in university teaching as a PGCE tutor at Bath University, in a department that wasn't really into research and publication very much at all at that time. And I went into higher education to support what the Institute calls 'beginning teachers'. I didn't go into it as someone who expected to be writing, researching and publishing. So I think it's important for some of our colleagues to realise that you can get into writing and get things out of writing even if it wasn't what you actually came into the business for (Geoff Whitty).*

Some identified, first of all, that they had had to learn to write. For example, in the following quotation the writer stresses that writing is not necessarily an inborn talent; rather, it is something that needs to be developed:

It took me time to learn that writing is a craft, a skill that needs to be learned. There is nothing innate about writing, there is no gift and so it has to be worked at (Pam Meecham).

On the same theme, another writer echoes the need for toil and practice:

Margaret Meek always used to say, 'I do write well, but that's because I do a lot of it.' So I think there's a lot of truth in that, that the more you write the better you get. And it is about the hard graft of sitting down and doing it (Jeni Riley).

Hazards of passage

Several accounts describe a period of insecurity, a phase of low self-confidence, a time associated with fear that one's writing, as a reflection of one's academic status, will not be 'good enough'.

The interviews highlight the vulnerability experienced at these times. In the following, the speaker imagines her writing is herself in print, making her feel exposed and a target of public scrutiny:

Ultimately you know that you're writing something for publication. Therefore people are going to read it and you don't know who they are or where they'll be and what they'll say about it or what they'll think about it and so you are exposing yourself. Even though you're sitting in your own room, now you're deferring the public appearance which will be only, not your face, but a black-and-white version of you. So I suppose that's what makes you nervous (Lucy Green).

Another speaker explains how she felt so insecure as to be unable to face up to or revise her own work:

I think initially I was so concerned about the process and so in awe of writers and writing that I was afraid to read my own writing. Many of the things that I wrote were not edited well enough because I didn't want to be confronted with my own work. I used to have the same problem (I think many artists do) when my work was up on the wall in an exhibition: seeing my writing felt like the same thing (Pam Meecham).

Another extract focuses on the writer's use of language at this self-conscious time and describes how, with emergent writers, there is an inclination to use dense language to 'prove' one's academic status. The same account suggests that over time with more practice, there is stage of letting go … letting go of 'me' and 'What does my writing says about me?' and moving to 'What does my writing communicate?':

When I was a younger academic, I was intimidated by feeling the need to always demonstrate that I was not an idiot. Therefore, I would sometimes use complicated language when I did not really need to. You need to develop the confidence to actually recognise that you do not have to have sentences that are 50 words long. If you say things in a sentence that is 20 words long, maximum, it is usually more accessible (David Gillborn).

Working at it – approaching the threshold

The accounts suggest that writers gradually increase the examination and analysis of their own work, particularly in relation to its power to communicate. The following quotation reflects that task:

My early fumblings and ramblings seem terribly complicated. I have tried to work towards a simpler way of writing, but also a way of condensing many ideas more successfully so that the reader doesn't have to do so much. My earlier pieces were just too long and too difficult for the reader and too demanding (Pam Meecham).

This exemplifies what Stephen Ball calls 'taking control' of one's writing. Taking control seems to be an important turning point for writers, after which their confidence increases.

While the accounts show that the writers draw on many resources to help them develop their writing, get published and gain confidence, they also suggest that that passage is as likely to be difficult as smooth: the struggle to become heard can involve facing criticism, unhelpful feedback and rejection.

The following comment describes the impact negative criticism had on the writer; criticism in the form of harsh red-pen slashing felt brutal, cruel:

I did actually once go on a creative writing course and it was quite an experience of savagery in that one was asked to write a description of something that had happened and then the person who ran the course would go through it with a red pen. I found that quite awful, actually, and she wasn't a very successful writer, so I don't know, really. I wouldn't call that a mentor experience (Ann Oakley).

Another writer describes the investment of self in putting together a research proposal and the disappointment experienced at its rejection:

I spent ages putting together that major research bid. It involved vast amounts of time and energy and we didn't even get past the first hurdle. So that was my first experience of rejection. Well, I guess you just have to swallow hard and then pick yourself up and try, try, try again (Barbara MacGilchrist).

The same comment focuses on maintaining motivation, a theme picked up in other accounts. Some of the interviews touch on the writer's need to harden, toughen resolve and hang on to self-belief. The following is an example:

I had a lot of difficulty in getting things that I was really interested in accepted, by the reviewers, before the thing actually got reviewed, from a proposal sent to publishers, most coming back with scathing reviews, so dealing with that at a personal level and steeling yourself against that sort of thing, and retaining the confidence, saying, 'This is what they say, yet I think there is something in there' (Gunther Kress).

Arrival

We traced in the transcripts a point in the journey that can be called arrival, i.e. the ability to be heard, at least in the sense of one's name and writing being published, 'known' and acknowledged by a readership.

The following quotation illustrates that this is a time of growing self-assurance:

One knows that while some of the things one writes don't get accepted, the great majority will indeed get published, so one has got more confidence, yes (Michael Reiss).

At this stage the writer feels able to take risks and be more experimental. In the following quotation, the speaker refers back to the journey's beginning – writing as a craft to be learned – and equates the writer's development with that of the fine artist:

Once you learn the craft then you can play with it, which I'm very privileged now to be able to do. It's like famous painters isn't it? Picasso was a very good classical painter and then he went on to abstract work because he knew the foundations. It's the same with writing: you have to get those foundations and then you can experiment. It's all about confidence really; confidence is the biggest block and the biggest help! (Heidi Safia Mirza).

Continuing the journey

The developmental process described in the accounts is continual. Although they have 'arrived' as successful published authors, the writers describe a lasting state of thinking about writing and learning from writing. They are experiencing 'a process of trying to think better' (Stephen Ball). In explaining this process, the same writer presents the view that all work can be seen as provisional and exploratory and thus available for review, amendment and new explanations:

I've come to view all of my writing as tentative. I increasingly try to avoid closure, and to recognise the limitations of my arguments, although that is not always easy to convey within texts or read as it is intended. But it leaves open the possibility of rewriting, revisiting, moving on (Stephen Ball).

Several other writers emphasise the ephemeral nature of the ideas and arguments in past pieces of writing … seeing them all as fragments to build on and stretch their thinking. The following quotation illustrates both the lifelong nature of learning and learning through writing:

If I felt I'd got it right, I would stop because 'writing is learning'. And that's another exciting thing about writing: you're going to learn something new … I think it's a mistake to think you've ever got it right. No, I think it's important to think that you're getting there, which is different (Ann Oakley).

Some writers explain how the construction of books can be a way of making sense of their experiences and an important way of bringing ideas together:

I suppose my book Sociology and School Knowledge *is the piece of writing I feel was most important in bringing my ideas together. It was written about ten years into my academic career and is actually based on a series of writings that I'd done over that time – some based on empirical research, some political pieces, some theoretical pieces. And I used the book to try and make sense of what I had done up to that point (Geoff Whitty).*

Here the interviewees described how they learned to become better writers. In the next section, they talk about the conditions and events that contributed to their growth.

3.2 Learning the craft

In the interviews, we find reference to a range of experiences that were important in the writers' development: the impacts of study, people and books are emphasised as is the learning gained from editing and translating the work of others.

Studying for a PhD

Several of the accounts referred to the part played by studying for a doctorate.

Working for a PhD is viewed as the 'apprenticeship' in academic writing (David Gillborn; Stephen Ball). This is remembered as a time of growth when the act of writing the thesis itself is a formative experience (Jan Blommaert). One account focuses on how, with guidance, the apprentice learns core skills (to organise, shape and argue) and to comply with the required conventions:

> *I think the discipline of doing a PhD helps you to learn to structure writing, but you're writing in an academic genre when you do a PhD, which needs practice, and that's a very particular learning curve....*

In the same account, the speaker claims that at some point in the process there is a turning point in learning to write – the knowledge is gained that allows the 'student' to emerge as upcoming 'writer':

> *... But after that I think you have the ability to structure an argument and the ability to develop your writing in terms of the compositional side (Jeni Riley).*

The theme of the PhD as a defining moment is echoed in another extract. For this speaker, the experience led to her taking up writing as work:

> *And doing that PhD was a watershed for me and got me into serious academic writing (Barbara McGilchrist).*

The part played by colleagues in learning to write well is raised in all the accounts and the benefits are stressed of taking guidance from mentors, receiving feedback on drafts, talking about and testing ideas with colleagues and students, and writing in collaboration with others.

Following models, taking guidance, seeking feedback
In many of the interviews the writers affirm the vital role of significant teachers or mentors in their development. They name and pay tribute to them in their histories. They define their contributions.

The importance of having a model to follow is the focus of the following account:

> *When I came here in 1970, I had the privilege of working under an exceptional person, Jack Tizzard ... Jack had a remarkably good writing style, I think he was a model of academic writing, and I think that it's quite important, when you're just starting out, to have friendly but firm criticism, not just about the academic content, but whether this is something anybody's going to want to read in the first place (Peter Moss).*

Continuing the theme, in the extract below, the writer unpacks what it was about the model that was worth imitating:

And then there was an author whose name people who've taught biology in schools will know, Mike Roberts, because he wrote a very successful series of biology textbooks, and I joined him in writing one of the later editions of an A-level biology textbook. Mike Roberts was just superb at things like structuring paragraphs, at the minutiae of grammar and syntax and punctuation, an economy with words, but the occasional, the occasional, stylistic flourish just to keep the reader engaged. And he was a completely ruthless editor in the best sense. So I got a lot from him (Michael Reiss).

Referring to guidance received during periods of study, the following speaker describes the approach to teaching that made it possible for her to get her ideas down on paper:

I had two excellent tutors when I did my Masters degree, Joan Tambourini and James Willig, and they were wonderful at, again, enabling me to write. And there was one thing that I never forgot, because only at the eleventh hour did they start looking at surface features. Up until then it had been helping me to develop my ideas and to get those ideas down on paper (Barbara MacGilchrist).

The writers are clearly open to the constructive criticism of others and the importance of oral and written feedback is mentioned in many of the accounts. For example, in the quotation below, the writer advises actively seeking feedback:

I'm happy to have people give me feedback and that's essential. I feel I've benefited hugely from in-depth one-to-one feedback from colleagues and I recommend that people look for that (Shirley Dex).

Following the same theme, another speaker recommends spreading the net wide and explains that the writer learns to understand more about the reader's perspective from the observations and commentaries of a diverse range of people:

… you get different kinds of comments from different kinds of people. Even if they are not expert in the subject, they can comment on the writing, or the clarity, or the structure. The more comments, the better. You don't have to respond to everything, but all of this makes you think about your writing and about your readers' reception of it (Stephen Ball).

Another account focuses on aiming high in the choice of rapporteurs and emphasises the value of sending drafts to experts in the field:

Robert Burgess said, 'As you write each chapter, send it to experts in the field, and get them to comment on it.' Now that would never have occurred to me. I was a new writer, and nobody had heard of me. I'd published very little, and this guy was saying send in your chapter, send it to them, explain what it is, and see if they've got any comments. And I was amazed at how many people wrote back – they gave detailed comments, they suggested new things, it was fantastic. I mean, some of them ignored it, but some really big names were interested and engaged, and that was brilliant (David Gillborn).

The writers recall episodes when the feedback tactics of others resulted in moments of clarity about their own writing. For example, in the following quotation, the writer reports that when a publisher told her what *not* to do, it made her more conscious of her preconceptions and overall style:

I think probably one of the most interesting things that the first publisher I ever worked with said was, 'You write as you lecture. You have to stop doing that, you must learn to write as a writer.' I didn't really understand quite what she meant at first and so I went back to read the chapter I was working on more carefully and of course I was writing as a lecturer, assuming a complicity on the part of my audience, which was a mistake. I was assuming that my audience were looking at slides and assuming a shared knowledge (Pam Meecham).

In another account, the speaker describes a procedure that involved no negative feedback, no feedback directly to her as the writer, yet offered her a new way of evaluating her work:

When I was a researcher and working on a project – it was a large project and we wrote some very long reports – and the project director wasn't working hands-on on the project, but came across from time to time and we wrote reports and fed back. And, I think for his own purposes mainly, he would annotate in the margins the main points from each part of the report. So each paragraph, or every few paragraphs perhaps, would have some sort of notes for him – tracking through what you were saying through the report, and I found that a very useful technique myself. I think it was to himself, to sort of track through what was being said and what the argument was. But it was making that explicit for me as a writer, how this was being interpreted for him as a reader. So I found that very useful, because it helped me see the structure of my writing more clearly, where it kept to the point, where it went off on a tangent and that sort of thing. And where there were gaps. So that was useful (Judy Ireson).

Testing ideas with other people

The accounts suggest that some of the writers develop an idea of what they want to say, then try it out to see whether it communicates what they were intending. For example, the writer quoted below emphasises the importance of rehearsing ideas in discussion with colleagues. He describes how ideas for writing are seeded in conversations with others:

Much of my writing happens after I've talked a lot. So, a talk at a conference or talking with students in a normal teaching session or with somebody who's doing a PhD. A lot of talking, and working out ideas, and testing ideas, and seeing how they're received. So going about writing is embedded in that. It comes out of a lot of interaction (Gunther Kress).

Following the same theme, the next quotation indicates how productive tutorials can be, revealing how one's writing and meanings come across to student readers:

One of my doctoral students came up with a neat device: WIRMI. 'WIRMI' stands for 'What I Really Mean Is'. And I had an example recently, while I was using the research review I wrote on classrooms as learning communities, and somebody said, 'I don't really understand what this bit's about.' And I looked at it and it was just an awful bit of writing, the paragraph needed a WIRMI (Chris Watkins).

The usefulness of presenting a paper to test ideas is the focus of another extract:

What I do to get the argument to come out, and the point of it, is always to give it as a paper. Because there's nothing like producing a set of overheads, or PowerPoint presentations for making you realise you can't go off onto that digression, or that really you need to move that forward earlier on (Diana Leonard).

Collaborating and co-writing

Almost all the writers have been involved in collaborative writing. They talk about learning from and with co-writers. For example, advantages have been found in working with more experienced colleagues (Barbara McGilchrist's interview) or with those taking a different theoretical stance (Heidi Safia Mirza's interview) or with those from a completely different profession (for example, Ann Oakley has worked with medical professionals).

The following extract emphasises reciprocity in the cooperative act and the learning benefits for partners with complementary skills:

I found that working with another person that I trusted was a huge help, partly because my flights of fancy were quickly brought into sharp relief by her sensible approach. She is also willing to press the delete key and doesn't worry about losing whole pages whereas I used to be a little precious about my writing. So working with somebody who I have confidence in, but who also had a much better writing style than I did, helped. I learned from that. I contributed to her writing in terms of the depth of my knowledge of the field so we worked symbiotically in that sense (Pam Meecham).

Most of all the participants see the importance of writing as a social activity:

Well, one of the things about my writing is that most of it is collaborative. I find that working with other people is helpful, not because they do all the work but because I feel the responsibility to colleagues, to put in the effort myself and comment on what they're doing, respond to their concerns. I prefer writing as a social activity rather than an individual activity (Geoff Whitty).

However, a number of participants point out that collaborative writing is not always easy or straightforward and that it throws up a number of challenges:

Collaborative writing really makes you think differently. I've written, of course, with Dave Gillborn here at the Institute, but I've written mainly with women, such as Diane Reay. What's challenging is to write so that it's seamless. We take responsibilities for different areas, but then we interweave so that the style seems seamless, and that's very hard to do, it takes time. Then there are the problems of ownership and that's where collaborative work can come unstuck ... I would say collaborative work is creative but it can be a minefield as well (Heidi Safia Mirza).

Editing the work of others

Some of the accounts emphasise the constructive role of editing. The process of revising the work of others is described as a learning process that encourages reassessment of one's own writing. In the following extract the speaker pinpoints specifically what can be learned from the task of paring down text:

What editing makes you have to say is: 'What can I cut out of that which will not affect the basic premise?' And it's surprising how often you can, and that makes you think, 'How much superfluous stuff, how much overwriting am I doing, and therefore losing the narrative?' So I think editing is quite important, I think you need to get up to a certain stage, but it's part of your development. If you start by practising, doing yourself, and then working on other people's, it's salutary (Peter Moss).

On the same theme, the following speaker explains that questioning why writing is 'going wrong' or going well is a learning process for the editor or marker.

I've also found that commenting on other people's writing helps me. Because I do a lot of marking now, of course, reviewing journal articles, marking students' work. And you can see where things are going wrong and what works in their writing and that makes it perhaps more explicit for you as a writer (Judy Ireson).

Reading

Within the accounts there are many references to the relationship between reading and writing, namely that reading works as a resource for writing as well as a source of inspiration for writing. The writers explain the importance they attach to reading, what they draw from their reading and the ways in which reading affects them.

The following quotation focuses first on the importance of writers being steady readers. Secondly, it points to the potential of well-written fiction to leave a mark on the reader:

I suppose I think (and this is quite unempirical) that it's very important to read good writers, and I don't just mean academic writers. So I personally, in my personal reading, I probably don't read enough academically, as I try and read other stuff. I read novels and things, and I think that rubs off as well simply because they're good things to read. So I think actually being a reader yourself is important (Peter Moss).

In the following account reading is likened to an imaginary debate, an opportunity to test run tentative ideas and arguments against powerful theories:

Formative experiences have been, on the one hand, great scholars that I've engaged with, in my reading, and from time to time I've got interested in particular great scholars, Richard Peters here, Jurgen Habermas, Ernest Gellner, one or two other people as well. And in a fairly concentrated period of time I've kind of given myself up to these people, one after another, as my interests have developed and changed. So I've, as it were, ground out my thinking and ideas, in conversation with others so to speak (Ron Barnett).

Following the same theme, another quotation stresses the function of reading as a stimulating and delightful interchange of ideas. The speaker articulates the reasons why books draw us into reading them again and again:

> *Why is it that we find certain books worth re-reading? Usually not only because they offer us significant intellectual input, but very often also because they are beautiful books, I mean they are beautifully written. There is an aesthetic quality to it that is charming and appeals and that gives you a feeling of being respected as a reader as well. It is what Roland Barthes said: the pleasure of the text, the joy that is brought into this dialogue we call reading (Jan Blommaert).*

Another account follows the theme of reading as a means of rousing strong feelings and emphasises that writing can also result from strongly felt emotions:

> *Ten years ago I was nominated to give the Lister Lecture … The Lister Lecture's very prestigious, it's awarded to an up-and-coming academic, and I wrote a very angry lecture. It was on racist pseudo-science and IQ. I looked at popularist right-wing academic arguments such as the Bell curve which linked race to low IQ. I was so angry about the stuff I was reading at the time and the revitalisation of Social Darwinism through the new genetics discourse. I look back on that essay now and I think how angry I was (Heidi Safia Mirza).*

In some accounts particular books are recalled for the influence they had on the writer and his or her writing. The following extract, for example, highlights the power of books to strike a chord with the reader. Here the writer explains how the content was startling in its resemblance to his own experience and this inspired him to carry out research and writing of the same kind:

> *My undergraduate tutor was Dennis Marsden, who wrote a very important book called* Education and the Working Class *(1962). That book was a revelation to me when I read it at university: it was about me, it was like reading about my own schooling. And it brought sociology alive, relating it to my own experience, and articulating the experience of working-class families. I was trying to do a similar thing with this book, which is about the lives of middle-class families and their struggles for social advantage for their children (Stephen Ball).*

Another underlines the capacity of some ('how-to') books to become indispensable props for writing:

> *A book by Howard Becker, called* Writing for Social Scientists, *which*

saved my life when I was doing my PhD and has some very direct tips about styles of writing, the use of the literature, which are just gold dust; it's a real goldmine of how to survive in the world of writing (David Gillborn).

In describing how they learned to write, the writers talk about how they make conscious and unconscious connections with other writing. In the following extract, for example, the writer describes scrutinising the work of others to recognise and learn the characteristics of a style she desires:

If I read someone else's work and I'm inspired – I would try to identify what made it 'inspiring' and try to use that style in my own writing (Heidi Safia Mirza).

On the same theme, another writer explains his practice of collecting words, phrases and expressions to use in his own work:

For years and years (and I still do it you know) I used to read things not only because of the sort of stuff that was in it, so it wasn't only reading for learning, but also for stealing stylistically. I ruthlessly exploited other people's oeuvre as a source of inspiration for particular turns of phrases – especially in English of course, which is my fourth language. But whenever I saw a beautifully worded argument or whenever I saw a nice turn of phrase or an expression that I found appealing, I used to make a note of it. And I really collected it like a sort of a butterfly collection – I still do, always with the explicit plan of at some point using it. I can say with confidence that I have used most of it. So there were authors that really, really have been masters to me in the sense that they provided me with examples of how to write (Jan Blommaert).

However, one writer refers to Graham Greene's warning: being in love with your own favourite phrases can lead to their use in ways that keep you on the surface of meaning and so they should be removed from your text:

... Advice from Graham Greene, who is a novelist that I admire a lot, and he said if when you're writing you have something that you really like, a sentence or maybe a paragraph that you're really, really fond of, cut it out. And I have so many times taken that piece of advice (Lucy Green).

It wasn't only the written word that is referred to as a resource, however. The following quotation describes how a writer drew on a different field – art – to illuminate educational issues in his own discipline:

The inaugural lecture I gave here started with a wonderful photograph by the photographer Andreas Gursky. And he's somebody who digitally enhances but only slightly, and I used that to get into issues of representation, and what the aims of science in general are and how this can connect with what the purposes of school science education should be (Michael Reiss).

Going about writing

4.1 Finding and managing time

The writers focus on time from two angles: writing for publication involves spending long hours on your own – and those hours need to be found and protected.

The essential solitariness of writing is referred to in the comment below, which points out the irony of that solitariness, since writing is about communicating with others:

I suppose for most people writing is a very private thing, isn't it? You do it by yourself. I mean, one of the things about being a writer: you have to be prepared to spend hours and hours on your own, in solitary confinement, without seeing anybody, speaking to anyone or having anything to do with other human beings. And of course what you're doing when you're writing is trying to communicate to others, but in order to make that communication you have to distance yourself from others. And so it is a very solitary thing to do in the first place (Lucy Green).

However, the dominant theme in the writers' responses is the importance of managing time in order to create a space for writing:

You have to sit down and just organise your time, to ensure there are spaces for writing. To give it the priority it deserves (Stephen Ball).

Others agree that writers need to be single-minded and even obsessive about time:

Writing is an activity for which you have to be very single-minded, you have to be very focused, and you have to be very unwilling to be distracted (Ann Oakley).

You have to be some species of hermit – and able to take a period out to do some writing, it has to be obsessive (Diana Leonard).

Often managing one's use of time is associated with clearing the mind and protecting a creative mental stance:

I have to start first thing. I have to have a fresh mind. It's no good if I try doing an email first thing, that's it, I won't be doing good writing for the rest of that day. Even one email destroys the kind of illusion that you have to get yourself into, of creativity. And so I don't open my emails first thing (Lucy Green).

However, while the professional status of the writers means that some are free to decide their own work timetable, this 'freedom' does not necessarily extend to women with young children:

Whereas before you just went with the flow and when you felt tired or you had enough you stopped. Well, now, children force you to have definite deadlines. At five o'clock or half past four, they have to be picked up or whatever it is. And however innovative and creative you feel [laughs] that's it: stop for the day … And you have to then … somehow resurrect it another time (Shirley Dex).

The difficulties of combining writing with caring for young children is echoed by the two comments below in which the speakers talk about the necessity of writing on the move:

I think because I was a mother … and because I've always worked full time, once the children were two or three, I had to multi-task when it came to writing. I have always had to work on trains, planes, at bus stations, a doctor's surgery – anywhere where I could find ten or 15 minutes. The notion of sitting quietly down in a study endlessly writing for days just hasn't been my experience (Pam Meecham).

I do it on the Tube, I do it on the bus. I'm dreaming about it. I think about it a lot and I might be sitting on the Tube with my eyes closed. People think I'm having some time off, but I'm actually writing (Lucy Green).

4.2. Planning and playing

We were interested in how the writers go about writing. In their descriptions, we discerned a preference for different approaches, ranging from, on the one hand, a systematic approach – working with a plan or structure – to an experimental, more 'organic' approach – setting off with a rough idea then playing with the writing, letting ideas emerge. One writer expresses the latter as: 'Never having a particular kind of endpoint in mind and just trying to stretch' (Chris Watkins).

The writers generally favour one approach more than another. For example, the following speaker avoids methodical organisation and describes an approach that involves a jumble of ideas jotted down in no particular order and at any time. The writer explains that this satisfies her need to 'ink the ideas' that come to her, no matter what she is doing:

I would like to say I had a structure. I would like to say I was methodical and I'd like to say I was consistent, but I am none of those things. My writing is much more a stream of consciousness, partly because I write while I'm gardening, cooking and doing a lot of other things. The computer will be on and I'll dash back to it and write something down. I'll often start with an idea on a book, a particular chapter that's formulated around an idea, so 'monuments' could be one. Then I will work fairly randomly to bring it all together and only at the end really put it into a structure. I find writing to a very fixed structure frustrating and limiting (Pam Meecham).

The following account follows the same theme of having no route map. Using the metaphor of a journey, the speaker compares making a start on writing with 'pitching into the unknown':

Writing for me is a learning journey. I very rarely know what the final message or outcome will be. I know the general themes that I want to write about, but I never know at the beginning exactly how it's going to pan out. I'm often pitching into the unknown. I like to develop. I like to move myself on in terms of my own learning as I'm writing. I know some people know exactly the beginning, middle and end and they've sketched it all out. I never do that (Barbara MacGilchrist).

As in the comments above, the writer quoted below enjoys the thrill of the unplanned approach. For these writers, plans are limiting and carry with them a sense of restriction:

I'm hopeless at detailed planning, and I think that's because I want to get lost in the creative experience – not lost, but I want to experience it as a journey and I don't really want to know the names of all the stations on the way. I want to find out where this is going to take me – and that's part of the excitement of writing, it's a journey we can go on and we don't know what's going to happen (Ann Oakley).

In the following extract, on the other hand, a systematic approach is strongly advocated:

I don't care if it's a chapter, a thesis, a 1,000 word article or an entire book, you sit down with a plan of what you're going to do, and then you start somewhere other than the beginning. Do not begin with the introduction, you begin with the first bit that you are confident of. Write that section, write another section, and write another section. When you have all that, write a conclusion, then go back and write an introduction. Because you cannot introduce it until you know what you are going to do, and as you are writing, you are changing the ideas (David Gillborn).

However, it is also the case that writers are sometimes required to follow a given structure. Psychology journals, for example, make strict demands about design and layout. The writer quoted below explains that this makes the organisational aspects of writing easier:

Journal articles in psychology have a very clear structure, it's a very standard structure. Once you've got used to it, it really makes life quite straightforward, because you know exactly what you've got to do, you know, that's quite helpful, I think. So I use that, particularly when I'm writing up some quantitative research. So that's fine (Judy Ireson).

5

Producing a text

In the transcripts we found references to the activity involved in reaching a finished text. On the one hand, while writing, the writers think constantly of their readers: they imagine their readers' responses, they go into matters of language and style in order to make meaning for the reader. The writers also talked about the strategies they use to ease the process of producing a text.

5.1 Considering and imagining the reader

The importance of the reader and the reader's experience emerges as a key construct in the minds of the writers. In thinking about writing, they think about the reader and about communicating and connecting with the reader. In the following extract the writer shows an awareness of the reader and writing as a social interaction and as a communication that emphasises the complexity of the task of writing:

> *I'm trying to understand my own sentiments, I'm trying to form coherent wholes, I'm trying [to] understand where my readers might be, I'm trying to reach out to them, I'm trying to have a sense of different audiences, I'm trying to have a sense of the authors that I'm engaging with, I'm having a sense of different time frames, different cultures. All of this is in my mind as I'm writing; that's hugely complex (Ron Barnett).*

The same awareness is articulated as 'thinking of writing for the experience of the reader' (Chris Watkins). In the following quotation the same speaker describes a back-and-forth activity of alternately surging ahead with your own idea and then imagining what the reader might make of it:

> *You think, 'Well, what do I want to do with and for the reader through this? What do I want to take them through, in what order and how will it engage them?' So I can sometimes think about that at the start, but normally what happens is I'll pile into something and then have to check,*

just say, 'Hang on, is this really thought-provoking?' (Chris Watkins).

Some interviews, more than others, emphasise the importance of imagining the reader's life and the reader's response to the work. The following quotation, for example, accentuates the writer's responsibility to visualise the reader and to try to identify with the reader's situation so that his writing becomes meaningful and significant to the reader and so that some kind of attachment is formed between reader and writer:

I'm trying to engage with my audience, so I'm trying to improvise for my audience, so I'm trying to engage where they are. I can't expect my reader to listen to me if I'm not listening to my reader. I can't expect to make connections, or the reader to make connections with what I'm saying, unless I make connections to where I think the reader is. So I have to be imaginative, I have to empathise with my reader. I have to reach out from myself. Imagine my readers, imagine what it is for them, imagine what their days are like. What their lives are like, in order for me to reach out to them. And so I think that partly counts for the disjuncture between how writers sometimes believe that they are intelligible and transparent, when the reality is that they are very often opaque. And incomprehensible. It's because there is that lack of connection being made. But the responsibility of that connection lies with the author (Ron Barnett).

In the excerpt below, the writer describes a fantasy conversation with his readers and sees them sharing the same passions as himself:

So I imagine the kind of person, or kinds of persons, with whom I might be talking … I'm imagining that I'm talking with the people, I never think about, let's say, the formal standing, but where I'm imagining a kind of shared interest, and a certain intensity of interest (Gunther Kress).

In the next excerpt the reader is envisaged as fired up, stirred by the writer's work:

I think to begin with that I thought it was just a question of choosing the right word to get the ideas across, but now I see it as much as producing the right emotions or concerns or … politics or passions in your reader (Diana Leonard).

A vision of the reader relishing the work, being gripped by it, distinguishes another account:

*There's very little redundancy in my text, so my texts – in that sense – are quite a big ask of the reader. Somebody said to me once that I don't let the reader off the hook. At least, they can't lighten or lessen their concentration of me. If they lose their concentration for a moment, they've lost the argument. **And** I keep the reader attentive as it were, that's what I'm trying to do actually, to keep the reader attentive. I'm trying not to let the reader off the hook, but I'm trying to take the reader with me all the time. So that's about pleasing the reader. But I'm also trying, if I can say so, to delight the reader. I want the reader to turn over the page (Ron Barnett).*

For another writer an important image is that of open-minded readers unhappy with conventional, unquestioned arguments and willing to look at old ideas afresh:

I've tried to strive more to escape from taking up obvious positions or deploying gross generalisations. Rather I have sought to make the obvious strange, to distance myself and hopefully my reader from taken-for-granted positions and arguments (Stephen Ball).

5.2 Language and style

Some writers, as exemplified in the quotation below, feel it is crucial to target a readership, i.e. to make an early decision about who the readers will be and then to imagine and use the language and style that will appeal to those readers:

You write for an audience, basically, and you have to know who the audience is when you start out and the style of writing that's appropriate. Learning to write for a specific audience is a sub-branch of learning to write at all … I think the principle of addressing the audience is one that all writing has to address upfront (Shirley Dex).

The same principle is expressed as: 'the writing is [done] with a sense of the client group that's going to make use of it' (Jeni Riley).

As an example of this, the following comment relates how the writer chose language and adopted a style designed to include all, but particularly some individual members of a public audience:

The lecture was almost like a rap poem, it had a rap beat, and it was divided up into seven stories or verses. I feel very strongly in my writing that I should be able to communicate and that it's accessible. You have to break down some of the academic language and concepts as it is a public audience where I knew some people, like my mum and my friends, have

*not got degrees and have never been to a university. This is a totally
unknown world to them and I wanted them to feel comfortable with what
I was saying, and not feel excluded. ... It took a long time to write, and
I'm very proud of that piece, because it made people cry, and it made them
laugh – it brought out emotions in people (Heidi Safia Mirza).*

In aiming to connect with the reader, other writers also describe different style
practices; for example, one writer combines an academic approach with a more
'popular' one (Ann Oakley); another avoids statement-making and is happy to
reveal the writer's processes, to create a 'writerly' text (Chris Watkins); a third uses
the first person, and gives an account of why she is interested in the topic and why
she wants to develop it (Diana Leonard).

All of this is intended to set up a certain relationship with the reader – like
talking with an acquaintance – and so the writers aim at a conversational style of
writing. This is explained by one of the writers in the following way:

*... because I see this as a social thing, I see it as continuous with talking
and thinking. I have striven for, I can say, since the mid-Seventies, which is
now a good time ago, to make my writing much more like my talking ...
to be conversational (Gunther Kress).*

This comment also implies that it takes effort and time to reach a style that is
more informal. This view is corroborated in the extract below where the emphasis
is on replacing overly academic language with something more plainspoken:

*What I was able to do in that lecture with the writing style was feel
confident that I'd reached a point, after all these years of writing, to write
as if I'm talking to you, and not hide behind the mask of over-articulations
and over-theorising (Heidi Safia Mirza).*

On the same theme, another writer describes a technique that helps him get
closer to conversational speech:

*I deliberately think about audience as I'm writing. I will have in mind, and
I know one or two other writers have this technique as well, of myself
actually speaking to three or four different kinds of people ... it's as if one's
sitting down in a bar or café, with three or four different kinds of people,
representing different kinds of interest and backgrounds, and one's just
talking to them. So the moment of writing approaches that – begins to
approach that – of the spoken word. It's more direct, it's more
straightforward (Ron Barnett).*

The writers we interviewed reveal a passion for language and its importance to meaning. For example, the writer below describes the excitement she feels about the technical challenge of composing a text, comparing it to creating a musical score:

The passion is about putting the words on the page, seeing the pattern of the words, hearing the rhythm of the words, punctuation. I think punctuation is like music. I tell you: not everybody has the same view as I do about semi-colons! It's just the best thing in the world to be able to do this, and there are so many words that you can use, and changing a long word or changing the punctuation changes the meaning (Ann Oakley).

Similarly, another writer takes enjoyment from restructuring and reorganising text to achieve the best way of expressing what she means:

I get a lot of pleasure from crafting language, from sort of moving text around and trying to streamline an argument and just using words in the best way that I know how to, to try to say something to a particular readership that I have in mind. That's a craft, which I think is very pleasurable when it's going well (Lucy Green).

5.3 Smoothing the way

In discussing their personal approaches to writing, the writers describe the steps they take to smooth the progress of their drafts. There are references in some of the transcripts to the importance of preparing oneself psychologically to make a start and to being organised. For example, in the following quotation, the writer finds a way of ensuring that writing is the first priority of her working day:

… the trick I've learned about writing is to leave something from the day before on the desk all ready to start the next day … Because I could spend all morning mithering around in my study, organising, doing and chasing, so if I say, 'Today I'm going to write the websites for the two current things', which is what I did this morning, then I need to have found everything and set it all out the day before (Diana Leonard).

Different ways of composing the text are described in the transcripts. For example, one approach (below) is to write freely, deliberately regarding first attempts as provisional, and consciously separating the writing task into two different, consequent activities, i.e. creating then editing:

It's important not to keep reading what you've just written. So, you don't go back and read it. You get hung up on the fact that there's a word that isn't working very well three sentences back ... that you just write it and you regard it a bit like a potter's clay – you've got something there that then can be moulded. I think that's what I've learnt, that is, the importance of distinguishing these different stages in writing: there's kind of an initial creative process and then the editorial one follows from that (Ann Oakley).

A completely different way of working is to regard creating and editing as concurrent processes:

I write directly onto the screen these days. I compose on the screen, and I give myself the challenge of composing good sentences, and good paragraphs straightaway. And this is extremely demanding, but it's compelling though. The composing of that sentence, getting the clauses right, getting the verbs right, is actually compelling me to think through what am I saying precisely (Ron Barnett).

Another course of action is to intentionally leave a period of time between creating and editing. The writers have found that this produces a certain detachment from the work, which helps them to approach the work more like a reader.

You write a draft yourself and you think you're reasonably happy. You wait a week, say, certainly a few days; don't do it the next day but leave a little gap, the longer the better in some ways – if possible, a good week. Go back and re-read it and you will then find many ways of improving it yourself. Just having that gap and then coming at it slightly fresher with a more objective view will enable you to improve your own writing (Shirley Dex).

The need for detachment and ruthless editing (despite the temptation to preserve elegant sentences and phrases) is emphasised by another writer:

You mustn't hang onto sentences that you like just because you like them – get rid of them. If they're somehow in the way, then they've got to go. It doesn't matter how fine the piece of writing you think it is, it just doesn't work, so chuck it (Ann Oakley).

Engaging in the process of writing

6.1 Academic writing and the creative arts

The writers referred to academic writing both as creative and as bridging the divide between academic writing and genres conventionally regarded as 'creative'. The comment below illustrates this in general terms in that it focuses on academic writing as performing a function similar to the practice of a creative art in an individual's life:

> *I can't sing well, I can't act well, I don't try and write fiction, so I think for me the writing satisfies that part of me that would otherwise feel one is not being creative (Michael Reiss).*

Many of the accounts referred to the striking metaphors that the writers draw on in the act of writing. The choice of metaphor, and the role ascribed to it, reflect different perspectives on the characteristics of academic writing. For example, in the following quotation, a view of writing academically that is primarily about situating oneself in a debate is presented as a process that demands the decisions and manoeuvres that are integral to writing a play:

> *… I see my writing sometimes as if I'm writing a play in which I have different characters, and I have to make judgements about which character is going to be on stage, at any one stage, and how they're going to come in and out of the picture, and what weight you're going to give them, and who's going to be talking at any one time. So that's another potent metaphor (Ron Barnett).*

In another salient metaphor, an emphasis on academic writing as requiring a distanced stance towards the personal is likened to the wearing of a theatrical mask:

The thing with academic writing is it can be like a mask. You can use academic theory and academic conventions to articulate, in a very objective and distanced way, something that you've experienced yourself, but you're not really naming or implicating yourself in it (Heidi Safia Mirza).

Another account emphasises the materiality of writing and draws a comparison between academic writing and sculpture:

…. I tend often to have a very broad idea of what I might want to say, and then it's a bit like working at a bit of sculpture: you chip away, you add a bit, you go back, you shift. So it's a different creative activity, or so I find it (Peter Moss).

Not all metaphors relate creativity to the arts, however. The following account draws on cooking. For this writer, writing is like producing a stew:

So I don't do this thing, which you get in low-level advice about writing, which is [pompous voice] 'Start off with a structure and a plan' and that sort of stuff. You get put off writing, I think. Most of that sort of advice doesn't work. So … I'm just kind of stewing, I think. Creating a stew, yes … So many things go on in the stewing: putting things together, trying out phrases, talking with people, letting it waltz all around, I think. Yeah. So I haven't got a very clear view of what the process of writing is, actually. Because it's just another part of doing what I do (Chris Watkins).

The transcripts call into question the duality found in many descriptions of academic writing, which imply a divide between rationality and creativity, mind and body. In such accounts academic writing tends to be linked firmly to the conventional idea of rationality: to, for example, critical thinking, or argument. While there are assertions that academic writing can be creative and can involve feeling and bodily responses to, for example, rhythm or the visual features of a text, this has not been explored in the literature on writing for publication (e.g. Murray, 2005) in the ways illustrated by the transcripts in this inquiry.

6.2 Feeling the process

A striking feature of the interviews is the way in which the writers articulate the emotions they encounter when producing a text – from the first seedling idea through the highs and lows, satisfactions and trials of developing the idea and transferring it into print. For example, the quotation below focuses on the sensations that come with the earliest stirrings of a hazy idea and the thrill of trying to harness and then frame it:

... the struggle and the feeling of vague excitement that there's something here, that I've got something new, that I'm wrestling with it and that it's somewhere in the back of my mind. And, then, I locate where it is and then I've got something to say (Shirley Dex).

It is the mere anticipation of starting a first draft that causes butterflies for another writer:

Something else I was thinking of to talk to you about, which I've often thought of but never spoken to anyone, apart from my husband, is the nerves that you feel. Particularly, if it's day one and I'm going to plan even an article, not necessarily a book, an article, and it's an article that I haven't actually drafted in any form before, but this is particularly when it's really a blank slate. I go to my desk in the morning and I actually feel nervous, as if I was going to go on stage and sing a song or play the piano or give a lecture. I think, 'So ridiculous, Lucy, I mean nobody's going to read what you write in this room today.' That's part of the deal with myself, of course, and yet I actually feel dry in the mouth, my heart's beating a little bit fast. It's crazy and I don't understand it (Lucy Green).

The writers recognise a stage at which the ideas are a 'jumble' (Chris Watkins) – an untidy, unclear heap of impressions – yet something that unites many of the writers is that they feel comfortable to leave all the ideas swirling around in their minds, until things take more shape. For example, the writer quoted below is content to muse on all the angles that come to her, although intuitively some may seem wild or unconventional at first:

Like now, the book is coming, it's a kind of cloud in my head. The kinds of ideas that I have are vague and structural. I've got to know that they might be completely wacky, totally wrong. I can't have detailed thoughts now, but they ... they're just sort of ... I don't know how to describe it. It's kind of general structural, possibly wacky things that I just feel might be worth keeping. And then gradually as time goes by, the thoughts that I have will get more and more detailed ...

In the same breath, the writer identifies a trend: developing a fixation with the idea (often to the detriment of other aspects of life):

.... and, of course, then I will get more and more obsessed by the whole thing and that's when it starts to eat up my life and it's ... it can get very oppressive. And then I am thinking about it, all the time, and I've had to

learn strategies to stop myself doing that when I'm with my family or with my friends, because it's not nice (Lucy Green).

Other writers experience the same thing: 'the idea' takes over. For example, the writer quoted below tells how it interrupts sleep and taunts the writer who is struggling alone:

Yes, it's obsessive, it dominates my thinking, I wake up in the night worried about an idea I've been working on and if it's not good enough. It's very difficult. You're always testing yourself, and it's lonely, and it's hard (Heidi Safia Mirza).

Several accounts emphasise the unpredictability of the quantity and quality of the text produced at different sittings. A common experience is that there are times when ideas flow and expressing them comes easily, but there are also times when thoughts are jammed or dammed and moving ideas from mind to paper is sluggish; hours can be spent with very little text produced. How those different experiences raise conflicting emotions is the focus of the following quotation:

I find I have very mixed emotions when I'm writing. Sometimes I get very frustrated, because I've sat down, and I've given up a whole Sunday, and at the end of the day I've written two lines, which is enormously frustrating. And the other extreme can be great, you know, exhilaration when you've been concentrating very hard and suddenly you find that new ideas … you've actually been able to capture them on paper (Barbara MacGilchrist).

On the same theme, another writer testifies to the disquiet of being 'stuck'. The challenge is in dragging yourself out:

Some days the ideas will just flow one after the other and it comes together well. Some days it's like wading through treacle, it's really, really hard. And I don't know the answer to that. I mean, I think the honest truth is you just have to stick at it and keep going, even when it's hard … usually I find you have to get through that pain barrier and it comes together later (Jeni Riley).

The metaphor of breaking through a barrier is continued in the next quotation. It is the ordeal that first comes to mind for the author, who describes a state of mental anguish that precedes any sense of satisfaction:

There's an awful lot of pain in writing and therefore when you mention writing, satisfaction's not necessarily the first thing one thinks about. The actual process of writing I find hugely difficult and hugely painful. Scary, you know, when I'm in the middle of something, I think 'I don't know where this is going' and 'it's not working out'. But I'm someone who writes myself into positions rather than sits down always knowing where I'm going. But the satisfaction comes when you break through that and you've got to the point, yes, that worked. So it's almost a satisfaction of the pain stopping (Geoff Whitty).

Writing is expressed as pain in other accounts. Wrestling, grappling or tussling with half-formed ideas is a 'huge effort' (Michael Reiss) and 'hard graft' (Jeni Riley).

In talking about the 'huge effort' of grappling with ideas, the writers describe how writing can affect the whole body. For example, in the following quotation, conveying thoughts to paper is likened to self-inflicted torture:

Why does writing cause me bodily pain? I think it's partly that one is drawing out from within oneself what is already there. This goes back to an old Greek idea that actually we know far more than we realise, and learning things is actually articulating what one already subconsciously knows. And I find writing is of that kind, one actually has a great deal stored up inside one in one way or another. And the challenge is of articulating half-formed sentences and values, and dredging them up, as it were, out of one's body. That's the sense I have; it's as if I'm pulling them out with wires, painfully, from within myself (Ron Barnett).

6.3 The love of writing tools

There was some discussion about methods of writing things down, e.g. handwriting, scribbling, word processing, transferring handwritten notes to the screen, and the effect that they have on the text and the writer. For example, the writer quoted below draws a link between 'the technology' used and the quality of writing produced. He also describes the materiality and physicality of writing and suggests there can be an emotional attachment to materials:

I think that the technology that you use ... in all sorts of ways [has an effect on how you write] affectively, I think – the tangibility, the sensoriness of paper, and the instrument with which you're writing (Gunther Kress).

Some of the writers expressed a partiality towards or even a soft spot or affection for particular tools. They associated different sensations with using different tools and found tools contributed to or facilitated the movement of ideas to paper.

Several of the writers preferred writing by hand. For example, the writer below condemns the computer as a tool for writing and sees it rather as an archive, his store cupboard. His preference is for moulding and building text through sketching and scribbling:

> *If I've got going from the completion of the sentence: 'The purpose of this chapter is' then I think, 'OK, how am I going to achieve it?' And then I use all sorts of things. I go to my computer and look through a thousand files and see if I've got anything on it already. Then I'll get off the computer because it's basically a bad instrument for writing. So I go back to pieces of paper and scribble. And the thing will slowly take shape and change shape all the time (Chris Watkins).*

In the following extract, pen and paper are preferred because they are substantial, real and can be touched; text can be controlled, cut up, reordered in a very concrete way. The body of work can be displayed all at once (and not in bits, as on the small screen):

> *I handwrite almost always, as I like to see the text in front of me so as I can play around with it. I don't use the computer. I like to be able to cross-reference, I like to be able to use Post-its, I like to be able to chop up the text, move it about, and yet I can't use the computer screen 'cause I can only see one piece, one wodge of text. Whereas when I've got it spread over the dining room table, with Post-its, I can physically move it about (Barbara MacGilchrist).*

The method described above has a monitoring function: the writer can keep more of a watchful eye on how the work is progressing, than if working on the screen. Everything is laid out for scrutiny. This advantage is echoed in another account where the writer is interested in the history of his brushstrokes and in seeing a record of his own journey towards producing a text:

> *Literacy is one of my interests, so I am fascinated by the way in which I self-correct, for instance, while writing, which of course is invisible when you work on a screen. I find that valuable because it reveals my own hesitations, my own quest for the right words to formulate something and so on. So, yes, I tend to value handwriting still, but it's not purely romantic, it is not purely nostalgia, but it really has a function – reminding me of my own developing thoughts and formulations (Jan Blommaert).*

The same writer finds that producing a text with thumb, index finger and pen works better with the brain's activity and the flow of ideas than a text produced by all fingers tapping keys:

Handwriting gives you, in a very weird way, a physical connection with ideas and with a particular textuality that you don't have when you are using a keyboard (Jan Blommaert).

Similarly, another writer prefers pen and paper because it captures the rhythm of thinking:

If I'm writing fiction or something a bit more reflective, then I handwrite, because there is something about the action of the pen and the ink and the page and the connection between the head and the arm and the hand which is important (Ann Oakley).

The benefits of using word processors are, however, listed in other accounts. Some writers find them indispensable to writing. For them word processors can be 'liberating', offer more control and can have more possibilities than drafting by hand (Peter Moss); and word processors make redrafting much easier (Michael Reiss). It is the cursor that makes a difference for the writer quoted below. He imagines a relationship with the cursor, which becomes an entity daring him to begin:

You've got to face up to that blinking cursor demanding words from you on that screen. And that's your challenge, demanding words from you on that screen (Ron Barnett).

7

The politics of writing for publication

As established writers, the participants can certainly be said to have authority: they have a wide readership and most are in senior positions at the Institute of Education. However, when we consider the writers' comments in relation to the politics of writing, 'power' – in its negative connotation of the differences in the possibilities it makes available – becomes visible.

7.1 The 'power' of publishers

The writers are very aware of the power of publishers – a power that they need to heed if their writing is to be published and their careers in academia are not to be damaged. One writer, mindful of this, stresses the importance of investigating the readership and specific requirements of different journals and then targeting those journals:

> *You need to be quite clear what the particular journal or publisher expects – and which journal or publisher it's best to target – for the sorts of things that you want to write about. So deciding whether or not you're wanting to write an article that really is going to be in a peer-reviewed, prestigious international academic journal or whether actually what you want to say is much more going to be geared towards practitioners and therefore you'd be better going for a well-known but accessible professional publisher (Barbara MacGilchrist).*

However, those interviewed also argued that less experienced writers can attribute too much power to publishers, which can inhibit their writing. The comment below draws on personal experience in aiming to demystify the mystique that can surround publishers for whom writers are in fact the primary resource:

I remember that with my first book, the story of the Shelley Potteries book. When I went for the first time into a publisher's office, I thought, 'Wow this is a scrappy old set up.' [Laughs] They were in one of those Georgian terraces and all they had was a few photocopiers and that made me think, 'Of course, they haven't got any resource themselves. Writers are their resource.' They don't act as though that's the case. They act as if they're the powerful ones. And that's a great shame. Because it puts people off writing that should be writing. Just talk to some of our students, grown-up teachers about writing for publication – they'll tell you how mystical they think it must be (Chris Watkins).

But the same writer argues that although getting published should be seen as a 'game', it is important to play the game well:

I've learned that if you are writing for publishers then you treat it as a game, but play the game well. I get a little bit of satisfaction about people like senior editors saying, 'Gosh, this is the best quality manuscript I've ever seen', you know, everything is in place. Just to get them off your back really (Chris Watkins).

7.2 Writing and publishing in English

Nearly all the writers in this inquiry publish exclusively in English. Working in a world-class research centre in education and the social sciences in the UK, they write from the centre of influence and material resources, not from the periphery (see Section 9.2). One of the writers in our inquiry, who is exceptional in that he publishes in three languages, reflects matter-of-factly on the economics behind the dominance of English in academic publishing in comparison with Dutch, his native language:

You see in Dutch … when you want to write an academic article there is no market, there are no journals in Dutch and as a consequence there is hardly any opportunity to write the sort of research article that is now the bread and butter of our profession in Dutch because of the simple fact that there is no academic market for that. In [these] universities as well the emphasis is very, very strongly on writing in English, writing articles for international journals means writing in English. As a consequence, what you have is simply that certain genres don't exist as real, practicable genres in that particular language [Dutch] and are of course over-developed in English (Jan Blommaert).

In referring to publishing in English in the United States, the same individual again emphasises the importance of place. Even when writers are mainly 'native speakers' of English, publishing in certain genres may not be possible for academics:

> ... *but it is really, really difficult for these people [American academics] to engage in the kinds of genres that I practised in my Dutch oeuvre, which are activist genres ... It is really, really hard for even a very senior academic in the US to get an opinion article in one of the major newspapers. It is really difficult and, as a consequence, you see that they don't really practise that sort of activist genre or the complex of activist genres, the small genres, the polemical ones and that very often the potential [political] contribution of their analytic work remains unused or not explored fully (Jan Blommaert).*

A further implication of the situation described above is that an 'outsider' may find that his writing experience and resources do not travel.

Another writer, a native speaker of English, criticises Anglocentric attitudes. She says:

> *But it's bizarre, isn't it, we never have occasion to pick up a French journal and read it. I don't even know where I would go to find journals in French or German. I'm doing a literature review for the HEA [Higher Education Academy] at the moment, and we said we'd look at French and German literature: we're the only literature review out of five that's going to be out of the English language (Diana Leonard).*

7.3 Gender issues and power

Power, in limiting the possibilities that are available, can also be seen in references to gender issues, which emerged as a strong theme.

Men and women in our study describe how their gender affects their space and time for writing. The common experience reported here is that finding time for writing is usually easier for men:

> *The lives of academic women and writers are affected by the familial responsibilities which they are expected to take up. Which, for the most part, men do not have to deal with, and if they do, they are praised for it. So yes, men in academia have enormous advantages in the very practical sense of time and the expectations of family life being different for them, as well as all the routine institutional sexism that goes along with that which women have to put up with and men do not (Stephen Ball).*

The experience of women writers is that women's writing work is seen as less important than their work as mothers and housewives:

I've had that, certainly, the double standard, whereby the man comes home and says he's got to work on something, that's fine. A woman comes home and says she's got to work on something – the children and the man will say: 'Ridiculous, you've got to cook our supper and do this, that and the other.' And I think that being the mother of small children is quite inimical to creativity in this field. Motherhood itself is creative, so this doesn't matter. It's very difficult. I found it possible to write 'narrow', academic things when my children were little, but very difficult to write anything more creative (Ann Oakley).

Well I don't think women ever get the 'waiting on' as the creative genius that various men do. Waited on by their spouses and partners, waited on by secretaries and other people (Diana Leonard).

7.4 Writing in higher education

There was general agreement that writing for publication has become an increasingly necessary part of an academic's life and has to be accommodated:

I see writing more and more as a taken-for-granted thing about what I do. It's not an extra thing. And I can imagine, if I could think back 20 years ago, it would have been seen as an extra. 'Oh god, I've got to write something.' It doesn't feel like that now (Chris Watkins).

The rewards and sanctions are highlighted:

As an academic more and more you live by virtue of your writing, not only by virtue of your lecturing, and that there are real rewards but also real sanctions attached to that … if you don't join that race, you might lose opportunities professionally and so on (Jan Blommaert).

The participants agree that making a space for writing is a struggle and the effects of excessive workloads and different pressures make academic life very difficult. Many of the writers mention that it is harder to get colleagues to read their writing as they are all too busy, and Peter Moss observes that, like others who work in the service industries, academics are being increasingly squeezed to become more productive. Stephen Ball and Diana Leonard talk about how increasingly time is taken up with non-academic tasks and that time for writing is lost even though writing is such a major part of their lives. Michael Reiss suggests that work overload stifles original thinking. Other writers like Heidi Safia Mirza talk about the frustration they feel as writing takes up so much of their time, especially at weekends:

> *To write you have to switch off and move into another mode. I used to work through the night, but now I have to work through the weekends as well to get that run. ... I'm using my own leave, my own time, my night time, my family time because of what I call the increasing bureaucratisation in higher education (Heidi Safia Mirza).*

However, a number of experienced writers talk about how they are able to combine their teaching with their writing:

> *I've made writing and research central to my teaching ... So I don't really separate out my teaching from my writing or from my research. It all has to mingle, otherwise I can't fit it in (Pam Meecham).*

7.5 The Research Assessment Exercise

The Research Assessment Exercise (RAE*) and its effects are mentioned in the majority of interviews. Some participants are ambivalent about the RAE, finding that it has both positive and negative effects:

> *The RAE overall has many very negative impacts. The one good impact is that it means that people's writing is seen as a serious part of their job (David Gillborn).*

> *What's helped me in my individual writing – pressure and deadlines, [laughs] the RAE, all those things which are helpful in a masochistic way (Geoff Whitty).*

However, for most of the participants the perceived dominance of the RAE and performance tables has resulted in an undemocratic, competitive and unhealthy culture. The RAE has 'changed the social climate around academic writing' (Gunther Kress).

Some of the participants comment on how the new 'social climate' has changed what and how they write:

> *It has affected the type of outputs that I focus on since the RAE has happened ... RAE outputs have to be given priority, because that creates funding for the university (Shirley Dex).*

While several participants complained that some of the writing they most enjoy doing does not 'count' for the RAE, others write for so many publications that it does not matter. The negative effects mentioned also include: the RAE reduces motivation (Ann Oakley, Chris Watkins); it intimidates and stops people taking risks with their writing (David Gillborn); it leaves no time for creative thinking (Shirley Dex); it is counter-productive (Jeni Riley); and journals publish inferior material (David Gillborn, Shirley Dex). The concerns of many of the participants are summed up by the following comments:

> *Most of the effects are appalling. It means a lot of people write a lot of things that are just not very good or not very necessary. Partly because they haven't had the time to think things through properly, there's a lot of haste ... And the general result is that there's too much writing. A lot of work is nothing more than re-inventing the wheel, the same ideas coming round repeatedly. What gets lost in the rush to publish is a sense of accumulation, building on other things, developing, and moving on. Most writing just stands on its own – 'I want to say this'– and too often the history of ideas, and concepts and analysis is ignored, in effect erased in the writing (Stephen Ball).*

Participants generally felt that academics were often placed under undue pressure by institutions to publish and as a result were not as creative in their writing as they could be or have the potential to be.

---

* The Research Assessment Exercise refers to the mechanism by which the UK government allocates funding for research to universities. The Exercise takes place every four to six years and requires that all universities submit a statement about research and publications. Subject panels of peers are appointed to evaluate the submissions and, on the basis of these judgements, differing levels of funding are awarded to the individual universities.

In the current (2008) Exercise, panels of specially appointed academic peers are making judgements on each submission in relation to the standard of publications, research environment and esteem factors. The criteria employed in making judgements are academic rigour, significance and originality.

The future of the RAE is being reviewed and may well lead to significant changes to ongoing UK government funding for research.

For more information see www.rae.ac.uk.

8

Writing, thinking and learning

In an earlier section we looked at the connections between reading and writing; here we examine what the experienced writers have to say about writing, thinking and learning. A number of views emerge about the act of writing and what is going on in the writers' heads as they write.

One participant sees her writing as an analytic process and can trace the development of her thinking across the different drafts of her work:

> *I'm the kind of person who discovers what I think by writing. Other people know what they think, and have a problem about getting it into words. For me, the process of writing is also an analytic process; it's a thinking process. So the first draft of something and the last draft of something, whatever it is, may not bear much relationship to one another (Ann Oakley).*

Another continues: 'the thinking comes through the writing. The writing, if it's serious writing, will provoke thinking' (Ron Barnett).

In another account one participant explained that writing forces him to test, construct and develop ideas, stories or accounts:

> *If I'm just sitting here, I can have a clever idea and I don't really have to test it. But when you're writing, you read it back and think, 'Really, I don't understand what I'm saying there' or 'That's incredibly banal', so it helps you to anchor, construct, develop an idea, a story, an account ... I see this really as a creative art form (Peter Moss).*

Others are more explicit about writing and learning. For example, one writer talks about a learning process, a process of 'trying to think better' (Stephen Ball). He continues:

> *If I was not learning new things, about the world, about myself, about*

theory, about the processes of writing, then perhaps I would stop writing. But I've never felt like that, I've always felt that there's more that I don't know than I do. The social world is still a mystery to me, theory still fascinates me … And I appreciate the opportunity to be able to rewrite things (Stephen Ball).

Others find writing exciting as they know they are going to learn through the process:

I feel very much that you should see writing as a learning process and, as far as I'm concerned, after 30-odd years, I still feel I'm learning, in the fuller sense. … The struggle and the feeling of vague excitement that there's something here, that I've got something new, that I'm wrestling with it and that it's somewhere in the back of my mind. And, then, I locate where it is and then I've got something to say (Shirley Dex).

Others describe how ideas come as they are constructing sentences. These need to be captured quickly as they may be lost:

And as I'm thinking about the verb, and the verb in relation to the noun, and the verb in relation to the subject, that's again opening up new lines of thought. And as I'm composing, I get two or three little rivers, riverlets, of thought running in my mind as I'm writing a sentence, and I kind of have to catch that very quickly, otherwise it will be gone (Ron Barnett).

And some of the writers have their own theories about the connection between writing and learning that they draw on. The act of writing is seen as transforming knowledge – writers are learning through writing:

What happens sometimes, at its best, is that as you write you realise that you are organising your thought in a way that is literally transforming it. So that your thinking goes up another whole level. That's really the best kind of writing. It all straightens out in your head as you write. And you realise that you're actually making new ideas for yourself, new theories and perhaps for others too. So I suppose that's the very deepest satisfaction (Jeni Riley).

In their interviews, participants referred to the work of Bereiter and Scardamalia to explain this process. Bereiter and Scardamalia (1987) suggest that skilled writers approach the act of writing as something which in itself enhances their knowledge and understanding. It is for this reason that they do not consider it any easier a task, since they are formulating more complex problems, advancing their knowledge still further, and so on, in a feedforward loop that generates better – but not easier – writing. Experienced writers construct effective texts by using many thoughtful processes, as well as the practical and organisational skills of getting the writing done. To illustrate this point, the same writer reports:

> *The way we think, our ideas and the kinds of ideas we're trying to express … start to change as we write and become more developed and more refined, so that the thinking changes a gear or two (Jeni Riley).*

By contrast, less skilful writers approach writing as a 'knowledge-telling process', in which knowledge is little influenced by its translation into text.

9

Learning from the writers

A primary aim of this research has been to help our organisation, the Institute of Education, and the individuals who work in it, to imagine a future that will be most effective in supporting academic writing and creating a collectively constructed vision to translate into best practices.

We collected and celebrated 18 stories of how academics approach their writing. We asked the participants about their best pieces of writing and we examined the unique conditions in which some of the best academic writing flourishes.

Through this stage of the research process we learned a number of things that informed the next stage of our task. We now summarise the main areas of our learning from the analysis of the interviews.

We have learned about what causes the 18 participants pain and pleasure in their writing, and about their passions and challenges. Writing is seen as a never-ending journey and it occupies a central role in the lives of the participants. As educationists, they are concerned about social justice and they desire to make a difference. We read of strong advocacy for the advancement of different subject areas and a wish to transform what happens in schools.

The 18 writers describe a developmental process – a journey, learning a craft and the need for toil and practice. In describing the hazards of passage there are poignant accounts of insecurity, low self-confidence and feelings of vulnerability. Some speak about how they were in awe of established writers initially and how they found it difficult to be confronted with their own work. Some describe how they had an inclination to use dense language to somehow 'prove' academic status, but that subsequently an important stage emerged when, with practice, they started to let go and think about what their writing communicates, rather than what it says about them. Their accounts suggest that they gradually spent more time analysing their own work and its power to communicate. We read of writers taking control of their writing – an important turning point that led to an increase in confidence. However, the writers still struggled to become heard as they faced the difficult hurdles of criticism, unhelpful feedback and rejection. But these writers did not give up. When they had difficulty in getting their work accepted, they toughened their resolve and tried to retain their confidence.

When these writers reached a point when they became known and acknowledged by a readership, they experienced a period of growing self-assurance which led to experimentation and risk-taking. As their journey continues, they have reached a lasting state of thinking about writing and learning from writing. This is described as a process of trying to think better. At this stage writing is seen as provisional and exploratory, available for review, amendment and new explanations.

The participants talk about the range of different experiences that were important in their development as writers, for example, the impact of their own studies, especially their PhD, and learning from other people and books as well as learning from editing (a process that encourages reassessment of one's own writing) and in translating others' writing. The most significant of these experiences seemed to be learning from their teachers and their mentors and the importance of oral and written feedback. Others speak about receiving observations about their writing from a diverse range of people and testing ideas with others in a variety of ways, for example, by presenting a paper or talking with students about their ideas. We were struck by their comments about collaborative writing, the reciprocity in the cooperative process and the learning benefits for partners with complementary skills.

We also learned about the importance writers place on reading – not just academic literature but novels and poetry – as a resource for writing as well as a source of inspiration. Good writing has the potential to leave its mark on the writers and in the accounts we noticed how writers make conscious and unconscious connections with other writing.

We were also struck by the way in which the writers talk about themselves as writers. Writing is part of the core that makes them who they are; they regard themselves as writers over and above, or alongside, any other role. Writing, for many of them, is about representing who they are and how they situate themselves in the world. The writers explain how their writing is strongly linked to the psychological effects it has on them. Some talk about its power to lift their spirits and how it has become an inextricable part of their lives.

We learned from the writers about important spaces that are favourable to their writing – both physical and psychological – as well as ambience. For example, a number of them report that their offices are not conducive to writing. Some, however, can write anywhere, and some learned to take any opportunity to write because of family and domestic responsibilities. New technology is creating new and different spaces.

The issue of time was raised in all the interviews. They writers talk about how writing involved spending long hours alone as well as how those hours needed to be protected. The latter point was linked to their professional lives and how some were free to decide on their own timetable (although this freedom did not necessarily extend to women with young children). Two of the women talked about the necessity of combining writing with caring for young children and writing on the move.

We were fascinated by the way in which the participants set about the task of writing. We discerned a preference for different approaches, for example, systematic approaches, working with a plan or structure, to experimental, more organic approaches, setting off with an idea and then playing to let the writing emerge. Their very different ways of writing reinforce the idea that writers themselves have to discover what works for them.

In producing a text, writers are constantly thinking of their readers and considering language and style in relation to making meaning. One writer talks about a back-and-forth activity of alternatively surging ahead with one's own ideas and imagining what the reader will make of them. It is the idea of the reader relishing the work that distinguishes another account. The writers try to make an early decision about who their readers will be and use the language and style that will appeal. Some talk about building a relationship with a reader and developing a conversational style which, it is suggested, requires more effort and time. One writer talks about how this stage of writing – of crafting language to achieve the best way of expressing what she wants to convey to a particular readership – provides great pleasure.

The importance of preparing yourself to make a start on each new occasion was highlighted. Some writers talk about the need to be organised. Others talk about writing freely, deliberately seeing first attempts as provisional and either seeing writing as composed of the different tasks of creating, then editing or, for others, doing these tasks concurrently. Leaving time between creating and editing was identified as useful, so that the writer could approach the work more as a detached reader.

We were intrigued by the way in which writers talk about the emotions they encounter when producing a text: the highs, lows and satisfactions. The anticipation of starting a draft causes butterflies for one writer, while others have grown to feel comfortable with ideas swirling around in their minds. Others talk about losing sleep and how hard and lonely writing can be. Some also mention the unpredictability of the quantity and quality of text produced at different sittings. Sometimes ideas flow and expressing them comes easily and then there are times when the writers become stuck and spend a great deal of time constructing very little text. Mental anguish and self-inflicted torture is conveyed in many of the accounts.

The methods of writing and the effects on the text was another fascinating area. The use of different tools – pencil, pen, word processor – and the way these contributed to the movement of ideas to paper distinguished the writers. Some saw handwriting as superior, while others sang the praises of new technologies for different tasks: many writers see new technology as indispensable.

The writers raise a number of issues in relation to the politics of writing for publication. Some talk about how less experienced writers can attribute too much power to publishers. Other issues include the importance of place, and writing in English. There was some criticism of Anglocentric attitudes. However, the most talked-about issue in limiting possibilities was gender. The common experience was that writing and being published are easier for men.

One strong theme to emerge was that writing in higher education is becoming increasingly necessary and yet excessive workloads and other pressures are making academic life very difficult. One writer comments that overload stifles original thinking. Others suggest it was more difficult to get colleagues to read their writing as everyone is so busy. The majority of the participants mention the effects of the RAE. Most comment on its negative aspects.

Another area of interest was how writing, thinking and learning are linked. Some participants see their writing as an analytic process and are able to trace the development of their thinking across different drafts. A number of participants talk about how thinking comes through writing, or how it helps them to think better, and how the process of writing forces them to test, construct and develop ideas. Some writers have their own theories about the connections between writing and learning. Writing continues to be exciting for these very experienced and successful writers, as they know they are going to continue to learn through the writing process.

These writers' stories are an endless source of learning, inspiration and interpretation. As can be seen in the transcripts and analysis, we welcomed emotional responses as well as intellectual analysis, and there was room for imagination as well as creative thought. Our approach is based on constructionist principles that suggest social knowledge and community outcomes are interwoven; inquiry and change are not separate but occur together – inquiry is intervention.

9.1 Building on the findings

We are now building on the strengths and wisdom that exist in individual writers and in the Institute of Education. At this stage of our task, we are creating statements to inform our future work (see Table 1).

The statements are intended to stretch, challenge and interrupt thinking about academic writing, whilst being grounded in illustrations that present the ideal as a real possibility. They differ from recommendations in that they are intended to create dialogue among people in the organisation. The statements are generative and present images of ourselves and the organisation that will inspire action and innovation, new ways of seeing, thinking, acting and being.

Table 1 Some statements prompted by the research

- Appropriate opportunities and support are provided so that both beginners and the experienced can achieve or continue to achieve excellent writing.
- The organisation shares a common vision to create openness, rapport and dialogue about writing.
- A range of social opportunities are made available to talk and test out ideas.
- Writers support other writers at all levels of the organisation.
- Writers are seen as publishers' resources and experienced colleagues give advice to less experienced writers to help them understand and gain control over the publishing of their writing.
- The role of the publisher is to disseminate and develop the author's writing.
- Writers do not feel isolated because they have the opportunity to belong to supportive writing groups.
- Institutions provide all staff with the opportunity to enhance their writing.
- Career structures and incentives in relation to writing and publication are transparent.
- The organisation demonstrates that it values a range of writing beyond what is required for the RAE.
- Writers are given adequate time and support, including financial, to foster their writing and there is unlimited access to continual professional learning support, including individual and group mentoring.

We will take the research process further by building on the successful mentor writing scheme that inspired this publication. We have learned from this study that successful writing is embedded in the daily lives of academics and must be sustained so that new and experienced writers are supported in changes to their practices.

Following other theorists (for example, see Webb, 1996, cited in Grant, 2006) we think that more support systems need to be set up so that writers can learn from each other through ongoing conversations and by developing further networks and communities of writers. These would provide intellectual as well as emotional support. As so many of our participants indicated, we need to support writers in trying to avoid the solitariness of individual writing, with all its pitfalls.

The retreat that Ann Oakley describes in her interview and those reported elsewhere (Grant, 2006; Grant and Knowles, 2000) suggest a learning process that needs to be ongoing, cumulative and interrupts the dominant culture of writing in isolation: 'They fly in the face of the "quick fix" culture that pervades institutional views of academic and professional development' (Grant, 2006: 485).

While some established writers suggest that retreats may not work for them, as familiar places and spaces are important for their writing, we would like to suggest residential retreats for less experienced writers. This could become part of a staff development offer to provide continued writing support, facilitated by the women and men in this study and others. The residential experience would allow for more creative approaches. For example, we like the idea expressed here:

> … *imagining may be understood to be a socially constructed capacity to be, a form of subjectivity which hails us and offers us a way to act. To be able to imagine ourselves as a writer (in our mind's eye), and to find pleasure in and attachment to being this writer, is crucial to 'be(com)ing' a writer (Grant and Knowles, 2000: 8).*

Many of the writers in our study expressed periods of insecurity: to be able to imagine yourself as an experienced and successful writer may be one way of overcoming insecurity and anxiety.

We would like to see gender issues addressed. There is clear evidence that, within the academy, women as a group occupy a broadly second-class position (Grant, 2006). Some surveys have shown that women academics, except for those few who are in senior positions, do not appear to write as much as men, particularly in the more prestigious forms: books, book chapters and articles in internationally refereed journals (Brooks, 1997; Lie and O'Leary, 1990; Wilson, 1986, cited in Grant and Knowles, 2000). Grant and Knowles suggest that because of the way in which academic publishing is counted, it is difficult to know whether women, on the whole, do not literally write as much as men. For example, there is research indicating that even when women do write as much, widely used peer-review systems are nepotistic, favouring men over equally productive women (Wenneras and Wold, 1997, cited in Grant and Knowles, 2000). In addition, the political economies of grant funding and academic publishing marginalise not only their preferred disciplines but also some of the kinds of research and writing that women do more frequently (Kim, Ricks and Fuller, 1996, cited in Grant and Knowles, 2000). 'If, overall, women do indeed write as much as men, only to have their work refused or unrecognised, it is unsurprising that many experience ambivalence about and resistance to writing' (Grant and Knowles, 2000: 7).

The academic culture is described here and elsewhere as competitive and individualistic and it appears that organisational practices are not becoming any less 'masculinised' (Skelton, 2005). Participants in this study, like those in Skelton's research, suggest that to access, survive and progress in universities, both women and men have to negotiate gendered expectations embedded in their cultures.

9.2 Reflections on the analyses

The section above relates to a primary aim of our study in that it refers to the organisational implications. Another aim was to offer perspectives and suggestions that might be useful to both beginner and experienced researchers. In seeking to meet that aim we now return to the theoretical perspectives and categorisations we outlined in Section 1.2 (under Collecting the writers' stories). We wished to develop their 'illuminative potential' (see Introduction), their significance and value as analytical tools, by putting them to further work in a review of our analyses.

In Section 1.2 we focused on writing as a situated activity – an activity-in-context – in which 'place' and 'space' are both actual and symbolic, i.e. laden with meanings and values. This interpretation of 'place' and 'space' reflects the increasing deployment of geographical concepts and metaphors in attempts to capture the sociocultural complexities of academic writing (see, for example, Thesen and van Pletzen's edited collection, 2006). Reviewing our analyses we now saw further potential in 'place' and 'space' as analytical categories: they enabled us to perceive in the writers' responses the numerous 'spaces' that carry particular meanings and values that are both socially and individually shaped: curricular and disciplinary spaces (e.g. psychology; sociology); spaces of collegiality (e.g collaborative writing); the spaces where people write (seldom in their offices; often in their heads); the page or computer screen or time as a writing space. Careers as time-space journeys, and place and space in relation to the politics of writing (see Section 7) were also discerned in the writers' responses. This opens the way to further work on our data (see 9.3).

Continuing to use 'space' as a lens that augmented our analyses, we noted spaces of particular relevance to the distinctiveness of the writers' responses: namely, the social categories, the identities, out of which the writers speak and write (Blommaert, 2005). We heard them speak not only as writers, but also, for example, as teachers who are learners, as subject specialists and, emphatically, as educationists or social scientists who, in their different ways, wish to 'make a difference out there' (Section 2.1). Some also speak on occasion as women (Section 4.1). We noted as well the fleeting identities, the momentary speaking positions, expressed in the writer-interviewer interactions through, for example, reformulations, shifts of tone or metaphor, and nuances of feeling (Rampton, 2005).

In planning the study we ascribed the identity 'much published academic' to the participants, an identity that has a 'real world validity'– the participants' voices are 'heard' (Hymes, 1996) in the academy where they represent authority. What we sought to uncover in our analyses was whether writing is also at the centre of an identity that the participants inhabit from choice and desire. What we found is that it definitely is. Gunther Kress expresses this widely held certainty in the following words in which he summarises his ideal view of himself as a socially concerned individual using writing to act in the world:

Writing is about a means of saying who you are, and locating yourself in the world, and representing yourself in the world … So my way of representing myself in the world has been through writing. So that it's been an essential part of me.

We acknowledge that our reading of the transcripts was influenced by our own histories and, like those we interviewed, by the disciplinary spaces we occupy. We recognise that for some writers who occupy different places and spaces (e.g. the 'hard' sciences), writing may be seen as simply a matter of getting the job done. However, we hope that the transcripts and analyses will encourage some readers, both in and outside education and the social sciences, to find the passion that can stimulate and inform writing in any field.

9.3 Future research

We begin this section by briefly situating our study in relation to other work in the field.

Published academic texts have been the subject of numerous studies (e.g. Hyland, 2000; Myers, 1991; Tadros, 1993), but writing for publication has been a comparatively neglected field of inquiry until recently. Not surprisingly, most of the existing studies are from the US where the teaching of writing and the formal encouragement of writing for publication occupies a long-established, and so far more central, space in US universities than it does as yet in the UK. However, selecting studies that bear some similarity to ours, we noted that they all seek, like ours, to bring about changes that look beyond the production of publishable academic texts to larger social concerns. Inevitably different national, institutional and disciplinary contexts, and the different positions the writers occupy in the university, lead to differences in the nature and degree of emphasis that is placed on challenging existing conceptions of writing in the cause of wider social change. In the US a primary emphasis tends to be on research that can lead to improved pedagogy on writing courses, with the writer's success as its goal. For example, Thaiss and Zawacki (2006), teacher-researchers who teach across disciplines, call for alternative discourses in the academy in research that challenges the perceived fixity of disciplinary boundaries. Jonathan Monroe, a director of a writing programme, has produced an edited collection (2002), in which very well known academics similarly argue that disciplines at the highest levels of scholarship and research are not as unchanging as is often assumed. The first-person essays in Casanave and Vandrick's (2003) interesting edited collection range more widely and touch on some of the issues raised in this book (e.g. power and position; identity and voice) as the contributors each describe an issue highlighted for them by their own experience of writing for publication. The editors and contributors are primarily concerned with English language education. This, together with the US university context, leads to differences from our study in the theoretical concepts the editors find most salient (e.g. 'legitimate peripheral participation' and membership of 'academic communities of practice').

Casanave and Vandrick's (2003) focus on English language education is also reflected in their emphasis on the growing importance to academics' standing and careers of publishing in English – a theme that occurs in a number of other publications, too, both in and outside the US (e.g. Canagarajah, 1996, 2003; Flowerdew, 2000; Lillis and Curry, 2004, 2006; Tardy, 2004). The point often made is that the 'periphery', in contrast to the 'centre' (i.e. mainly the US and the UK), may lack English language and material resources. However, Canagarajah (2002) directly addresses the politics of writing for publication in English by challenging an emphasis on uncritically meeting the centre's norms. This is a perspective which is touched upon in our study (Section 7.2) and deserves to inform future research.

Taking our cue from that last sentence, we next consider our transcripts as a source of topics for further research before making specific suggestions based on what we could not investigate within the constraints of a small-scale study.

The transcripts and recordings are a rich source of data that could provide material for further analysis from different perspectives, including a multimodal consideration of tones of voice, facial expressions, gestures (recorded in field notes). In addition the thematic headings we chose to organise our text can carve out spaces for innumerable further studies in different locations and across disciplines, institutions and countries. To give just three examples: published writers' discourses about language and style are relatively unresearched; so are the metaphors writers use to describe writing, and the institutional politics around writing for publication. The significance of 'place' and 'space' as metaphor-concepts could also be further explored. However, to conclude our study, we offer below suggestions for future projects that look beyond our data.

Talk about texts

We asked the writers we interviewed to talk about which of their own publications they liked best and which least, but we did not study the actual texts that they mentioned. A further study could focus on the texts selected by published writers. The texts might be discussed not only with the writers, but also with readers, including research students working in the same field.

From early thoughts to published text

Another study could involve tracing the journey of a paper: the responses to it and changes made, as the paper progresses from an initial idea and develops, through drafts and advice, submission to a journal, and readings by publishers' reviewers and editors, into a published journal article. If the journey involved a book and not a paper, the inquiry might also include reviews of the book and the writer's response to the reviews. The process involved in writing for e-journals or the web is a similar area of research waiting to be investigated.

Published writers as teachers

Taking our cue from the Americans Thaiss and Zawacki (2006), but extending their remit, we suggest a study that focuses on how perceptions of different audiences (including students) inform the ways in which the much-published writers in our study talk about or, in some cases, write about writing for publication. Such a study could be extended to involve other published academics, including those in different institutional, disciplinary or national spaces.

The perspectives of inexperienced/beginner writers-for-publication

We concentrated on much-published academics. But what of beginner/inexperienced writers (including research students and postdoctoral fellows)? Research that treated them as voices to be heard (Hymes, 1996) would be a major contribution to research in its integration with teaching. The mentor scheme would facilitate the researching of these voices.

Small or occluded genres

Small genres (Blommaert, section 7.2) or occluded genres (Swales, 1996) are kinds of writing that are linked to publication but operate behind the scenes. Examples include reviews of published books and of papers submitted to journals, articles about one's research for 'popular' journals or for TV. Blommaert (section 7.2) mentions these small genres and, in linking his comments to the possibilities – or constraints – of different national places, he opens up new directions for research, both nationally and internationally.

The editing and reviewing process

We suggest a detailed study of the editing process, which would include all the documentation (notes, memos, doodles, etc.) made by editors and reviewers of a submitted article for different purposes and audiences (including themselves); the discussions that take place around the article with different audiences; and the final report.

Socio-political autobiographies

What we have in mind is a study similar to ours, but with a much less structured schedule so that the 'story' of each person is allowed to emerge through an autobiographical 'sharing' (Heidi Safia Mirza, in correspondence with the authors). Such a study would be based on an appreciation of the different histories of the writers and the potential influences on their writing of their backgrounds in terms of race, gender and class. Prospective readers could be inspired as writers and/or as teachers of writing.

To conclude: 'globalisation' and 'internationalisation' are beginning to be more than generators of fine rhetoric. Our own institution, like many in the UK (and many, increasingly, in the US), is anxious to enable its academics' and students' voices to be heard as different and valuable in their difference. To borrow and adapt Fox's (1994) phrase, universities and publishers are beginning to substitute 'listening to the world' for colonialist discourses that emphasise certainty instead of dialogue across differences. This returns us finally to a central concern that the participants in this study express so loudly: a concern with addressing inequities and promoting social justice institutionally, nationally and internationally. It is that concern that we would like to see at the centre of research and organisational initiatives.

References

Ahearne, J. (1995) *Michel de Certeau: Interpretation and its Other.* Cambridge and Malden, MA: Polity Press.

Barthes, Roland (1974) *S/Z.* London: Jonathan Cape.

- (1976) *The Pleasure of the Text.* London: Jonathan Cape.

Bereiter, C. and Scardamalia, M. (1987) *The Psychology of Written Composition.* Hillsdale, NJ: Lawrence Erlbaum.

Blommaert, J. (2005) *Discourse.* Cambridge: Cambridge University Press.

Brooks, A. (1997) *Academic Women.* Buckingham: Society for Research into Higher Education.

Canagarajah, A.S. (1996) '"Nondiscursive" requirements in academic publishing; material resources of periphery scholars and the politics of knowledge production'. *Written Communication*, 13 (4), 435-472.

- (2002) *A Geopolitics of Academic Writing.* Pittsburg, PA: University of Pittsburgh Press.

- (2003) 'A somewhat legitimate and very peripheral participation'. In C. Casanave and S. Vandrick (eds) *Writing for Scholarly Publication: Behind the scenes in language education.* Mahwah, New Jersey and London: Lawrence Erlbaum Associates.

Casanave, C. and Vandrick, S. (2003) (eds) *Writing for Scholarly Publication: Behind the scenes in language education.* Mahwah, New Jersey and London: Lawrence Erlbaum Associates.

Certeau, Michel de (1984) 'Walking in the city'. In S. Rendall (trans.) *The Practice of Everyday Life.* Berkeley, Los Angeles; London: University of California Press.

Flowerdew, J. (2000) 'Discourse community, legitimate peripheral participation, and the nonnative-English-speaking scholar'. *TESOL Quarterly*, 34 (1), 127–150.

Fox, H. (1994) *Listening to the World: Cultural issues in academic writing.* Urbana, Il: NCTE.

Gee, J. (1996) *Social Linguistics and Literacies: Ideology in discourse (second edition).* London: Falmer Press.

Glaser, B.G. and Strauss, A.L. (1967) *The Discovery of Grounded Theory: Strategies for qualitative research.* Chicago: Aldine.

Grant, B.M. (2006) 'Writing in the company of other women: exceeding the boundaries'. *Studies in Higher Education*, 31 (4), 483-495.

Grant, B.M. and Knowles, S. (2000) 'Flights of imagination: academic women be(com)ing writers'. *The International Journal for Academic Development*, 5 (1), 6-19.

Hyland, K. (2000) *Disciplinary Discourses: Social interactions in academic writing.* Harlow, Essex: Pearson Education.

Hymes, D. (1996) *Ethnography, Linguistics and Narrative Inequality: Toward an understanding of voice.* London: Taylor & Francis.

Kanuka, H. and Anderson, T. (1999) 'Using constructivism in technology-mediated learning: constructing order out of the chaos in the literature'. *Radical Pedagogy*, 1:2. http://radicicalpedagogy.icapp.org/content/vol1.1999/issue2/02kanukal_2.html Date accessed 27 January 2007.

Kress, G. (1989) *Linguistic Processes in Sociocultural Practices.* Oxford: Oxford University Press.

Lie, S.S. and O'Leary, V.E. (eds) (1990) *Storming the Tower: Women in the academic world.* London: Kogan Page.

Lillis, T. and Curry, M.J. (2004) 'The imperative to publish in English: Negotiating interests, demands and rewards'. *TESOL Quarterly*, 38 (4), 663-688.

- (2006) 'Professional academic writing by multilingual scholars: Interactions with literacy brokers in the production of English-medium texts'. *Written Communication*, 23 (1), 3–35.

Monroe, J. (2002) *Writing, Revising the Disciplines.* Cornell: Cornell University Press.

Murray, R. (2005) *Writing for Academic Journals.* Maidenhead, Berkshire: Open University Press.

Myers, G. (1991) 'Lexical cohesion and specialised knowledge in science and popular science texts'. *Discourse Processes*, 14 (1), 1–26.

Rampton, B. (2005) *Crossing: Language and Ethnicity Among Adolescents (second edition).* Manchester: St Jerome Press.

Scott, D., Brown, A., Lunt, I. and Thorn, L. (2004) *Professional Doctorates: Integrating professional and academic knowledge.* Berkshire: SRHE and Open University Press.

Skelton, C. (2005) 'The "individualised" (woman) in the academy: Ulrich Beck, gender and power'. *Gender and Education*, 17, 319-332.

Street, B. (1985) *Literacy in Theory and Practice.* Cambridge: Cambridge University Press.

- (2003) 'What's new in new literacy studies?'. *Current Issues in Comparative Education*, 5 (20), 1–14.

Strauss, A.L. and Corbin, J.M. (1997) *Grounded Theory in Practice.* Thousand Oaks, CA: Sage.

Swales, J. (1996) 'Occluded genres in the academy: the case of the submission letter'. In E. Ventola and A. Mauranen (eds) *Academic Writing: Intercultural and textual issues.* Amsterdam: John Benjamins.

Tadros, A. (1993) 'The pragmatics of text averral and attribution in academic texts'. In M. Hoey (ed.) *Data, Description, Discourse.* London: HarperCollins.

Tardy, C. (2004) 'The role of English in scientific communication: Lingua franca or Tyrannosaurus rex?'. *Journal of English for Academic Purposes*, 3, 247–269.

Thaiss, C. and Zawacki, T.M. (2006) *Engaged Writers, Dynamic Disciplines: Research on the academic writing life.* Portsmouth, NH: Boynton/Cook; Heinemann.

Thesen, L. and van Pletzen, E. (2006) (eds) *Academic Literacy and the Languages of Change.* London and New York: Continuum.

Turner, V. (1974) *Dramas, Fields and Metaphors: Symbolic action in human society.* New York: Cornell University Press.

Part 2
Transcripts of the interviews

Stephen Ball

I: Can I ask you just to start by saying something about how long you have been at the Institute, and what you do here?

SB: I came to the Institute in 2001, to take the position of the Karl Mannheim Professor of Sociology of Education. In addition, I was Director of the Educational Policy Research Unit.

I: As the Karl Mannheim Professor, what does that mean exactly, are there any particular responsibilities that come with that title?

SB: Not specifically. Apart from leadership in the field of sociology in education. So, in my School we have a sociology section. And on occasions, I have tried to mobilise other sociologists in the Institute – to speak together as sociologists. I've had many research students, and I've taught on the MA in Sociology in Education.

I hold an ESRC Research Fellowship. So, what that means is that for three years the ESRC pay my salary. I am still employed by the Institute, but the ESRC pay my salary, which buys me out of all of my teaching and administrative responsibilities, which then allows me to concentrate on my research and writing. I have a research agenda, which I'm working on.

I: Can you tell me about the best piece of writing you've done, or the one that you feel most pleased with?

SB: Given that I've written so much – I'm a compulsive writer; I write too much – that's a very difficult question to answer. So, there were two possibilities. One is a book *Class Strategies in the Educational Market* (2003). The other is a Scottish Educational Research Association lecture, which was published in their journal (2005).

I: We'll look at both, but let's start with Class Strategies in the Educational Market.

SB: I'm pleased with that for a variety of reasons. One is that it draws on four different ESRC research projects that I was involved in through the Nineties and beyond. It pulls together a set of issues involved in the achievement of class advantage, looking particularly at middle-class families. Social class has been a main preoccupation throughout my career, from when I first got involved in sociology as an undergraduate. My undergraduate tutor was Dennis Marsden, who wrote a very important book called *Education and the Working Class* (Jackson and Marsden, 1962). That book was a revelation to me when I read it at university: it was about me, it was like reading about my own schooling. And it brought sociology alive, relating it to my own experience, and articulating the experience of working-class families. I was trying to do a similar thing with this book, which is about the lives of middle-class families and their struggles for social advantage for their children. And the basis of that: in their anxieties and concerns about the future of their children in the current context of politics and economics, the labour market, etc.

In recent years, I've experimented with my writing to some extent, and there's some degree of experiment in the writing of the book. I've tried to write in a way that ensured it was lively and it uses a language which, although it draws from sociological theory, was equally as vital as the lives I was trying to represent. It doesn't mean I necessarily succeeded, but I enjoyed the attempt to do that.

I: And you mentioned the lecture.

SB: Yes. The lecture is slightly different. The lecture is about teachers and the way in which policy is changing teachers' lives and practice. And I was arguing that it's making them inauthentic, that policy requires teachers to be responsive and flexible, rather than to be thoughtful. And I argue in the lecture that

being professional fundamentally rests on having a reflective relationship between principles and practice, that practice is subjected to the interrogation of principle. And I suggest that policy is destroying that relationship, making constructive reflexivity increasingly difficult for teachers, with the result that practice is experienced as inauthentic and the self of the teacher is diminished.

One of the other things in my writing in recent years is that I've tended to rewrite things a lot, developing, adding, extemporising, elaborating. The lecture, and the journal article based on it, were about the fifth version of the 'inauthenticity' argument. I was initially pleased with the first version but then became dissatisfied with it, and with the subsequent versions, or at least I want to extend and refine the arguments and the analysis. And I appreciate the opportunity to be able to rewrite things. Indeed I've come to view all of my writing as tentative. I increasingly try to avoid closure and to recognise the limitations of my arguments, although that is not always easy to convey within texts or read as it is intended. But it leaves open the possibility of rewriting, revisiting, moving on. Although that rather goes against the discursive norms of social science.

I: That's interesting, the notion that even with your wealth of experience as a writer there's always room for improvement, hence the revisiting and reworking.

SB: Absolutely, although I see two categories of rewriting. On the one hand, there will be those pieces which I rewrite because I see the possibility of further development, and it's not that the first version is bad, it's not that I'm displeased with it in terms of its quality, perhaps I'm displeased with it in terms of the extent to which I've been able to develop the argument. But, on the other hand, I do have things that I've written that I am simply displeased with as pieces of writing. Things I could not get right within the limitations of their production – like deadlines. For example, a paper published this year in the journal *Forum*, which as soon as it came out, I thought just wasn't very good. I am still very capable of bad writing.

I think the arguments are simplistic. They're easy arguments, too glib. They're not well thought out, they're superficial. They make a number of fairly easy points. Several people have read it and said they liked it. I think they liked it because it confirms prejudices. And that's a sort of writing that I have been trying to move away from. I've tried to strive more to escape from taking up obvious positions or deploying gross generalisations. Rather I have sought to make the obvious strange, to distance myself and hopefully my reader from taken-for-granted positions and arguments. The article is also clumsily structured.

I felt it hadn't engaged with the complexity of the issues that I was trying to address. One of the other things, generally, that I've struggled with in my writing, and perhaps it's something about ageing, is that increasingly the social world seems to me to be more and more complex, and I'm trying to grapple with and represent that complexity. Almost any single or parsimonious argument or single position about the social world is bound to be wrong, or at least incredibly partial. Two arguments, two theories, coherently presented and related, are usually better than one. And I'm not talking about a kind of 'on one hand/on the other hand' formulation. Rather what I mean is that the 'social' is complexly constituted through structures, discourses and interactions. We need accounts of the social and analytic tools which enable us to grasp the work of those different constituents. And that may mean dealing in paradoxes as well as recognising the partiality or limitations of our accounts. But this also means accepting that our interpretations are just that – interpretations. We can hopefully work with criteria which allow us to decide that some interpretations are better than others, but accounts which claim to be definitive always have to be viewed with suspicion.

I: Is part of your pleasure of writing to do with the engagement you have with your readers, having conversations with others and rethinking earlier ideas?

SB: Yes. The *Class* book, in particular, is situated in a very lively area of debate around class analysis and class theory. And it deliberately engages, in a fairly affirming way, with the work of a number of people who have been writing recently about class, people like Mike Savage, Diane Reay, Tim Butler and Rosemary Crompton. And I've been able to talk to them about it and get reactions from them. And it's pleasing to be able to be part of a community of

writing. Although I recognise that this also carries dangers of sliding into the comforts of orthodoxy.

The SERA paper's slightly different, although it does address a set of issues related to performativity that other people are interested in. I presented the paper initially at a conference and one of the things that I often get comments about, especially when I write about policy and about teachers, is that I'm very pessimistic. People say that when they come to my talks that they always think I'm going to be very depressing. A transgression of enlightenment norms about the relationship of knowledge to humanism and progress. And in that paper I started out by accepting that this was going to be grim and desperate stuff, but that's the way it is, and that's how I'm going to deal with it. So, it was almost an engagement, an anticipation by the audience that those were going to be the terms of engagement.

Perversely, they responded very positively. A lot of feedback in academic life … it's very formal, people write reviews of books or there are formal ways of commenting on other people's work, people write critiques, etc. Which is fine, and can be pleasing. But sometimes it's the small things that actually give you more pleasure. I gave an earlier version of the Scottish paper to a mixed group, which involved teachers as well as academics, and a teacher came up to me afterwards, she was in her late forties I guess, and she said, 'I've recently left the teaching profession, and I want to thank you for your paper because I now know why I left.'

She thought it was very positive. She said that she didn't really understand why she was unhappy and why she had to leave teaching. And my paper allowed her to understand why she was unhappy and why she had to leave. So, she felt pleased about that, she could understand herself better and it provided her with a kind of closure. The paper provided her with tools for reflection – and that is exactly what I hope to achieve through my writing: to help people to think. Not to tell them how to think.

I: You mentioned that through your study of sociology you read something that resonated with your life. What brought you from there to here, that writing journey?

SB: It's quite a difficult question. I have never planned

my life, I never aimed for a life in academia. I almost didn't go to university, I got a place and then decided to go out to work, and so I started later. But I did decide ... I wanted to do an MA because I wanted to explore these issues around class and schooling. I wanted to look inside schools to see how class was played-out and class reproduction was achieved. But I certainly wasn't a good writer when I was an undergraduate, I don't think I was a good writer when I was a Masters student. I suppose most people would say in academia they learned to write when they did their PhD. And I think that was certainly true in my case, although I don't think my PhD is very well written either. When it was turned from a thesis to a book (*Beachside Comprehensive: A case-study of secondary schooling*, 1981), it was back in the days when you got real desk editing, I had to work hard on the writing for publication. I received a huge bundle of papers back from Cambridge University Press, with queries and questions, asking about sentences and structure, and the use of verbs, this sort of thing, and I learned a lot. And I think that was the first time I'd ever been made to think systematically about the way I wrote, rather than simply what I was writing. And it had quite an impact on me, and I think from that point on I was increasingly aware of the importance of how I wrote. And, in fact, as a result of that process with the book manuscript I changed the way I write. I increasingly became aware of the relationship between how you write and what you're trying to say.

I: So, are you saying the kind of editing support that you received from Cambridge University Press doesn't exist today?

SB: Well, certainly from most publishers these days it doesn't. They've cut back on the costs of production, and I haven't come across any kind of real editing for a long time. You get basic copy editing. But I've just had a book come out this month, and I think that in the production process they asked about three sentences in the whole book. So, yes, that's no longer available.

For many students the process of PhD writing is their apprenticeship in writing. And as a supervisor I try to respond to my students' writing as part of my engagement with their work. With some students it's not necessarily always wise to do that, if they're

having other kinds of problems with their work. But if they are beginning to develop and manage their work effectively, then I will also respond to how they write, and I try to get them to think about how they write and their role in the writing, their role in the text. They often take up, as I did myself, positions about writing, which they've never really thought about. A lot of students are still very wedded to the third person, for instance. And I think in the social sciences, the third person is inappropriate. Because social science is an interpretive science. And that means the author, the writer, is active in constructing their account of the world. So to take yourself out of that stylistically, by talking about 'the author' or 'we' or just avoiding any first person usage is, I think, both a conceit and a deceit. Because what you're saying, implicitly or explicitly, is there was no human hand or human mind at work here, this is simply some kind of mirror reflection of a reality that's out there, and you as reader are being told how it is. And I think in the social sciences that's untenable.

I: Because I think that is a difficulty for most people coming into academia, particularly if they're coming from the classroom, and suddenly having to write in a particular genre – where do they start? Whom do they turn to? And, I suppose, there is a limit to the number of times you can ask a particular person to look at a piece of work, without feeling that you're imposing.

SB: It's difficult, and that is getting more difficult I think, because the pressures on academics' time are increasing. We spend more and more time on things that are nothing to do with being an academic, but to do with the RAE or the latest restructuring or whatever it happens to be. It is more difficult to find people to read your work – whoever you are. And overall, students are ... not necessarily good at helping one another in their writing. But I think they should, and they should try harder. And in some ways, you need to work hard to recruit people to read your work. Because it's a problem. I'm in the latter stages of writing a book now, and I'm trying to get people to read chapters. And it's the same problem, because they're very pressured, but you can build up a kind of relationship – you read my stuff and I'll read yours. And you get different kinds of comments from different kinds of people, even if they are not expert in the subject, they can comment on the writing or the clarity or the structure. The more comments, the better. You don't have to respond to everything, but all of this makes you think about your writing and about your readers' reception of it.

I: You mentioned the RAE; what do you think about the RAE and writing?

SB: Well, I'm not a good test case, partly because I'm a writaholic. So I could have stopped writing two years ago and still had enough stuff for the next RAE. So, in one sense it doesn't matter to me, I just get on with what I want to do, but as the editor of a journal, I think, on the whole, most of the effects are appalling. It means a lot of people write a lot of things that are just not very good or not very necessary. Partly because they haven't had the time to think things through properly, there's a lot of haste. More and more, people are emailing and saying, 'Can you tell me when my paper's coming out?' or 'Before I send a paper can you tell me how long your turnaround time is?' Which is also a pain as a journal editor, because you don't really want to be fielding that sort of stuff. But the RAE puts people under pressure. I'm sure there are a few cases where it animates people who would otherwise be happy to be moribund, but in the vast majority of cases, I think the impact is, on the whole, a negative one. And the general result is that there's too much writing. A lot of work is nothing more than re-inventing the wheel, the same ideas coming round repeatedly. What gets lost in the rush to publish is a sense of accumulation, building on other things, developing and moving on. Most writing just stands on its own – 'I want to say this' – and too often the history of ideas, and concepts and analysis is ignored, in effect erased in the writing.

I: If you weren't in academia, would you still write?

SB: I don't know. Probably I'd still write because I can't stop. I've toyed a couple of times with the idea of writing a novel, and a lot of academics try that. But actually I find it quite difficult to switch out of the social science mode of writing, to a novel style. I did write half a novel, many years ago, a detective story, where a sociologist was solving the crimes, very unoriginal. But, yes, I probably would find some

outlet for writing. I'd like to write more for newspapers.

I: What's helped you with your writing? What's helped you choose the themes, and decide this is what I'm going to write?

SB: I suppose at one level it's the classic sociological position of critique. And responding to the problems of the world, things you see to be unfair and unjust, and wanting to address them, to understand and explain them, and use that as a basis for achieving some sort of change. One of the writers who made me think about how I write is Michel Foucault. In one of his interviews he says the first task each day is to decide that which is the greatest danger. And in some senses, I think the sociology that I do is about seeing danger where others don't. Making rather than taking problems.

Foucault also saw his writing as very personal, that it was about responding to and addressing things that he saw as 'cracked'. And again, I think that's what almost always drives me to write. To fill in gaps, or to engage with things that people are not attending to properly. I want to say, 'Hey! Look at this, this is happening, we need to attend to this, we need to think about this, these are important things. This stuff is going on, and it's having effects, and we should be paying attention to it. This is cracked.' There are many more things that I'd like to say than I ever have time to write, I'm often frustrated that there isn't infinite time.

I: Is there a process that you follow when writing?

SB: I can't write here in my office. I tend to write almost all the time in my room-in-the-roof at home. I write best in the mornings, between nine and 12.30. Over many years I've got rid of most of my frittering, so I'm quite good at sitting down at nine o'clock and starting at one minute past.

In terms of process what I tend to do is to make lots of notes, I'm usually working with bodies of data, and then bodies of theory, so I read the theory and I read the data, and move between the two in an iterative and cumulative process. One informing the other. To improve and amend and adapt theory in relation to data, and to explore data using the tools of theory. So there comes a point from that, when I think I have a sense of what I'm going to write in a chapter or a paper or some headline ideas or themes, then I start to write. But I don't usually have a sense of what a whole book or paper will look like before I start. And I like to write drafts, so for each piece of writing I do I have a notebook, which I use for thoughts, reflections on data, comments, ideas and key quotations from literature, fragments of analysis and other writing, possibilities to explore. I go through the notes and I put together a very rough draft. So some bits would be written out, some bits would be notes, some bits would just be headings. But once I've got the whole thing mapped out then I print it out and will rework it, and then produce another draft, which is a much fuller draft, and that may involve moving things about, dropping things, bringing new things in, elaborating and refining. And then when I've got that, I usually go through it again and, given the time that's available, I will do that again and again until I'm at least temporarily satisfied with the outcome. So, I see writing as a continual reiteration process, drafting and redrafting, until a draft stands as finished, at least for the time being.

I: In the last 18 months with the ESRC grant, it freed you up to do more of what you want to do. How did you manage in the past to combine a busy work schedule and writing?

SB: By cutting out segments of time well in advance. Actually going through my diary and drawing in it with a highlighter, putting borders around days or mornings, and then rigorously keeping to that. Because if you don't write them in, if you're looking for spaces next week or even next month, you're probably too late. So, what I used to at the beginning of each term was to make sure there was some time every week to write. And it was partly a necessity for me because I was working as director or participant in funded research projects, and you have to deliver. You have to produce, if you want to get more research projects, you have to produce. So there's a level at which you have a commitment and an obligation to write. So it's discipline in terms of organising of time. You have to sit down and just organise your time, to ensure there are spaces for writing. To give it the priority it deserves.

I: Writing for publication: any tips for those new to writing?

SB: There's so many opportunities to publish now, as I've said, we've almost got to the stage where there's no excuse not to get published, because there are so many outlets. Although the world of publishing has changed in other ways, publishers, particularly in the social sciences and education, want things that are more practical these days, rather than research monographs, which is a shame. But in terms of journals, there are so many varieties of journals with little niches that you can almost guarantee to find some outlet for your work, however esoteric it might be. So one thing is to have a sense of what's out there. Look in the libraries, look at the journals, see what sort of things they're interested in. Look for matches with what it is you want to do and how it is that you write. But don't succumb completely to the suasions of convention. As a journal editor, one of the pleasing things I find is when you get a paper that's relevant to your journal, but is also actually different. Maybe different in terms of it's looking at areas that are not well-worn territory, but also different perhaps in style. Something that's not more of the same. So there's a kind of balance between finding where your stuff will be well received and, on the other hand, not delivering more of the same. Clearly, there are still a few very conservative referees around, and they won't tolerate any move away from convention, but they're a small minority, most people are quite open to something new, something fresh and something different. And all that means thinking about how you write. I think the problem is that most, even experienced, academics don't think about how they write, they just do it.

I: Is it confidence that we're talking about here? You know, getting to that point where you feel that you can take a risk?

SB: Yes, you're absolutely right, it is about confidence, about being in control of your writing, rather than it controlling you. Which, I appreciate, for a young, newly fledged academic or PhD student is a big challenge. But at least if you start thinking about those things from the beginning, as you build up confidence it gives you more opportunities to write differently or write better, to make your case more effectively. And PhD writing is getting more experimental in some fields and disciplines. In the United States in education research, there's now a lot of very, very interesting PhD writing. We're a little more conservative here in the UK, but I think there is still room for experiment in PhD presentation. There is one I'm reading now as an external examiner, which is a very personal piece of writing, but at the same time very theoretical. Which is very engaging and very sophisticated. When PhDs come thudding through the letterbox, you think, 'Oh my god, it's huge, is it going to be a good read, or have I got to grit my teeth, wade through it?' And it's so nice if the writing's interesting and you actually want to carry on rather than die. [*Laughs*]

I: *What does your writing say about you?*

SB: You probably have to ask somebody else about that. For a long time I would have said, not much. Because for a long time I think my writing was very traditional and it was like a lot of other writing, I could have been an academic clone, so you wouldn't necessarily have learned much about me as a person. More recently, I have tried to relate the way I write to the way I think about social science. So perhaps the way I write tells people something about at least me as a sociologist. That is an openness and tentativeness, leaving space for the possibility of other interpretations, and recognising the role of interpretation itself. That might tell people something. But I don't know if it reveals anything deep about my psyche.

I: *How would you like to be remembered in terms of your writing?*

SB: I would like to be remembered as having provided opportunities for at least some people to think differently about things, to think otherwise. I would be happy with that. Even if only a handful of people, like the teacher I mentioned, said, 'Now I understand.' If people say, 'Yeah, that's helpful, I can use that', then that makes me happy. I want people to do things with my writing.

I: *And you will continue to write because …?*

SB: I still feel I'm learning things. In one of my books, I borrowed a phrase from Goya. When he was 82, not long before he died, somebody asked him a similar question, why did he keep painting, he'd been painting for 60 years, and he said: 'I'm still learning.' And I feel the same way. If I was not learning new things, about the world, about myself, about theory, about the processes of writing, then perhaps I would stop writing. But I've never felt like that, I've always felt that there's more that I don't know than I do. The social world is still a mystery to me, theory still fascinates me, and so it's a learning process, a process of trying to think better.

I: *The fact that you've said there's still something to learn is refreshing to all writers out there. To know that even somebody who's a prolific writer still feels they can learn something.*

SB: But, it's also a sense of modesty, I think, in terms of what it is that you're able to say about the world. I need to do a lot more work to be able to say anything sensible. I'm involved in a process of developing strategic knowledge, just building up little bits at a time that may eventually illuminate or clarify social problems and contribute to change or to the sapping of power.

I: *Do you ever think, 'Gosh, I've come a long way, from where I thought I might be to where I am now?'*

SB: Well, I had no idea of the possibility of being where I am now, from where I started. One of the concepts that I used in the *Class* book is what I call 'imaginary futures'. Social actors in different class positions have access to different imaginary futures. And for working-class young people, while there's always the possibility that you become a doctor or a lawyer or a teacher, if none of your family are doctors, lawyers or teachers, or if they don't know any lawyers, doctors or teachers, it's very difficult to actually construct a realistic account of the path from where you are now to that imaginary future and to know what is necessary, how to overcome obstacles, who can help you, how you have to be to get on. You can't really join up between where you are now and where you want to end up. The distance between them is just a void. Whereas for many middle-class families, those sorts of positions are things that their parents, their friends, their relatives are familiar with, and they become part of the way they think and what they know. My imaginary future never involved becoming an academic and certainly not becoming a professor. It was all a process of making it up as I went along. And there are still moments when I feel, or am made to feel, that I am in the wrong place.

I: Did you have, say, a mentor, a significant other in your life?

SB: At certain points in time, yes. When I was an undergraduate, and other points in my career, there have been people who've been enormously supportive, who have made an important difference, in terms of social and cultural capital. But I suppose it's also a matter of getting to certain points, and then having to make a new set of decisions, rather than planning in the long term. I suppose I see my career as a lot of small, short-term segments, so I get to a certain point and then I have to make a decision about what I do next. So part of that has involved constant surprises – some bad, mostly good.

I: You're talked about class, but do you see gender, or any other factors, playing a part in one's success as a writer? When you're trying to juggle writing with your family, etc., it can be difficult. I'm thinking as well as class, is there also a gender thing, as to how one becomes more successful?

SB: Oh, absolutely, yes. And both in a research sense and in a personal sense, I have a stark awareness of that. In the research I've just finished we were looking at middle-class families choosing childcare: one of the things that almost all of the mothers talked about was having these equal relationships and equal partnerships and dual careers, until they had a child. And then suddenly they are responsible for childcare and the husband goes off to work. We couldn't find any of these supposed 'new men' who were involved in childcare. So the women's lives changed and, yes, the lives of academic women and writers are affected by the familial responsibilities which they are expected to take up. Which, for the most part, men do not have to deal with, and if they do, they are praised for it. So yes, men in academia have enormous advantages in the very practical sense of time and the expectations of family life being different for them, as well as all

the routine institutional sexism that goes along with that which women have to put up with and men do not.

When I was at university I became quite interested in how novelists wrote, and I read a series of interviews in *The Parisian Review* with people like Ernest Hemingway and Scott Fitzgerald and Evelyn Waugh, and they were asked about how they write. And I think that if you read about how other people write, then it makes you think about how you write, and I think that is one of the things I've been saying all through this interview: if you think about how you write, then you can take control of it. If you don't think about it, you haven't got control; it's controlling you. There's a column now in *Time Out* every week called 'How I write?' and the practical and psychological differences between writers are striking.

Ron Barnett

I: *Thank you for agreeing to be interviewed. First of all: how long have you been at the Institute and what are, and have been, your roles?*

RB: I've been at the Institute since September 1990, and my roles have been that of an academic, and having various management and leadership roles. So far as the academic side is concerned, I was course leader for an MA course, which we built up, the MA in Higher and Professional Education as we titled it. At one time it had over 70 people registered on it. And so far as my more management roles are concerned, I've been Dean of Professional Development, that's all our Masters courses across the Institute. I was Dean from roughly 1995 to 2001 or 2. And more recently I've taken on the role of Pro-

Director for Longer Term Strategy. So far as my academic work is concerned, I've primarily been a scholar and writer, my field being that of theoretical understanding of higher education, and there I've been trying to work out an educational theory of higher education. In addition, I've undertaken consultancy for most of the major higher education organisations in the UK.

I: *Thank you. I know you've published a great deal, and won awards. I don't know how this next question strikes you, but it is: tell me about the best piece of writing, or best pieces, you've done or tell me the pieces you've written that you've been most pleased with, and what pleased you about them?*

RB: The work that's probably given most pleasure is indeed my first major book, *The Idea of Higher Education* (1990). It grew out of a PhD that I took at the Institute of Education itself, so it had a long gestation period. Having done my PhD, I then put my PhD aside, and attempted to write a book based on it, and might say in actually writing my PhD I had in mind that I was riding two horses at once, that I was writing a PhD, but also writing the draft of a book manuscript. But it was quite clear as soon as I finished my PhD if I wanted to turn it into a book I had to write a completely separate text. I closed the PhD and set about that task afresh. What I was trying to do there was to do two things, which I've been continuing to do: trying to develop or set out the beginnings of an educational theory of higher education, which hadn't been attempted up till then, and there was very little in the way of theoretical literature on higher education. So I was really, frankly, if I can say so, breaking new ground. But also I wanted to write a book that would reach out to wide audiences, and not just be of interest to a small coterie of academics. In writing the book I had in mind the challenge: could I write a book or could I frame a text that would be of interest to, say, an engineer who'd never read a book on education in their lives? A few weeks after the book had been published I had a phone call at my desk – I remember it very well. One afternoon, the phone went, 'Is that Dr Barnett? You don't know me, but I'm the senior partner in an international firm of consulting engineers. Would you like to come and speak to our partners, please?'

I: Do you think consciously about the audience when you write?

RB: Absolutely. And this is a crucial part of the challenge of writing for me. In education, we're privileged but challenged, in that many people are interested in education, and in so far as higher education is concerned, there are all manner of groups – doubtless there are in other fields of education as well – but it is true of higher education. So one has the possibility, but also the challenge, of reaching out to multiple audiences, plural, as one is crafting a sentence, crafting a paragraph … Can one actually produce a text that will be of interest to leading edge academics around the world? And to be of interest at that level one has, of course, to have peer review mechanisms in mind these days. But also reach out to wider audiences: I'm trying to reach out to senior managers and leaders in universities, who either haven't had a chance of reading academic or educational works of any substance or haven't really got the time to do so, but I'm also trying to reach out to wider audiences as well. And it's a great delight to me to know my work is, in fact, being read by wide audiences around the world. And I do get news from time to time of senior people referring to my work on public platforms, in all sorts of organisations all round the world. But I'm also trying to write texts that offer resources for work, and it pleases me too that I see evidence that people are not just reading my work with pleasure, but also picking up and running with it and trying to see what cash value they might find in the ideas for practical development.

I: So how has audience affected your style? Was the PhD style very different from the style you've developed now? Or if you were writing philosophy papers now, would you use a particular choice of language, or structuring, a way of explaining concepts that a lay audience wouldn't also know?

RB: Well, these are crucial matters, and complex matters, and quite difficult for a writer to, I think, articulate. However, I am quite keen on writing, I have reflected on all of this to some degree. But I haven't read the literature on writing, so this is all very amateurish by way of self-reflection. What I will say is that, as I say, I deliberately think about audience as I'm writing. I will have in mind, and I know one or two other writers have this technique as well, of myself actually speaking to three or four different kinds of people … and it's as if … and I talk to my students in my way, when they're trying to write for audiences, it's as if one's sitting down in a bar or café, with three or four different kinds of people, representing different kinds of interest and backgrounds, and one's just talking to them. So the moment of writing approaches that – begins to approach that – of the spoken word. It's more direct, it's more straightforward. People say of my work that it's quite complex, it's quite theoretical, and it's packed with references. Somebody wrote a book review once of one of my books, in the *Times Educational Supplement*, said it was terribly scholarly, it was packed with references. He sent me the draft, and I said, 'Peter, whatever criticisms you might make of my work, you can hardly say that. I invite you to open any of my books at random, and you can't help but be struck by the fact that there are hardly any other references to any other author.' So there's a paradox here that my work gives the appearance of being heavily scholarly in a formal sense, without it actually being covered in lots of references. I'm trying to write straightforward texts – they're clearly not straightforward, given some of the responses I'm getting from some people. But nevertheless, that's what I'm trying to do, I'm trying to speak in a direct way, talk in a direct way, so those are the verbs I would use, 'speaking' and 'talking', in relation to my writing, and I'm speaking to particular kinds of audiences, particular kinds of persons, who are sitting there in that café or bar, having a drink with me. So the style is much more direct. This means the sentences are relatively short, and even though people say I have very long words and, of course, I make up quite a lot of new words – even have a glossary or two in some of my books – nevertheless, the average length of my words is quite short. The average length of my words is five characters. And the average length of my sentences is just over one line of A4 script. So I'm using short sentences, short words; wherever I can I use a straightforward, accessible English word. I'm also keen to exploit the English language, we're talking about education here, and I will deliberately draw on the full extent of my English vocabulary. And I will both use straightforward, almost colloquial words, and I will use the broadest range of my vocabulary in order to bring colour and life into my text, so that it is lively, it is accessible and it is clear. And clarity is also another important consideration to me, which I can talk about.

I: That's fascinating, Ron. Well, the next question on the sheet is: what piece of writing that you have done are you least pleased with?

RB: I don't know that there's a piece of work that I can easily say I'm particularly unhappy with. Writing is important to me, and I try to come to each writing task afresh. You won't see long lists of references to Ron Barnett's work in Ron Barnett's bibliographies. That kind of style just drives me up the wall. Many of my books have no references whatsoever to my work. So I'm trying to come at each work afresh and trying to say new things each time I write and trying to make it interesting to myself. If I'm reproducing even work I myself have produced, it's not terribly interesting for me, I get bored, so the reader's going to get bored.

I: And other kinds of writing, book reviews and such things, do you do that as part of your role, do you like doing it?

RB: Well, I think this is crucial to me as a writer. I'm in the first place, before anything else, before being an academic or a scholar, I think I'm a writer. I'm trying to reach out to people, to communicate to people, trying to bring all the different ploys that I can in order to communicate, and I can talk about that too. So I deliberately set out to write in different genres, and that means, of course, writing in slightly different styles. My writing style any way, even in my main books, has developed and changed, I like to believe it's improved, but you could actually say it's become a little bit more impenetrable as my books have gone on. Impenetrability, if it's there, has come about because of the development of my ideas, as a result that even though my words are still short, and my sentences are still short, there is now a density of conceptual matter coming into the sentences. That was always the case, I have to admit. But now, even though I'm trying very hard to make my writing accessible, I'm conscious that many do find my work taxing. And I think that's how I would account for it, that even though … well, I think another reason for this density is my determination, paradoxically, to be clear. And so I pare my writing rigorously and savagely. Certainly my books – I'm quite disciplined for myself, I won't let a chapter go over six thousand words, and if a first draft is seven thousand words, I then have to junk a thousand words. And that means that everything is pared and pruned, so you get a very spare kind of text. There's very little redundancy in my text, so my texts – in that sense – are quite a big ask of the reader. Somebody said to me once that I don't let the reader off the hook. At least, they can't lighten or lessen their concentration on me. If they lose their concentration for a moment, they've lost the argument. *And* I keep the reader attentive as it were, that's what I'm trying to do actually, to keep the reader attentive. I'm trying not to let the reader off the hook, but I'm trying to take the reader with me all the time. So that's about pleasing the reader. But I'm also trying, if I can say so, to delight the reader. I want the reader to turn over the page. I'm conscious with wider audiences that reading books … they're reading on trains and buses, tiny spaces of their busy professional lives, and I'm trying to please them, delight them. One reviewer said of my work, 'Barnett writes with wit', and I'd like to think that might be the case, but one's got to do that with an extremely light touch, it can't be heavy handed or even obvious. I like to be, when I write … a wry smile that might come across.

I: I think it does. And if some people complain about the density, perhaps that's more their fault than yours, because obviously you do get to a wide audience. So what can you think of that has helped you, along the way, that has shaped what you do? Was it people you worked with, was it collaborative writing, was it reviews you've had, was it advice you've been given, on the PhD for instance?

RB: Well, I had a lovely supervisor here, Terry Moore, who's still alive. He used to urge me to write clearly and simply. That was in the philosophy department, and it was part of the Philosophy of Education department. And I am embarrassed now when I think back to the pretentiousness of my early draft. So that was one formative experience. The discipline that came about there. But other formative experiences have been, on the one hand, great scholars that I've engaged with, in my reading, and from time to time I've got interested in particular great scholars, Richard Peters here, Jurgen Habermas, Ernest Gellner, one or two other people as well. And in a fairly concentrated period of time I've kind of given myself up to these people, one after another, as my interests have developed and changed. So I've, as it were, ground out my thinking and ideas, in conversation with others so to speak. I think it's very important that

students do get stuck into individual people, but I fear that they don't do that so much these days. Another formative aspect of my writing, of course, has been the – by-and-large – wonderful reception that my writing has received around the world. This, of course, bucks one up enormously, helps one to believe that one's got something here, and it's worth keeping going. I find writing extremely challenging. Cardinal John Henry Newman who wrote the great book *The Idea of a University* wrote about the bodily pain that writing caused him, and I used to have this phrase stuck up by my word processor at home. And I resonate with all of that, again, I can talk about that, why does writing cause me bodily pain? I think it's partly that one is drawing out from within oneself what is already there. This goes back to an old Greek idea that actually we know far more than we realise, and learning things is actually articulating what one already subconsciously knows. And I find writing is of that kind, one actually has a great deal stored up inside one in one way or another. And the challenge is of articulating half-formed sentences and values, and dredging them up, as it were, out of one's body. That's the sense I have, it's as if I'm pulling them out with wires, painfully, from within myself. And so the formation of those ideas and sentiments, from whisperings and values, into clear sentences and paragraphs, well-ordered sentences and paragraphs, which follow each other so that the reader can see the links between them, is extremely arduous and, as I say, for me extremely painful – also, indeed, a bodily process.

I: Yes, I think a lot of people see writing as painful, even if, like you, they've published a great deal. The next question is: how have you managed to keep writing a major part of your life?

RB: Well, if one wants to do something, one does it, as they say. It's a matter of one's own values and priorities. I think writing has become crucial to my own identity, and of course it has given me enormous satisfaction. It's helped me develop an academic identity and profile around the world. It has enabled me to do what I want: as I say, I'm trying to communicate to people, to reach out to people, people I'll never meet on the other side of the world. And to be able to do that, and to have people suggest that one's actually managing to achieve that, is hugely satisfying.

I: And then, you've talked about the pain in writing, but what kind of satisfaction do you get from it? Does there come a stage when you've got over the pain, the uncertainties perhaps, and there's a sense of something shaping up?

RB: Well, as I say, pain and pleasure are different aspects or moments of the writing. The pain is the process, the satisfaction is the sense of realising that one's actually achieving one's aims, of reaching out to people. And, of course, hopefully having good reviews and that kind of thing. But as I say, I'm also ... if I was to put it pompously, what I would say is that what I'm trying to offer the education world are resources for new policies and new practices. And so it's a great joy to me to know that my work is being picked up and read by those in influential positions, but also being picked up by course leaders, programme managers, curriculum developers, academic developers, and actually being picked up and run with. And people are trying to work through implications and possibilities that my ideas are opening out, so they are becoming real live resources for new kinds of practices. I'm trying in my writing to imagine a new kind of future, but not a future that is totally imaginary – I'm trying to imagine a future that is a feasible future. I'm trying to put into the world ideas that could, in the best of all possible worlds, have a realistic chance of being achievable. And it's a great delight to know, have a sense, that perhaps groups are being formed in universities and other places in which people are looking at my books and saying, 'Well, this looks interesting, where do we go from here?'

I: So would you say that in some ways, the kind of writing you do and fiction writing are not so far apart, both involve imagination, imagining new possibilities, new worlds?

RB: I'm not a fiction writer, to my shame, and I'm not a poet either. But I do see that my writing is story telling. So that's one metaphor that I would use. But I also see a parallel metaphor in the writing of plays. I see my writing sometimes as if I'm writing a play in which I have different characters, and I have to make judgements about which character is going to be on stage, at any one stage, and how they're going to come in and out of the picture, and what weight you're going to give them, and who's going to be talking at any one time. So that's another potent metaphor.

I: And who's going to be the villain! [Laughs]

RB: Indeed. But I have other metaphors as well. There's that idea of an impressionistic painter. One can go on for ever with an impressionistic painting, presumably, it's never quite finished, one could say that you have at some point to walk away from it and say, 'This is it for now.' And I think that is the case for my writing. I don't know whether it's of interest, but having done a first draft, my first draft is basically a sketch, it's as if ... I'm working on a book right now, and I feel that although I'm writing the first draft, such that if anybody was to pick it up, they'd think, 'Gosh, this is a really well-worked-out draft of a book.' Actually, for me, it's just the assembly of materials. And I feel I'm like a painter who's got a huge project in front of them, and I'm just getting all the materials ready, and I'm just beginning to sketch out the lines on the canvas, a few hazy, sketchy lines, and nothing is at all fixed. I'm still actually assembling all the paints, the pots, the brushes, all the materials that I'm going to need. This is what I'm doing, I'm assembling materials at this early stage. Then, having got the first draft done, it's really just raw material for me to work on, and I can go on working on that and polishing it. And the real hard work often comes about draft three or four, when I've got into it, I've done a few tidyings, and then I'm beginning to get under the skin of it all and I'm looking at the whole of it in its entirety, its structure. And then I'm beginning to realise that some chapters aren't working or some chapters are clashing with others or some lines of argument are inconsistent with others, and I've really got to get hold of it and restructure it. It's like seeing a figure in a painting and thinking, 'Gosh, that shouldn't be there, or it should be on the other side of the painting.' Or an arm is completely out of kilter with the rest of the body and it's got to be moved or just hidden from view. So you have to take a whole red pen to a whole chapter, and you have to excise great chunks of text. And that's why the phrase 'the body of the work' is very important to me, because once I start hacking around with my text, I feel I'm hacking around with my own body. And again, I feel more pain coming into me as I'm doing that, but you know it's got to be done, it's like the surgeon with the knife, you know it's got to be done. So the work goes on, refining, pruning, restructuring and, of course, that work could go on forever, there's no end to that work. But there is actually, because now I've got in my mind a sense of structure of that kind of process. But my chapters will go through ultimately between ten and 15 readings, every chapter. So I'm reading over and over again, and I could talk more about that, how each time I come at my work, sitting, on my knee with a chapter, or a whole manuscript on my knee, I'm doing it for a particular reason, with a particular task in mind, and because my mind's so feeble I can only take on one task at a time, so that's why I have to go through ten to 15 readings, because each time it's a different kind of task I've set myself. It might be just fiddling with the commas or it might be fiddling with the references. It might be actually hugely major, as I say, it might be the actual structure of two chapters, how they relate to each other. So each time I come at the text, it's for a different purpose, a different task.

I: And before you do the first draft, to be very mundane, do you make notes? Do you have a notebook, and when an idea comes to you, you write it down? I remember a colleague saying she always had a notebook in her handbag.

RB: I used to. Perhaps I don't anymore because ideas come to me so irregularly these days, getting somewhat old in the tooth. But what I do find is, and it's where I've developed from my writing, that ideas come in the writing, and that's why – again, wearing another hat – I never allow in this room the phrase the 'writing up of one's research' to be heard. That phrase is meaningless to me, the thinking comes through the writing. The writing, if it's serious writing, will provoke thinking. So I have notes, and so

for each chapter I'm writing I will have sketchy notes. But I have already challenges in my mind. So, for example, the chapter I'm working on at the moment … of course, I've got the previous chapter which should set things up a bit for this chapter … so I've got as it were ideas in that chapter which I'm now trying to build upon in some way or other. I've also got some notes about this chapter, and I've got the overall theme of the book. Then I start to write an introduction, and as I write the introduction, I say to the reader what I'm going to do in this chapter, and the writing of that introduction itself sets up some additional tasks. So straightaway I've got three or four fairly major tasks, all swimming around. Now that's much more than my mind can handle, so I don't need any more notes, thank you very much!

I: And does it matter where you write? Virginia Woolf said a woman needs a room of her own and a thousand a year, but can you write when you're abroad, for example, or do you have a particular place where you write?

RB: Well, I do have a particular place, it's where I live. So wherever I happen to be living, I will try and create a computer workspace for myself, which is my space. As I think back, it's characteristically a corner of a room. I'm not very computer literate, so it wouldn't be easy for me to try to write in other places. I like to have my texts around me, the books that I'm particularly working with and from and arguing with and articulating with and my notes. But I don't need a lot of material. I say to my students, often I say to them, 'You've done enough reading, stop reading, and put aside all the papers you've accumulated, now just write – bring yourself to write.' You've got to face up to that blinking cursor demanding words from you on that screen. And that's your challenge, demanding words from you on that screen. The arrival of the computer and word processors has completely changed my life. One of the best things I ever did was teach myself to touch type, so I'm now, in that sense, completely independent as a writer. And I would give my publishers a perfect text. When I say it's perfect, I'm immodest to say that, but it is pretty well perfect in the sense that I can engage with copy-editors, and if they want to start changing my text, I want to know exactly what they're doing. And I will go through every single point with them, and I require now of my publishers that I see the marked up copy from copy-editors, so I can see exactly what they're trying to do. And sometimes I simply don't agree with the line that copy-editors are taking or their approach. So the writing place is very important to me. But also the ambience, I like listening to classical music and I will have classical music playing when I'm writing. But it has to be familiar classical music, has to be music that's not imposing any additional psychological load on my brain, requiring new information to be processed, it has to be familiar music that I'm comfortable with.

I: And do you write any of it by hand?

RB: No, I write directly onto the screen these days. I compose on the screen, and I give myself the challenge of composing good sentences and good paragraphs straightaway. And this is extremely demanding, but it's compelling though. The composing of that sentence, getting the clauses right, getting the verbs right, is actually compelling me to think through what am I saying precisely. And as I'm thinking about the verb, and the verb in relation to the noun, and the verb in relation to the subject, that's again opening up new lines of thought. And as I'm composing, I get two or three little rivers, riverlets, of thought running in my mind as I'm writing a sentence, and I kind of have to catch that very quickly, otherwise it will be gone.

I: It would be wonderful for students, and I'm sure you do share these ideas with students. Returning to the question sheet: I think we've talked about how you go about writing, but could you summarise what you have learned about the process of writing and about writing for publication?

RB: Well, as I say, the most important thing for me is being clear about the audience and reaching out to that audience. My books are about education, but even so, very often, the main audience shifts slightly. So the tone, the character, what you can get away with, as it were, the pitch, the scenes, will vary according to the audience. So sometimes I'm writing books that are much more oriented towards vice-chancellors and senior managers, policy makers. Sometimes I'm writing books which are more oriented towards teachers and those much more at the sharp end of things. And this means that the tone, the character should change. The actual words that you use may change, the limits of the vocabulary may change subtly. One doesn't do this all consciously, one just gives oneself up to it as one's trying to reach out to different audiences. But this requirement of mine, on myself, to reach out to audiences, is absolutely crucial. And, again, I could be intemperate and reflect on my feelings about the character of much so-called academic writing these days, which I fear doesn't seriously attempt to reach out to audiences, even texts which proclaim virtues of equality and equity and democracy.

I: And what do you think your writing says about you, or what would you like it to say about you?

RB: That's a very challenging question, liable to lead one into embarrassing admissions if one's not careful, I guess.

I: No false modesty please …

RB: No, no, I mean why is it that somebody wants to write, seriously wants to write, seriously wants to reach out to others on the other side of the world that they'll never meet, to make contact of that kind? That is a very serious psychological process, which I suspect we don't understand. I have my own understandings of why I'm doing it personally, but I'm not sure I want to go fully down that road at this moment.

I: I think you've really answered the next question, which is: if you were not at the Institute, but perhaps at another academic institution, do you think you would still write? Is it so much a part of you, and who you are, of your way of being in the world?

RB: Well, I confess that one reason for me to anticipate and look forward to retirement is that I can then write even more. That's really what I want to do when I retire, to take writing really seriously. Up until now it's been the evening job, and not even that, it's been pretty spasmodic. But I would like to ... I would also like to become a scholar, I've never had a chance to become a scholar, to actually go into libraries and read some books and do some digging ... certain kinds of scholars that I'm just getting into, I'm just getting into a whole new literature around existential philosophy, which is mind-boggling and confusing and terrifying. But it needs time and space to do that seriously and properly. So yes, I think I'd write wherever I was, I think if I was on the desert island, I'd really want my word processor with me.

I: Is there anything you'd like to add to what you've said?

RB: Well, what I would say is, from my experience, is that writing can give one enormous satisfactions, you can reach out to people through one's writing in a way that is otherwise largely impossible for many of us. And what I've also found, as I've touched on, is that I think I've grown and developed as a human being, as a person, through my writing, which is a pretty uncanny thing, that blobs on a piece of paper can both reach out and delight others on the other side of the world, but they can also have an effect on oneself as a human being. So I do feel that to be the case. So writing is a hugely powerful human tool, used well. And it can be enormously enriching both for ourselves and for others.

...

The interview then continued.

RB: I do find the concept of integrity tricky, but I do like to feel that I'm being honest with the reader, I'm not hiding behind other people, behind other scholars or anything else. It's just me and the reader, and I'm trying to engage seriously with the reader. And I think that is also an important set of values as far as the writer is concerned.

I: You said you have various ploys which you use to communicate with others?

RB: I don't want to reveal all my trade secrets, but it is speaking directly. So I will ask questions, but it's

important to ask questions in order to answer questions. I will use quirky English words, quirky at least in the context of conventional academic writing on education. And I will use deliberately short sentences sometimes, I will mix up the pace and rhythm of my sentences and paragraphs. I will have a two-word sentence, for example. I will have a two-line paragraph. But I do it deliberately and carefully and precisely.

I: So you like saving hard copies of what you write?

RB: I will print out what I've written that session, it might only be a couple of paragraphs, but I print it out, so I've got the latest version in front of me, and I'm adding to the Lever Arch file, so I see the book building up day by day in front of me. So that gives one a great deal of confidence. In the last few months I've drafted ... appeared as it were, out of nowhere. But you know, building it up physically is very important.

It's very important that when I have a big writing task like a book I set myself ... crazy demands. So I will form a schedule. In fact, I'm just coming to the end of a first draft, so this is my schedule of work for the term, basically, under different headings. But over here, under the heading, 'Writing home', I've got the chapters, so Chapter 9, Chapter 10, Chapter 11, Chapter 12. And I've got the dates. So 8th January to deliver myself that chapter, and so on down the page. So I'm working on Chapter 9 at the moment, and I've got to deliver that to myself 29th January. That date's just passed and I haven't quite finished it. I have a good reason for not being on target, my computer was actually taken away for two weeks, but I've always caught up with the target again, always back on schedule. So I've got this schedule, that's giving me three weeks per chapter and that's quite relaxed. I have had schedules where I've given myself just two weeks to produce a draft chapter for a whole book. So the whole first draft is completed ... well, two weeks for each chapter, so that's six months for writing the whole first draft. This is slightly longer because I've got other things going on at the moment. But a definite timetable is crucial, that's what I say to my PhD students, I want a timetable; if you slip from it, I want a revised timetable. So they're always producing new timetables. But the timetable is crucial: you've got to have that sense of closure. But this is the first step, just producing this first draft, for some people; it's a first sketch for me.

I: It's interesting that other interviewees have also referred to what one called mechanistic aspects of writing – having the paper definitely plotted out and planned in advance. Because otherwise everything else …

RB: … I'm trying to engage with my audience, so I'm trying to improvise for my audience, so I'm trying to engage where they are. I can't expect my reader to listen to me if I'm not listening to my reader. I can't expect to make connections, or the reader to make connections with what I'm saying, unless I make connections to where I think the reader is. So I have to be imaginative, I have to empathise with my reader. I have to reach out from myself. Imagine my readers, imagine what it is for them, imagine what their days are like. What their lives are like, in order for me to reach out to them. And so I think that partly counts for the disjuncture between how writers sometimes believe that they are intelligible and transparent, when the reality is that they are very often opaque. And incomprehensible. It's because there is that lack of connection being made. But the responsibility of that connection lies with the author. And I know a lot of postmodern debate about the death of the author and all that sort of thing, but that is nonsensical to me. There are huge challenges and responsibility on the author. Of course, once they're out in the world, their works will be picked up and used in all sorts of ways, and interpreted in all sorts of ways, in ways we never conceived of, in ways contrary to our intentions. OK, but we have the responsibility in the first place, I think, to try and reach out, to try and be clear, and that is extremely demanding. And again, we haven't had time to go into it, but that's why again the writing task is so challenging and so painful, because it is again a whole cluster of different writing tasks. I'm trying to understand my own sentiments, I'm trying to form coherent wholes, I'm trying [to] understand where my readers might be, I'm trying to reach out to them, I'm trying to have a sense of different audiences, I'm trying to have a sense of the

authors that I'm engaging with, I'm having a sense of different time frames, different cultures. All of this is in my mind as I'm writing; that's hugely complex. And I remember having a conversation with my publisher once, and it was at the fairly early stage in one of my books – I think I'd just produced a first draft – and I felt at the time it was just getting out of hand, that the challenges I'd set myself were enormous. I just wrote them down, listed them in bullet-point fashion on one side of A4, and they scared me. Writing is enormously challenging.

… clear the desk, just you and the computer. Just you, only you.

Jan Blommaert

I: *Thank you for agreeing to be interviewed. How long have you been at the Institute and what are your roles?*

JB: I am very new, I only joined the Institute last September, and as for roles, I am the Chair of Languages in Education here in CLC [Culture, Language and Communication]. I supervise students and also teach in the TESOL Programme. I am also Deputy Head of School for Research and Consultancy. There are my roles.

I: *Please tell me about the best piece of writing you have done or the best pieces – the one or ones that you are most pleased with and, of course, why you are pleased with them?*

JB: The best paper is always the next paper, but there are two pieces that I still like to reread. In general, I am the sort of writer who becomes disappointed with his own writing as soon as it is in print, but the two pieces that still appeal to me and that I would still firmly defend *(long pause)* there is one article that I wrote in 2001 on asylum seekers' narratives, which was called 'Investigating narrative inequality'. It is a huge article – I think printed it is over 35 pages. It is extremely dense, with all kinds of data and so on and so on, but I remember that I was very happy to see it go in print because I put my heart in that thing. For me it was a blending of academic skill and responsibility. I mean, I really had to go to the very extreme of what I was capable of as a professional analyst, but also as a public intellectual – as an intellectual who wanted to address issues in society, forms of inequality. In this particular case, it had to do with asylum seekers and it was the right connection between brain and heart, so to speak. That's one piece.

The other one is a little book that eventually came out in 2004, which is called *Workshopping*. I wrote the first draft of that in '96 (if I get it right) and it was a reflection on three workshops that I had attended on discourse analysis. For me it was a moment in which I was really, really ordering my ideas on methodology and also reflecting on my own professional practices in a way that again offered me the sort of, I would say, crossover between what we call professional skill and my own identity, my own role as an academic to some extent and the sort of capacity that you have to intervene in public debate.

I would say that the two publications would be similar in the sense that they offered me more than just an opportunity to display academic skill, but also offered me a way of using academic skill for clarifying my own role as an intellectual in the wider sense of the term.

I: That's very interesting. I wonder if this is the point at which to ask you about your writing in different languages? Are the article and the book both in English?

JB: These are both in English, but apart from that I have written several books and lots of articles in my native language, Dutch, and I have a few publications in French, which I also have authored. My writing in French is never easy, because it's the language in which I have least written proficiency and in which the codes of academic discourse are most alien to me. On the other hand, writing in Dutch to me always was a way of addressing local audiences in Belgium. As a consequence, a lot of it was explicitly political, but I used academic techniques to make political arguments. In fact, some of my most successful publications are things that I wrote in Dutch in the sense that they really had an impact in society and that they really were taken on by the audiences that I would like, or that I had in mind, as the preferred audiences.

I: That might bring about change?

JB: That could bring about an effect in society – visible and real effects in society. Also having the strange sort of effect of *(short pause)* celebrity is the wrong word, but being a name with a reputation, so to speak, with all the pros and cons attached to it … people sending me hate mail and things like that because I used to write on things like multiculturalism, immigration, nationalism and so on and so on. In a society like Belgium, which is not very different from the UK, well, evidently that means that you enter into probably the most sensitive domains of political life or public debate, in which you very often bump into *(short pause)* not conspiracies, but normalcy, a particular rejection of diversity, which is not seen as rejection of diversity, but as a rational way of handling all these different people in your society. As a consequence I made enemies out of very sensible people – people who had a heart in the right place and who had the most noble of intentions, but who, at the same time, shared a number of assumptions with, for instance, the extreme Right without knowing so, at least without realising it.

I: You spent time in the States. Do you think there is a certain amount of lip service there to multiculturalism? Are they more into it or do they say all these right things, but …?

JB: It is not easy in the US to be an activist academic, one reason being that the political system is not built around opposition, it is built about individual voice. The political environment is a fragmented one in which the opposition is an individual opposition. If, for instance, you are opposed to the foreign policy of the US as an intellectual, you find yourself very much alone. There are no large movements, there are no trade unions (for instance) that could be a voice in public debate and so on and so on. So what you have there is – you do have academic work and outstanding academic work, of course, on diversity and multiculturalism and so on, but it is really, really difficult for these people to engage in the kinds of genres that I practised in my Dutch oeuvre, which are activist genres, small genres like the polemical essay or squib, or the written debates or opinion articles in the newspapers and so on. It is really, really hard for even a very senior academic in the US to get an opinion article in one of the major newspapers. It is really difficult and, as a consequence, you see that they don't really practise that sort of activist genre or the complex of activist genres, the small genres, the polemical ones, and that very often the potential contribution of their analytic work remains unused or not explored fully.

I: *Does that also say something about difficulties presented by the actual ways of writing, the different kinds of academic discourse in different languages? You referred earlier to French as having a particular code of academic discourse.*

JB: Well, it might be an experience that many have – I mean if you read that, let's say translations of Foucault or Bourdieu, you would find it hard to read because it has a certain wordiness to it. There are differences in the structure of chapters or the way in which you lay out your argument and so on. And, of course, there are significant differences in terminology and rather fundamental ones – I mean, things that only exist as nouns in English – for instance power – only exist as verbs in French and so on and so on. So what it means to write in French to me is a struggle not only with language, but also with the way in which I need to order in my own mind – I have to construct my argument, the way in which I have to organise my own thoughts around particular topics. But I haven't written much, four or five articles, I think, in French, but I take pride in the fact that I didn't give them to a native speaker to have a look at it, I really worked day and night to get it right using basically inspiration from things I had read as my only guideline or yardstick. I am not going to say that they are particularly good articles, but when I did it, I found it an amazing accomplishment, a great achievement in my life.

I: *And Dutch and English: would you say they are fairly similar in terms of …?*

JB: By and large, yes, but then again the genre distribution would be different. You see in Dutch there is no space for academic writing. When you want to write an academic article there is no market, there are no journals in Dutch and as a consequence there is hardly any opportunity to write the sort of research article that is now the bread and butter of our profession in Dutch because of the simple fact that there is no academic market for that. In Belgian universities as well the emphasis is very, very strongly on writing in English, writing articles for international journals meaning writing in English. As a consequence, what you have is simply that certain genres don't exist as real, practicable genres in that particular language and are, of course, over-developed in English. So there isn't really a sort of equivalent mapping of the genres in the two languages. I am not trying to look for a sort of asymmetry in the other direction, but there would be genres in Dutch that do not exist as such in English. There is more essayistic writing, I would say, in Dutch in the sense that there are several good, significant journals for political debate or public debate on big issues, and in which you can actually practise an essayistic genre – you know, a genre in which you make or defend a particular or elaborate a particular position with an intellectual instrument. You deploy academic skill, in what is basically political argumentation and I think that this, or at least in my own experience, is slightly more available there than it is here. I can be wrong on this, of course.

I: *For what it's worth, I do not think you are. This is all very interesting. To continue with the questions: what pieces of writing are you least pleased with and why?*

JB: My PhD! I guess, like everyone, my PhD. I wrote a 658-page PhD on *Swahili Political Style*. I had to do it in Dutch because it was obligatory and I found myself – while I was actually printing the final version – disagreeing with almost every major point that I had made! As a consequence I think I only extracted two or three articles directly from that PhD. There was one offer at some point to have it converted into a book, but I declined that offer. There were valuable elements in it, and it was a very formative sort of writing and so on, but yes, that's definitely a thing that I hated while I was doing it, but even afterwards that I would look upon with skepsis. I will always be very hesitant to borrow it. It is not a good read, it's awfully written and so on and so on. But apart from that, there are a number of other articles (for instance) that were editorially massacred and one book, my very first international book, which came out in '91, was an edited collection, which I did with a friend of mine and it was called *The Pragmatics of Intercultural and International Communication*. I still think it is an excellent collection of articles, but John Benjamins (and I'm going to use their name now) managed to print a different version of the title on the cover so it read *The Pragmatics of International and Intercultural Communication*. There are no words that can explain the disappointment that I had when I saw the first copy of that book. It was going to be the most beautiful moment in my life and the first thing I saw was a huge typographical error on the cover. So again, there was reason for enormous disappointment, for unhappiness, but it was an editorial thing, I mean it was a thing in which the printer in this particular case, or the publisher, hadn't been or had been less than careful.

I: And you couldn't get it changed at that stage?

JB: No, it was printed, it was bound and, as always, with academic books, they print seven hundred copies and if you say, 'I refuse to have it on the shelf', then the book simply disappears. We are not the author of Harry Potter, of course! And a number of other articles in which (you know) editors unilaterally decided to, say, reduce the length by five hundred words or forget to print particular tables and so on and so on, and evidently this involves dissatisfaction with particular stages of the writing trajectory. It made me realise that no matter how good you think your own work is, you are never alone in the production of that work. You also need a publisher, an editor and so on, and that even if you think that you have written a good piece of work academically, it can look awful and it can miss every effect because of the way it went through the other stages. It made me very, very meticulous in the preparation of my own manuscript, I am really – again I say it with a degree of pride. It is part of my self-definition as an author, I really always try to follow guidelines. I never try to take any liberty with the instructions given by

the publisher or by the editor with respect to the length of papers or with respect to the layout of tables or manuscript administration and so on because I know that if I don't do my part of the work, the chance that others will also make errors or mistakes afterwards is simply increased. So this is a good piece of advice for the young authors, you know. Follow guidelines and be strict on yourself.

I: I think that is very good advice. Next question: what has helped your writing? Have you written with a more experienced writer? Is it advice from others, is it reviews or …?

JB: Well, I think two things. The first, in the beginning of my, let's say writing career, I did a lot of joint writing with an experienced colleague, Jef Verschueren, who was actually a very good writer as well. He was also Belgian, but with a brilliant style in English and a way in which he could organise (you know) the argument in such a way, it was both readable, but also appealing intellectually and had all the sort of features of genre that would make it acceptable to the publisher and so on. That was a massive help because in the space of like one year I learned all the tricks, including, for instance, looking for good swinging titles. He was a master in finding very nice and appealing titles that were, as we used to call it 'sexy' in the sense that they never lied about what was in the article or the book, but at the same time also gave them a sort of marketing appeal. So in that short time span I went through high school when it came to academic publishing.

I: You've continued to write with him, haven't you?

JB: Oh yes, since about … I have done like …

I: Quite recently?

JB: Twenty articles with him and one major book, *Debating Diversity*, published in 1998. That was one major influence, the second one has always been reading [*long pause*] I mean, in the way of advice to the younger authors, you might not have the opportunity for meeting a very experienced fellow like I had, but you might have the opportunity of using reading as a source of inspiration. For years and years (and I still do it, you know) I used to read things not only because of the sort of stuff that was in it, so it wasn't only reading for learning, but also for stealing stylistically. I ruthlessly exploited other people's oeuvre as a source of inspiration for particular turns of phrases – especially in English, of course, which is my fourth language. But whenever I saw a beautifully worded argument or whenever I saw a nice turn of phrase or an expression that I found appealing, I used to make a note of it. And I really collected it like a sort of a butterfly collection – I still do, always with the explicit plan of, at some point, using it. I can say with confidence that I have used most of it. So there were authors that really, really have been masters to me in the sense that they provided me with examples of how to write. One example is the historian Eric Hobsbawm whose style of writing I still find a mixture of endearing and charming features with authority and academic robustness, which I find amazing. There are several others as well, E.P. Thompson is one, Johannes Fabian, Dell Hymes: people who have a very literary way of writing (you know) who don't produce aridly factual accounts of things, who don't also attend very much to rules of politeness and indirectness in their writing. Very often they are writing offensively and are extremely outspoken when it comes to formulating their opinions. In that sense they violate quite a few criteria that we now would offer to our students as models for academic writing. But those would be my sources of inspiration and reading them was a part of the discipline that I developed for myself as a writer. I realised that English was a weak point for me, that it was a slowly developing resource and that I needed to be meticulous about the way in which I would prepare myself for particular forms of writing.

I: I think you're raising an important point. So often in seminars we concentrate or, rather, I concentrate on the content rather than on discussing how a recommended reading text is written. I do that even though I have often advised students to find a journal article on a relevant topic that they think is well written and to look at how it is put together, how the ideas are expressed, the transitions handled …

JB: Yes, the aesthetics of things. Why is it that we find certain books worth rereading? Usually not only because they offer us significant intellectual input, but very often also because they are beautiful books, I mean they are beautifully written. There is an aesthetic quality to it that is charming and appeals and that gives you a feeling of being respected as a reader as well. It is what Roland Barthes said: the pleasure of the text, the joy that is brought into this dialogue we call reading.

I: And so often that's left out of courses for students on how to write, isn't it? Instead students are given a set of … of rules and structures and …

JB: Of uniformity. I still believe, using myself as an example, that it need not be a matter of sheer talent. That attention to aesthetic detail, to the way in which you stylistically elaborate your artefacts, was in my case a rather rigorous sort of discipline in which I said, 'Well if you write, you might as well write nicely, you might as well write a beautiful book, you might as well try to make a readable article, an article which would be readable to an audience beyond the five or six people in the world who are really interested in your stuff.' And one of the effects is that some of these items are, indeed, read by more than five or six people in the world and might be easier to consume than a number of others.

I: This is all interesting and relevant. How have you managed to keep writing a major part of your life, if indeed you have?

JB: I have written a lot. You must realise that I come from within an economy of academic writing in which a senior professor would be somebody who had published one or two books in his life and would, if he was prolific, publish one article every year. I am in the generation in which academic writing has tremendously accelerated, in which we are now expected to produce a book every three years and five or six international journal articles per year. In other words, every three years we do as much as the previous generation in a career. I have always been aware of that pressure, I have always been aware of the fact that as an academic more and more you live by virtue of your writing, not only by virtue of your lecturing, and that there are real rewards but also real sanctions attached to that. That if you don't join that race, you might lose opportunities professionally and so on.

Now how have I managed that? I always wonder and other people also wonder because I have always had rather busy professional lives in which I combined several functions and in which I was active in an extraordinary number of activities, all at the same time. I think the two points that might be important in explaining this is, on the one hand, a desire to write. I like writing, I enjoy it, I don't consider it a burden and writing is a thing that can fill dead moments, if I have half-an-hour in-between a class and a meeting or something. Writing is not a thing that requires a lot of preparation for me. I can essentially sit down and start writing and I enjoy it. It is a thing that I like as an activity, that's one thing. Secondly, but that is not a recipe for others, I am a fast writer as well. I don't have difficulties composing an academic written document – a report, a discussion memo for a meeting, an article, a lecture. It can be anything as long as I have the main line of the argument in my head. And I have my notes – I have used notebooks all through my life. As long as I have these basic elements, these conditions fulfilled, I can sit down and start writing and I can write very fast.

I: And can you write anywhere or do you have to be in a special place? If you are abroad can you write?

JB: Yes, I can, I do write wherever I can. I can imagine that you need a certain environment in order to produce a certain type of text and evidently there are places and circumstances that are far more favourable than others. There are places where I like to write more than in others. For instance, my own study at home is definitely the preferred sort of environment for serious and sustained writing, but at the same time, in the sort of job we do and with the pressure on us to actually write and produce, I need to be able to write in-between things – you know, in-between phone calls, in-between meeting students – using a stolen five or 15 minutes (you know) to complete a section or to complete a list of references and so on. I write whenever I find an opportunity.

I: Is writing for you …?

JB: I can't write on a 'plane, that's one place where I can't write.

I: There's too much going on around you …

JB: Yes, it's far too hectic and it's uncomfortable as well.

I: Do you write on screen or do you write by hand? Do you use your laptop?

JB: Yeah, for finished products. An article would be immediately written on the computer screen, the same goes for a book manuscript indeed. But as I said, there is a discipline that I developed since very early on: I still keep handwritten notes. So I don't use my laptop as a notebook, my notebooks really look like actual notebooks. They have a sort of archaic quality to it that reflects an earlier regime of academic literacy, with a contents list at the back, numbered pages, cross references, 'see Note 45 in Notebook 11' and things like that. And I insist on handwriting because handwriting gives you, in a very weird way, a physical connection with ideas and with a particular textuality that you don't have when you are using a keyboard. Literacy is one of my interests, so I am fascinated by the way in which I self-correct, for instance, while writing, which of course is invisible when you work on a screen. I find that valuable because it reveals my own hesitations, my own quest for the right words to formulate something and so on. So, yes, I tend to value handwriting still, but it's not purely romantic, it is not purely nostalgia, but it really has a function – reminding me of my own developing thoughts and formulations.

I: And it's also very well organised too and usable?

JB: It is usable and it also forces me … I mean I do make a lot of notes while reading and that slows down the pace of reading. It forces you to reflect on particular bits of reading for the time that you are making a handwritten note. Sometimes that can be as long as half-an-hour or an hour or several hours and, in that sense, it's an important way of truncating rapid consumption, rapid production, it creates a space for slowness, for reflection and for constructing an individual archive. It represents my own memory over an extended period, which I harvest. And it is safer than a computer. I would have a heart attack when I would lose my notes because of my laptop being stolen or the hard disk of my computer being damaged or something like that. It would break my heart because it would mean the loss of my memory of – oh well, how many? – a thousand readings that I have done and 30 or 40 articles that I have written of which the initial ideas are there. It would really break my heart.

I: I certainly understand that. What kinds of writing do you most enjoy? Do you ever write fiction? Have you ever tried to write fiction?

JB: With regard to satisfaction, in general I like writing as an opportunity of committing yourself to an idea, OK? Going on record as being somebody, for instance, who asks a number of questions, a specific type of questions in a specific way and so on. And it's not a matter of display, I genuinely see academic writing as a form of dialogue, probably the only real form of dialogue that we have with one another. We meet scholars at events like international conferences and so and, of course, with email these days you do have a form of engagement, which is new and sometimes very intensive. At the same time, nothing beats the academic book or article as a way of engaging with each other's work and with each other's ideas as well as with the history of ideas. That's another aspect of which I am aware. With every article that you write you create a bit of history, your article will be one article that at one point will end up in a list of references, representing a particular historicity to a question or to an academic field, which in itself is an extremely interesting aspect of writing, the fact that you insert yourself into intellectual history.

There is also the aspect of vanity, but I think it counts for everyone. It's what's known in French as '*le plaisir de se voir imprimé*' – the pleasure of seeing yourself in print. As I said, I have written quite a bit, but every time a new book comes out, it comes with a childlike form of excitement and of satisfaction – of actually seeing and holding the book (unless, of course, when it's a bitter disappointment like I told

you). It is the real pleasure of seeing this text written on my computer in Times New Roman 12, etc. etc. now converted into some exotic font in an archaic form, with artwork and a cover. It is a real form of enjoyment, but I would say the main aspect of motivation and satisfaction would be the aspect of dialogue, the opportunity you get to insert yourself into the history of ideas.

Let me add to that that I don't write to declare things or to proclaim things. Most of my writing is inquisitive and is essentially a question that I throw up for debate by others.

So the volume of my oeuvre in no way reflects the certainty with which I write. On the contrary, it reflects the ongoing self-questioning process and the fact that you always need another article to be more precise about something or to be more firm about something or to be less firm and less certain about things that you were uncertain about in a previous publication. This is, of course, the burden of the writer, of the academic writer. The perfect article, the perfect book doesn't exist because it would silence you. Fortunately we are absolutely not perfect and there is always another opportunity in writing to correct your own mistakes.

I: Have you ever written fiction?

JB: No, never fiction, but I have practised small genres and I still do. For instance, columns in magazines and opinion articles in newspapers are quite a significant oeuvre, also political squibs and reviewing. And I do value the small genres because very often they offer you an opportunity for doing things, for expressing yourself in a way which is not possible in the more prestigious, the bigger genres. It is very unfortunate to see that in our field reviewing is going really down as a genre that has prestige, has value – it is not seen as a form of achievement. More and more you get sloppy reviews.

I: Yes, they don't count for much in the RAE, in fact, hardly at all.

JB: Well, exactly, I mean they don't count at all. I do a lot of reviewing and, in fact, after this interview I am going to write a review of a significant new book by Ben Rampton. I do value it as a form of engaging with a particular bit of work, and of articulating a sense of responsibility within the field. If people consider you a voice of authority it creates a responsibility: significant developments require your attention in order to be appreciated as a significant event or a significant development in the field by others. So I do feel that every once in a while I have to practise these other genres as a way of service to the rest of the community and the different audiences we address. But I have never written any literary stuff.

I: *Another interviewee said that when he was 18 he wrote an historical novel. It never saw the light of day of course, but …*

JB: Apart from occasional verses for birthdays and anniversaries and so on, I have never written any dilettante poetry or something like that. I did write for high school, the vaudeville sort of evening for which I would write scenarios and things like that.

I: *The next question is: what have you learned over the years about the process of writing and also about writing for publication?*

JB: It's a very interesting issue. I give all sorts of advice to my own students which I never followed myself. I was very much an intuitive sort of writer – I mean, I never worked in a planned way like, you know, I need to write a particular type of article for a particular type of journal for the benefit of my career, which is what people now have to do. Basically, I think the most important lesson that I have learned is that writing has become a specialism in its own right and, as a consequence, that we in our academic programmes do not spend sufficient energy and intellectual attention to it. We simply assume that you do research and when research is over, you write. You write it up and it will (as if by a miracle) become an article in a very big journal or become a book with Oxford University Press or whatever. Now it doesn't work that way. It is really a thing that requires preparation: you have to do your homework if you want to start writing. You have to read, you have to explore the so-called market. For instance, what kind of articles appear in some of these journals? Do I feel that my material is up to that sort of thing? And you

have to go stealing – how do I look at these publications as a model for mine or as an example of achievement that I could also use for my work and so on?

So what have I learned? That we need to be far more precise with respect to what we tell our students about writing. If I were a junior researcher now and if I would use the same sort of approach as I used 25 years ago, I would never get published other than by accident – somebody believing that it might be worthwhile and helping me out on the editorial stuff and so on and so on. But I would never get anywhere with my material.

I: *In Chicago at the 4Cs – Conference on College Composition and Communication – I was invited to participate in a round table discussion. There were six people at the table, all young academics who want, and need, to publish. They had brought along ideas about what they might publish and their queries and anxieties. They received feedback from each other and from a senior American academic who could suggest American journals which they might consider, and from me. I think they found it very helpful. We asked: 'What's your intended audience: just what is your message here?' etc. and the American would say: 'Well if that's your focus and that's your audience, these are journals to go for. Have a look at them, study them …'.*

JB: We now need to think about things that are, at first glance trivial, such as the key words that you choose. When you choose key words, it means that you will show up in electronic databases as an author in a particular field using a particular framework. I remember that when I started out none of these advanced electronic indexes were available; as a consequence, it was rather more an old-fashioned way of going about your text. It needed to be a solid piece of research and it needed to say exactly what it had to say and so on, whereas now you are obviously more in the marketing business, which again imposes more and more pressures on our students. I am not saying that it is harder to get a thing out in a journal, for instance, because there are a vast number of journals that didn't exist 20 years ago – there is an inflation of the number of journals. But it is hard to get an article into the exact journal where it belongs, to be read by exactly these and these and these people that you have in mind as your audience. In other words, it is harder now to make an impact with your articles than it was 25 years ago. And again, this is a matter for training, it is a matter for serious attention, yet we simply take for granted that writing will be like riding a bike – try it and you see that it works. No, I don't think we can maintain that sort of line any more.

I: You say times have changed a lot …

JB: They have.

I: And if you were not at the Institute or another academic institution, do you think you would still write?

JB: My father was a butcher and he went to school until the age of 14, so he was a man with very little education and very little opportunity in life to read. He used to say to me, 'Oh I would love to read' and I always thought 'Yeah, of course, but you will never read.' The day he retired he became a voracious reader and he literally read everything, from yesterday's newspaper all the way to eight hundred-page novels and historical works. Whatever he could lay his hands on, he would read. I guess what I am saying is that I enjoy writing, I find it a form of expression that allows me to be more precise, more versatile, perhaps clearer as well than ordinary genres of conversation or human interaction would allow me to be. And so my feeling is, yes, I would write like my father read. I don't know what I would write, I don't know in what capacity I would write, but minimally I might be somebody who would keep a diary – a kind of big one you know, a multi-volume one, not a short one!

I: One question which perhaps hasn't really been addressed so far is: what does your writing say about you – or what do you hope it says about you?

JB: The writing is not uniform of course and I might be the odd one out in the sense that I work in different languages and across a range of genres. I like that diversity in the sense that I can be things in

specific forms of writing that I don't need to be in others. I can, in that sense, create different little worlds in which I am this rather than that, and I can either keep them separate or I can allow them to blend and so on and so on – ad lib. It may speak to the nasty things about me, the fact that I tend to be highly critical of everything, notably of myself, and the fact that I never consider a job finished which, in a number of instances, drives people crazy. At the same time it's a thing for which this multilingual and multi-genre writing offers me exactly the sort of space to articulate. So in that sense it maybe tells the story of a typical late modern individual who is fractured or, at least, who moves through different worlds each time being different individuals: not only Dr Jekyll and Mr Hyde, also Mr Jones and Mr Smith and Mr Brown. Sometimes they like one another and sometimes they hate one another. [*Laughs*]

I: This has been fascinating, but is there anything you would like to add?

JB: Well, I mean, as an advice to young people: take your writing seriously, so if you write, write to kill – OK? Don't consider it a sidekick of other things. It really, really is a massively central ingredient of your job. In addition, it really does offer you opportunities that you don't have if you don't do it. It allows you, as I said, ways of expressing yourself that have a flexibility and fullness, a rigour and a lasting dimension to them that other forms of expression don't have. So do elaborate it, do work on it. Start by reading in a particular way, reading also as a way of looking at stylistic hints and look at the beauty of texts. And if you write, try to write well. My advice to my students is always: when you write a book, try to write the sort of book that you would love to read. In that respect, very often people appear to like to read extremely arid and extremely boring books, but even so, the attempt must be to create a textual artefact that is appealing, that has a beauty to it. There is no opposition between intellectual work and an aesthetic drive or ambition, and your intellectual product deserves a golden lining in order to shine the way it ought to shine.

I: Wonderful metaphor – thank you very much. It has been a really fascinating interview.

Note

Jan Blommaert is now Finland Distinguished Professor of Linguistic Anthropology, University of Jyväskylä, Finland, and Professor of Linguistic Anthropology, Tilburg University, The Netherlands.

Shirley Dex

I: *If we could start by just getting you to say something about what you do at the Institute, your role, responsibilities, and how long you have been here.*

SD: I came to the Institute in October 2002 as a research professor to build up a programme of research around the British Birth Cohorts, and then one year later in October 2003, I became Head of the Bedford Group of Life Course and Statistical Studies and that requires me to undertake a lot of management and committee work in the Institute as well as supporting the development of the whole group, which is up to 100 staff of various kinds. So I try to combine research work alongside quite a lot of management and administration work, and it is quite

a juggling exercise and the administrative management aspect of my work pushes out the research if I am not very careful.

I: *Could you start by saying something about either your best piece of writing or one that you feel most proud with the result?*

SD: Well, I feel very pleased with several bits of writing and a recent book, which I've edited, but I've written quite a lot of it as well, with Heather Joshi, on the Millennium Cohort Study. But that is a certain type of writing, which is not a peer-review journal, it's a book, which has got an academic publisher but is also aimed at being accessible to policy makers and other interested parties.

And I suppose what I think is that you have to divide up writing into the various genres that occur within academic life; for example, there's peer review journal articles, which have a specific format and are geared to particular journals. They have customised elements relevant to journals and certain disciplines, with different traditions. Then there's books, which might be more academic, and other books that are more populist. Then there are short pieces in pamphlets or briefings that might be specifically aimed at very busy policy makers whom you want to communicate to – people who will only read two sides of A4 and therefore you want to get across your main findings.

There are also research reports, which we do quite a lot of in the Bedford Group, for government departments or specific funders, and they again impose a format. They can be longer than an article in a peer review journal and have all the details in and can come across as sometimes quite boring writing, but nonetheless are read avidly by the people who paid for them.

So there are these different genres and I think in my career I have had to learn how to write, and I have learnt how to write for the different genres at different points along the way.

Therefore, I started out, after my PhD, learning a bit about academic peer review journal articles. I then got thrust into a phase, which was quite a lengthy phase of my career, doing contract research for government departments, in which the outputs were always research reports.

I did not bother too much about the outputs in my early career because nobody had to think about that. Then these quality assessments, the RAE started to be talked about and so I went back to writing more specifically for peer review journals and had to learn a lot more about doing that. Then more recently I have been involved in whole research programmes where there is much greater emphasis on communicating with practitioners, policy makers and lay audiences. Then the format is short bulletin reports or writing press releases. So there's a whole range of things that I've learnt, in different orders, but I suppose the one thing I'd say is, on all of these things, I've had to learn how to do them better and I think I'm still doing that. Nevertheless, although I have improved enormously in

my writing, I can still see that there are improvements that I can make.

I feel very much that you should see writing as a learning process and, as far as I'm concerned, after 30-odd years, I still feel I'm learning, in the fuller sense. And the other thing that is crucial, is that you write for an audience, basically, and you have to know who the audience is when you start out and the style of writing that's appropriate. Learning to write for a specific audience is a sub-branch of learning to write at all.

I: Do you have any writing that you are not so pleased with or feel that you could do better?

SD: Well, I think I can look back on a lot of my writing [*laughs*] like that, unfortunately. That is part of the process of improving. However, when you look back to see the earlier things you think, 'Whoa, that was dreadful.' I certainly did think that. I looked back on my own writing looking for examples for several teaching sessions I did on 'writing journal articles' on a research methods course.

I taught a couple of sessions on academic writing, a few years ago. And I picked out examples of my own writing to use. These were mainly introductions to peer review articles. I had various drafts of an article and I got the group to critique the first one and then I brought along the better one and so on. So I can find quite a bit of my older writing that, you know, I think could have been hugely improved.

I: What, if any, is the satisfaction you gain when writing on your own or with others?

SD: Well, if it is a joint project, it is different from if I get feedback on my writing from somebody who is not an author. I do think it is valuable to get feedback on your own writing from other people who bring a fresh eye to it. I'm most often writing with junior colleagues where I'm helping them develop their writing skills, so that can be satisfying in the sense of supporting a new colleague. But, it's also important to give your own objective eye to a piece of writing. Be self-critical.

I see that as part of my job so I am happy to help. However, it is sometimes frustrating the amount of work that needs to go into it, but you know, that just has to be done. If I were to write with senior colleagues, there are some struggles and frustrations, particularly as not many people approach writing in the same way as you do.

Either you have to allocate things within sections or somebody has to do a complete first draft of the piece. There has to be an agreed division of labour up front, and that's fine. If I do the first draft then I'm all right. [*Laughs*]

If I came to somebody else's first draft, you know, I'm often quite critical and there are diplomacy issues to face and things like that. But you know, on the whole, fortunately, I've never found serious problems about this, but one feels slightly tense about editing other people's drafts, as to whether they'll agree with you. But you work through it.

I: *How about a few tips about writing? Like asking others to comment on drafts?*

SD: Oh, that's essential and that's been crucial to the development of my writing. After I finished my PhD, I wanted to turn some of the PhD into peer review articles.

I had a first job in Exeter as a tutor, and I was lucky to have some colleagues there who were happy to look at my drafts and give me what turned out to be very extensive feedback [*laughs*] on more than one draft. In addition, they went through with me some of the principles of writing that they felt were important, which I was completely missing. I could see you need a structure, that you want a beginning, a middle and an end. If your article was about data analysis you'd discuss the data and the methods and then the results in the middle bit, and then the conclusions.

But one of them suggested to me that every paragraph had to be complete in itself and he showed me through examples what he meant. So that the introduction had to go through the whole article saying what the subject was about, why it was important, whether it filled a gap or what its contribution was going to be (draw on some new data for example), ending with a summary of the main findings in a sentence. That is all within one paragraph.

So that you the writer had to lead the reader

through this mini-story of what the rest of the whole thing was about. And then similarly within sections each paragraph should have a sort of rounded feel to it and be complete in itself. Then you move on to another paragraph topic which you introduce and you say why, what's going to happen and you fill it out. This sort of detailed mentoring *showing me* how to do it was very important in my writing development.

But then comes the detailed sentence-by-sentence editing within paragraphs. I had to learn to avoid the use of shortened terms, concatenated concepts and putting adjectives in front of everything to try and shorten it, sort of thing, you know, where it makes a very disjointed feel to your writing.

Flowing sentences and flowing paragraphs were something that I had to work quite hard on and somebody had to keep telling me, 'Well, this doesn't read well' and I had to go back and try again. So, I had that quite intensive one-to-one feedback on a number of pieces of my early writing, which really helped me make a mega-jump.

Then later on I've had more feedback from editors that funders have employed to edit research reports, because they wanted them to be accessible. They've gone over them with a fine-tooth comb, the writing that we've done, and I've been shocked and horrified when the thing's come back with all their editing on the manuscripts. I mean, some editors that publishers employ hardly do any work on the script, but some funders really think communication is very important and they'll spend money getting everything completely right and accessible and clear. And having had that experience, my first reaction was: 'What a pain in the neck, I'm going to have to go through and edit on this sort of scale.' Usually you think, oh, editing, it'll take you an hour or so for a large document maybe. But, this was days of work, altering all the sentence constructions. But, you know, there was no question it was better [*laughs*] so that was a very big step towards my improvement and better writing. And after that gradually you start to write like that in the first place.

So getting people who will do detailed editing and give you detailed help is not easy, and more so due to the pressure people are under these days to do their own writing. Reading other people's writing and giving that sort of detailed feedback is hard to find.

But if you ask someone to edit your work and give you feedback, they need to know that you are ready for detailed feedback. So if somebody really wants to improve their writing, they need to say to the person, 'Look, I really want honest and detailed feedback. Can you give that to me? That way I will improve.' You need to indicate, signal up front, that you're open to a serious level of feedback and not just general comments.

You can help yourself though. You write a draft yourself and you think you're reasonably happy with it. You should then wait a week, say, certainly a few days, don't do it the next day but leave a little gap, the longer the better in some ways, if possible, a good week. Go back and re-read it and you will then find many ways of improving it yourself. Just having that gap and then coming at it slightly fresher with a more objective view will enable you to improve your own writing. Ideally I would do that twice before I show it to anybody else. Now I know pressures mean that you don't always do it like this and, you know, I'm often writing to deadlines and that isn't the ideal. And let me stress that if you want to develop your writing you certainly don't do it by writing to deadlines. So, if writing improvement is one of your aims you need to be doing it away from specific deadlines.

Then, show it to somebody else and encourage them to look at your writing as well as the content of what's being talked about. But you obviously need to choose wisely. You need somebody who writes well [laughs] and somebody who will agree to give you the time that's needed. And, if all else fails, you could employ, pay a professional editor to give you detailed feedback on a one-to-one sort of basis, because they will. People who do editing for a job are usually excellent writers. But they tend to specialise in a certain type of writing, so you need to identify what sort of audience it is you're addressing and writing for and find an editor that specialises in that audience.

I: *When do you write?*

SD: It's not a time of day thing, with me, although maybe it is with some people. Usually my other timetable – for example, meetings – sets the time I have for writing. Although, I suppose, if I was starting out a new piece, I would choose the morning

probably. The first step is sitting in a chair with a piece of paper and a pen and thinking about it, asking myself, 'What do I want to say in this?' I make some notes of the key items that I want to get across. And then I would fairly soon go to the computer and start writing. If I'm writing to a known format, which is most of the time really, I would then just start typing, and I would work from the beginning to the end. I've tried not doing that, but somehow I find it very tense or unsatisfactory where I haven't written a complete introduction, which I sort of think to myself is silly, but anyway. [*Laughs*] Although writing the introduction does focus you on what the paper or writing is about.

But I don't always follow it beginning to end. I do sometimes digress. If there's a section of detail that's going to go in an appendix, I might leave that till the end. There will be a lot of rereading and rejigging. I find, you know, I don't write coherently the first time. I'll find I've sort of got sentences or paragraphs in the wrong place that should've followed or gone earlier. I constantly read the printed version and cut and paste.

I: *And what about the background reading? Literature searches?*

SD: Well, with difficulty. [*Laughs*] Reading's a real luxury these days.

I: *As you know, refereed journals require this.*

SD: Yes, that's right. Well, in a peer review journal article and a lot of other genres, as book chapters, they will want a sense of the literature in a summarised form that's relevant to the topic that you're writing about. And even with dissemination leaflets as a type of writing, the policy maker will still want a sense of where this fits in the scheme of things.

There needs to be communication about whether this writing is filling a gap or whether it's totally new. Or are you just adding new data or confirming earlier findings? All of those things have to be summarised. It's as if you are saying: 'There is a body of literature that says this, but I'm going to tell you it's not like that.' [*Laughs*]

You have a main storyline, so you do need to be immersed in the literature of the field. You don't need to tell everything about it. You have to do a judicious summary of what's leading up to what you have to say about this subject. So it's enough to show you know the literature. If it goes through a refereeing process and you have missed, you know, the central things about the literature, the referees will come back saying 'doesn't know the literature' or something like that. But equally, in an area where there's a lot of writing already, you can't possibly reference everything. So you're really telling just enough. It's the beginnings of the story that you're going to carry on, pick up the beacon and carry, walk forward a bit down the line. And that's the story aspect and narrative to the whole thing – which is very important, even for peer review journal articles. You're in a way telling a story. But the story then has a format. You are saying: 'There's this body of knowledge or debates on this, I'm going to extend it, fill a gap' or 'I'm going to broaden the understanding or widen the theoretical framework, or completely overturn former thinking on this' etc. So, your story through the rest of the writing is important. But, yes, juggling the writing with reading and with my other work is a real problem.

I: *How on earth do you manage to be a head of a school and all that entails, and still find time to write?*

SD: Well, unfortunately you have to take shortcuts. And the shortcuts can be in the form of reading grant applications that are on the field, because they tend to fill out the literature for you and you get a flavour of things. I go to some conferences where there'll be papers there that summarise the literature and I'll set junior researchers who work for me, the job of conducting literature reviews. So, you're doing it by proxy almost, without having time to read all the stuff yourself as you did at PhD level. And you hope by that way to rather pick out things that are really vital that you need to read and, sometimes, you just have to squash reading into every spare moment that you have.

I: *How does the RAE contribute to your writing?*

SD: It doesn't contribute to the quality of my writing, I don't think, but it has affected the type of outputs that I focus on since the RAE has happened. So whereas in the past I just went along with the flow of my career, which was that I kept getting approached by government departments to do research contracts for them – and they were quite interesting things. I felt I was offered the chance to do quite innovative work. But this all ended in research reports for the funder. These were not rated highly by the RAE. So I had to switch to writing more peer reviewed journal articles.

But when I first switched to peer review journal writing, somebody said to me that my papers all sounded like research reports. And I had to learn to change it. So, that was another step in the learning, shifting genres and writing for different audiences. And you really do have to focus on highly rated RAE outputs.

So although I've done quite a lot of other writing, RAE outputs have to be given priority, because that creates funding for the university. I have a much more strategic and ruthless view of whether I'll do writing now of a particular sort. I mean if I've got limited time I have to make sure I've got my quality peer review journal articles first. The irony is that you're then tempted to think: 'I've now got the four quality RAE outputs, so I can now do some other writing.' So the RAE can inhibit and constrain [to four papers] a productive researcher.

The RAE creates such a pressure – yet the good thing about it is that it's focused on quality. But the bad thing was that it also creates this pressure to publish, which for people earlier in their careers, they might feel they have to publish rubbish. And certainly in terms of the quantity of papers that people produce these days, and the number of new journals to accommodate all this writing, not all of them really need to be published. But people feel that they have to have publications on their CV and the more, the better. But a lot of things that happen further down the line are not necessarily good quality and we'd be better off for the system as a whole if we didn't have such a lot of things published.

I: *So what have you learnt about writing, based on what you've just said?*

SD: I don't think the RAE has taught me very much about writing. It's just created a pressure that you have to write certain sorts of things. But I don't feel it's entirely bad. In the past, the system had its own defects. This one's got some defects as well. In the past, there were people who didn't feel under any pressure to write and have outputs from their research or to do research at all. But you do need to communicate your research in some form or other, or why do it at all?

So, you know, there is a sort of bottom line of quality, which the RAE has flipped the coin to focus on. But what it doesn't do is to allow space and time for more creative thinking and longer-term views and projects. Instead of that there's a dread that I must get a publication *now* because of the RAE, you know, and I think the group of researchers who've entered academia since the RAE in general have a much more instrumental view of what they're doing and not a creative excitement about it in the same way.

I: And the audience for the RAE?

SD: The RAE has added pressure to write for a particular type of audience, other academics, and a certain writing style goes with that.

I think the principle of addressing the audience is one that all writing has to address up front: 'Who are the people that I want to communicate with and how do they expect you to communicate?' I learnt another thing about writing and communicating with audience through doing research in a Business School: that if you want to reach employers, for example, you have to write in a different way than for the government, civil servants. Even the outlets vary, and the words that you would use in the headings. So if, I wrote something on 'family-friendly policies', this is not a title that attracts employers because of 'family'. I would need to use a different title if I were targeting this research at employers, for example, work-life balance or flexible working arrangements or SME employers' policies.

The audience also influences the choice of venue for a conference if you want people to attend. Employers will come to a conference at the DTI, CBI or a business school but not an 'Institute of Education' or a 'Family and Work Institute'.

So, the writing ideally needs to be presented at -

different outlets according to the audience.

I: I'm just wondering where this all leaves the creativity in writing; what happens to it?

SD: I don't think it's totally absent from any of the writing I do. I think that, being creative isn't in a vacuum. You always have some sort of target and framework. If it's to reach employers, you can be creative about that in your style of writing. And if it's to be a good peer review journal article, the creativity might be more in the excitement, for an academic, in the content of what you're trying to communicate rather than necessarily the creativity of the writing. You can still be very excited by the results, the research you've done. Within each genre of writing, I've felt pleased with the writing when I've finished it, although creative isn't always how I would describe it. But the research work that goes into it, always has creative elements.

I: Would you be writing if you weren't in academia?

SD: I certainly will write some things. I think, as I look towards retirement [*laughs*], there'll be unfinished projects and things that are going round in my head that I've no time for now which I certainly think I will want to write up. I've done other sorts of writing, which are letter writing, but letters about problems and other things I've got involved in, such as arbitration – setting out what I've thought about two sides of an argument. And you know, I've had people tell me that my writing was very clear. And that was satisfying to think that it's communicated clearly and that I've been involved in helping resolve disputes. So I imagine I might do more of that.

I: Do you think there's an element of gender imbalance, in terms of working in academia? To what extent are women able to achieve, on the publication front, as much as their male counterparts are?

SD: Well that's certainly true at our house. [*Laughs*] I do the managing of our home's domestic affairs. My husband does bits of jobs that I can get him to do. He's happy to do certain jobs – fix electrical goods (TV, video, MP3 players, burglar alarms, cars). But he doesn't want to organise the whole show. Sociologists call this home management and emotion work, and I end up doing that. I'm the gatekeeper, manager of what domestic work gets done at our house.

And I do find it difficult to combine that with certain sorts of writing. So if I'm initiating something and it's not just straightforward through x, y and z, I do need space, time, and somewhere quiet and free of people to do that. And I can't do it at home, unless everybody's out. But if they're pottering around, I just can't settle to do that. I can pick up pieces of writing that are already started and reasonably straightforward and add a bit when I'm in-between doing other things at home. But I need really an hour minimum to initiate a piece of writing and plan it out. I can't really settle down to do it in only 15-minute gaps. You just gear yourself up and then you have to stop [*laughs*] and it's very frustrating. However, I have trained myself over time to make the most of short periods of time. Otherwise, you don't fit in anything. If I've got an hour, I can make some headway in something and I will get down to it. And if it's just bits of writing, notes or memos kind of thing, obviously I can do that in shorter spaces of time. But anything that has real thinking to it, I need more dedicated and quiet time. And it's very hard to fit in these days.

Writing stimulates ideas. I often make notes down at the bottom of the page, and use it to remind myself that there's something to slot in.

I: So there is the need to be very disciplined.

SD: Yes, definitely disciplined. And that's something I've had to learn. It is learnable and it's the arrival of children that really makes you have to learn it. Whereas before, you know, you just went with the flow and when you felt tired or you had enough you stopped. Well, now, young children force you to have definite deadlines. At five o'clock or half past four, they have to be picked up or whatever it is. And however innovative and creative you feel [*laughs*] that's it: stop for the day.

And you have to then, somehow, resurrect it another time. I've talked to my husband about this, because he often doesn't come home at the time when I've expected him. And he'll say, 'Well I just had to

finish something.' And I say, 'Well, you know, I could have felt like that but I had to stop.' [*Laughs*] He has no concept of having to stop, and even when he's due to pick up the children. When the children were little, and he was meant to pick them up from school, at a certain time, he would invariably be late. He found it very hard to stop working until he'd completely finished something. He wants to stop when he has a feeling that it's a good point at which to have a break. And we had many rows about that. But I think women do learn to be very disciplined, pack it all in, use small amounts of time and they discipline themselves to cut off the flow when they have to.

But there probably is a cost to that. I think the fact that I've learnt to stop work when I have to do other things, and not go with the flow when I'm interested in doing it and feeling stimulated, means I probably don't have so many flowing occasions.

I: Does your writing say anything about you? Is there a sense of identity in your writing?

SD: Well, it's said different things about me over time, I suppose. It might have said I was struggling to write [*laughs*] at one point. Well, I do think it is part of me and part of it says I'm disciplined and organised and I like to be in control. And it says I can see the importance of clearly communicating; it says something about my values. I want it to be honest and have integrity.

I: How would you like to be remembered through your writing?

SD: Well, I think this is a difficult question and the response is something that comes off the cuff. I suppose I want to be remembered for the things that have given me the most satisfaction. And that would be seeing my ideas come together and then being able to communicate them. And that's been quite a struggle sometimes. I've had an idea that there's something here and I just can't get my head around it and then, sometimes, suddenly it happens and I realise what it was I wanted to say. These are special moments and it feels like a discovery.

It's not just the writing that makes it special. It's the bit that's gone before, the struggle and the feeling of vague excitement that, there's something here, that I've got something new, that I'm wrestling with it and that it's somewhere in the back of my mind. And, then, I locate where it is and then I've got something to say. But there's a lot of writing I do which I don't feel like that about at all. I just get on with it, I know what I've got to do, I just do it. But those other occasions where it's been special, you know, relatively few, I would point to those as being real insights that I've had and, therefore, I had something special to communicate.

What has helped me, is to realise that writing is a learning exercise and that, even after 30 years, I still feel there are things to learn and I'm happy to have people give me feedback and that's essential.

I feel I've benefited hugely from in-depth, one-to-one feedback from colleagues and I recommend that people look for that. I've also benefited from people saying to me, 'Who's the audience?' as a general refrain or a question. Because some of the pressures that you work under and write under, sometimes you forget to think about that. And it should be the question at the beginning of any writing. And I think writing is something that you can enjoy. There's a lot of satisfaction in writing something.

You also need to have a good process, which suits you, when you do it, where, how you start and how you cope with the stimulation that it creates, of making notes to yourself, etc. There's a need to build in time gaps where you can have a break and then go back objectively to correct your own writing – you should expect to do that at least twice.

I: Did you always feel that you would be a writer?

SD: No. I didn't really think about it at all. I realised I had to write my PhD, so I knew I was going to do that. I didn't know I was going to be an academic when I did that, and I drifted into it. And I found out that being an academic was about writing almost along the way. So, I didn't start out being a good writer. I can look back and think I was dismal. So, you know, you can be helped to get to the top of the profession if you're motivated to do it.

If you're not so good at the outset, you don't have to think you're always going to be like that. You just have to be motivated to improve. And take any

critical feedback on the chin and just get on with working at improving it.

David Gillborn

I: *David, Can you say something about how long you have been at the Institute, and your role?*

DG: Yes, I have been here since September 1992. Joined as a lecturer in sociology of education, and then got a readership in sociology of education, and I think about 2000 got a personal chair in education. I am currently the Head of the School of Educational Foundations and Policy Studies, and I am Chair of the Race Equality Committee.

I: *Can you tell me about your best piece of writing, or one you feel really somewhat satisfied with?*

DG: I do not think I can point to a single piece and say, 'That is the best piece I have ever done.' The thing I am about to start writing is usually the thing I am most excited about. I suppose the thing I am proudest of is the book I wrote with [Deborah Youdell], *Rationing Education* (2000), because it is very hard-hitting, it is a radical analysis. But despite that, it won quite a prestigious prize in the UK for the best book in education that year. In addition, given that it is radical, given that it is based on qualitative research, it was quite nice to be recognised. Because quite often those prizes go to statistical books and large-scale surveys, so that was quite nice. However, it was unusual in the sense that it was co-written; I tend to write by myself. In addition, I couldn't actually point to one thing and say that's the best thing I've done, because you know, a book is so different to a chapter in a collection. I mean, some of the things I write are meant for a very broad audience, so they are very different pieces of work.

I: Can you say what it was like working with somebody else?

DG: I haven't co-written very much. If I were to go through my CV there's probably only about half a dozen people that I've actually co-written with. Moreover, I think each person that I have written with, I have written with in a different way. Therefore, sometimes we will agree up front who is going to write different sections, and we will write them individually and then put them together and somebody will edit it. The kind of co-writing that does not work, for me, is when you try to write something together as a team. That is really, why I tend to write by myself – I can work to my own deadlines. I think the best work that I do is work that I have written and then had many people look at. One of the best tips I got from anybody was to show my work to other people before I publish it. That is a good idea. However, the vast majority of stuff that I do I write by myself.

I look back at some of my early stuff – there are a few papers in journals, and some conference papers that I have written – where I have been trying out new ideas or new approaches, and they just did not work. When I was a younger academic, I was intimidated by feeling the need to always demonstrate that I was not an idiot. Therefore, I would sometimes use complicated language when I did not really need to. You need to develop the confidence to actually recognise that you do not have to have sentences that are 50 words long. If you say things in a sentence that is 20 words long, maximum, it is usually more accessible. So if I look at the very first paper that I ever published, there are big chunks in that, that I'd want to rewrite now, simply because it's badly written.

I: What has helped you with your writing?

DG: When I started writing my first book, it was in an edited series and the series editor was Professor Robert G. Burgess, who at that time was professor of sociology at Warwick, and is now VC at Leicester.

Robert Burgess said, 'As you write each chapter, send it to experts in the field, and get them to comment on it.' Now that would never have occurred to me. I was a new writer and nobody had heard of me, I'd published very little, and this guy was saying send your chapter, send it them, explain what it is, and see if they've got any comments. And I was amazed at how many people wrote back – they gave detailed comments, they suggested new things, it was fantastic. I mean, some of them ignored it, but some really big names were interested and engaged, and that was brilliant. And in a way, I try to do that for people that send articles into my journal. The referees that I use and re-use are the ones that don't just give a recommendation, and a line of print, they're the ones that give a page, two, sometimes three or more pages of detailed comment, so that often, somebody submitting a paper to the journal, whether or not it gets published, they're almost having a tutorial with two of the leading people internationally in the field. That can really help, so I would definitely advise people to do that, just bite the bullet. It is a lot easier to send these things through the post than to approach people at conferences, although I would also recommend that.

The other thing that really helped me was a piece of editing software which is now part of Microsoft Word. And it was fabulous, it was the best teacher I could have. You went through it, and you changed the rules specifically for things that you found were difficult, whether it was a letter, or a chapter, or a book, this piece of software looked at it, told you how readable it was, flagged split infinitives, and flagged sentences that were too long. What I found was that academic writing uses long sentences, so I had to tell it not to flag the sentences that were only 20 words long, but the sentence that was 30 words long. And for about three or four years, I used that on everything that I wrote, even memos to people in the department, and that really taught me how to write directly. How not to make things complicated because you think it makes you look clever. Because all it really does is to make it difficult for people to follow you. After about two or three years it became redundant, there was no need for it any more, because I had learned. The things it was going to flag, I knew as I was writing.

And another thing that helped was a book by Howard Becker, called *Writing for Social Scientists* which saved my life when I was doing my PhD and has some very direct tips about styles of writing, the use of the literature, which are just gold dust; it's a real goldmine of how to survive in the world of writing.

I: Can you say something about the journal you mentioned earlier?

DG: I edit a journal called *Race, Ethnicity and Education*, which has been going for, nine years now. In addition, it attracts work from all over the world, looking particularly at issues around racism in educational policy and practice.

I: How does it work?

DG: Well, let us start at the beginning. Somebody submits something to the journal. As long as it is not ridiculously long or short, it will go out to at least two independent referees. Some journal editors read things and only send out things that they think are any good. I do not do that, because that would introduce a bias, so I send everything out to referee. Then I am guided by the referee's guidance. And that means sometimes I publish things that I do not think are terribly good, and sometimes I have to turn down things that I think are perfectly fine. However, that is the nature of a refereed journal, very different to an edited collection. But finding referees can be very difficult, because it is a thing that people do free of charge, they get no kudos for it at all, but I have a group of people that grows every year, that do a good job. People recognise the support that they are getting through the journal, so then they tell other people. So there has been a good word of mouth.

At the American Educational Research Association, they have what they call round tables, where they invite journal editors who will just sit at a table for 45 minutes, and anybody who's interested in that journal comes up and sits at the table. And editors are encouraged to explain how the journal operates, what they are looking for. But people are free to ask anything. And I have done one of those every year since they first started, and they have been great,

because people can come up and ask questions that they would be afraid to ask elsewhere.

A supervisor or a mentor's job, I think, is to tell you what it's really like, to tell you how journals operate, how do you go about submitting, how do you network with people, how do you find out which journal is full for the next three years, and which journal is looking for articles? These are not state secrets, and unless we share them with people, it is going to be the same old groups publishing the same old thing.

I: So, how do you manage to continue to write with your other roles and responsibilities?

DG: It's easier since I became a professor, in the sense that when I say I'm working at home tomorrow, people don't look at me as if I just said something outrageously disgusting. There is a sense that professors are expected to work at home. I don't know if people assume that professors actually just sit in their garden and smoke pipes, but … when I used to say that as a lecturer, people used to look at me like I was skiving off. There was definitely a sense that if you were not visible five days a week, you were not standing in front of a class or meeting students, you weren't working. But I have always seen the writing as one of the most important parts of my scholarship, because it addresses a much wider audience. I can get at people with very different life experiences, in different nation states.

When I arrived, I spoke to my head of department and my personal mentor at the time, and I said, 'I am finding it difficult to write.' And he said, 'Well, don't come in every day – you have to manage it so that you're at home at least one day a week, and you write. Otherwise, you are not going to produce anything.' It took me about two or three years to realise that what that means is you have to start saying 'no' to things. And you can only say 'no' to things if your boss backs you up.

So it is not one of these things where oh, if it was only as easy as people learning the strategies – it is about power. You do need line managers who understand that you cannot do everything. And line managers who will talk with you honestly about what the priorities are. And sometimes you are not going to get any writing done at all. I try to work at least one day a week at home, writing. But even now, there will be weeks when I am in every day. There will be weeks when, even though I do not come in, what I am doing at home is more admin; I am sitting there writing a policy paper.

For many years, the only way I could possibly get any writing done was working at weekends and into the night. And that is not healthy. I would not have produced the steady trickle of publications that I have, if I had not been working regularly at least one full day every weekend.

The demands are absolutely upon your family, and because of the way things work, in terms of structuring of power in our patriarchal society, it is usually much easier for men. Society is built around supporting them and exploiting the unpaid labour of their partners. But the whole family is implicated in it. If one partner, whichever one it is, comes home and says, 'Well I've got to work on this, the deadline is next Tuesday', they don't see you, whether it's the mother or the father. One of the most important publications I have ever done was a thing I wrote for Ofsted in the mid-Nineties. And in order to have the breadth of data that we wanted in it, but also to hit the publication deadline, for about three months, two days a week during the week and every day at the weekend, I was working until half past two in the morning. But it was the only way to do it. It is hard on everybody, it is horrible. Really horrible. However, you do the things because you are committed to it, and you tell yourself it is not going to be this terrible all the time.

I: What about the RAE and writing?

DG: The RAE overall has many very negative impacts. The one good impact is that it means that people's writing is seen as a serious part of their job. When I got my first proper job at a university in 1998, there was a culture among some of my colleagues that … one colleague referred to another colleague's list of publications – I haven't got the exact phrase – but it was something like a 'brag rag', that basically somebody's list of publications was them showing off. Now, that was it. People that published were seen basically as arrogant show offs. Now that is

not a very healthy academic outlook. The RAE has definitely put that right, but I think it has gone way over the top. I think it has completely intimidated many people. And I think in a way, well in several ways, it has actually made it more difficult for young scholars to break through. Because of the time constraints, you do not have time to take a risk. It would be really good to send it to that prestigious journal; however, your chances of getting in that prestigious journal are not as good as this less prestigious – given the time constraints, send it to that one. Now that is not healthy for anyone – it is not healthy for the person, it is not healthy for the journals. So I think the RAE has been a sledgehammer to crack a small nut. And its impacts have been clearly the worst for people who are the most exposed. I am sure its impacts have been felt most amongst research staff, amongst people on short-term contracts, and particularly amongst members of staff from minority ethnic groups.

I: You touched on earlier about the satisfaction you get from writing: can you say a bit more?

DG: [*Pause*] That is a difficult question. Because I am acutely aware of the time lag between finishing a piece of writing and it appearing in print. So I think there's a lot more instant gratification from teaching and supervision. And from presentations – I mean, if I present at a conference for parents or I do something for a government department, even if the room is full of people who think I'm a complete idiot and who are only there because they've been told they have to listen to these alternative perspectives, you're in the moment, you're seeing the reaction. And you could be frustrated, you can be galvanised, whatever, it is instant.

Whereas writing, even if you think, 'My god, that is brilliant, that is cogent, it's original, that's really going to put the cat amongst the pigeons', it's not going to put the cat amongst the pigeons for at least nine months, because it's going to take that long for it to come out. You are never sure who is going to read it, how's it going to be received, the world will have moved on. So quite often, I'll be sitting at the word processor, thinking. 'Well I want to make an argument along certain lines', and realising that this is way better than an argument that I made similarly in something that's coming out next week.

So a book's going to come out, there's a chapter by me in it, and I'm already looking at it and thinking, 'Well, you know, that's like a first go at it and, god, I hope nobody's reading that – they should really read this one I'm going to write tomorrow.' And that's weird, because then you'd go to places and give a seminar, and they say, 'But surely in that thing you wrote last year, you said x and y?' And I am saying, 'No, because that thing that came out last year, I wrote three years ago, and it has been delayed at the publishers, and I have changed my mind, things have moved on.' So, it is weird. It is a strange kind of thing.

I suppose the most pleasure I get out of writing, is when I talk to someone who I've never met before, and they say, 'I read x by you, and that was great.' If your work has been important to somebody, that is great. Because then you feel like we are not just going through the motions, we are not just addressing a bunch of policy makers who really do not give a damn about equity. We are also addressing people who are fighting these battles in other locations and are using my work constructively. So that is the pleasure from writing, and that can happen years after you have finished.

I: Is there a particular type of writing that you enjoy?

DG: I suppose it would be chapters in books, in edited collections, because although I do a lot of writing of smaller pieces for specific audiences, like evidence for the Select Committee or a little piece of writing for the Stephen Lawrence Charitable Trust or the Runnymede Trust or something like that, you're really limited – a small piece of writing like that, two thousand words, you can really only put one decent idea across, because you've got to hit them, you've got to explain it, it's got to stand up with some evidence, then you shut up, you're finished. So, those are too short. Books are brilliant, sole author books are fantastic, because you can throw everything in there, but they take a hell of a long time to write. Articles in refereed journals can be fun, but because it's refereed, I always feel like you've got an eye over your shoulder. Whereas a chapter in a book, you've really

only got to convince the editor that this stands up, you can take risks a bit more. You can say, 'Y'now what, I'm just going to go for this argument here, and I'm going to marshal these things, and you might not recognise this as what I was going to write about, but stay with me and read it to the end, and then tell me what you think.' So those can be the most fun, because you can do things a little bit different to other styles of writing. But they do not count for very much in the RAE.

That is the real frustration. I mean, my eyes have been opened on this over the last few years. I've been working with people in critical race theory in the States, and this particular perspective, critical race theory, started in legal studies. Now I had always assumed that law journals would be full of stuffy tracts about this case and that case. Some of the writing in the legal version of critical race theory is incredible. Stories, parables about invented characters going back in time, meeting with the founding fathers and arguing with them about the way the constitution was written, and then using that to open up a whole set of issues about the current forms. I mean, really amazing stuff. And I am reading this and looking at the bottom of the page and it says *Harvard Law Review*. And that's just opened my eyes, I can't write like that, I'm not good at flowery writing, I have a certain style of writing, which I hope is clear, and also marshals a lot of evidence. The kind of short story version of writing, I cannot do it. But I can appreciate it. [*Since this interview was conducted I have written a new book and experimented with storytelling! The lesson is – have a go! If it doesn't work, what have you lost?*] And one of the other things about critical race theory is its directness. It is a real corrective to things like the kind of European social theorists, especially in education, who you read and they will take six pages to say something that they really could have said in three pages. It's difficult when ideas are translated, so there are some amazing ideas in Foucault or Bourdieu, and Basil Bernstein is probably the Institute of Education's greatest ever scholar, but I think he would have been even greater if he could have written things that people would have found more accessible. I think his ideas are more powerful than his writing.

The book I mentioned by Howard Becker, *Writing*

for Social Scientists, the first chapter is about a discussion between Howard Becker, who's one of the leading American sociologists of the twentieth century, conducting a seminar on writing that he ran for graduate students. They took a piece of writing and went through it and crossed out all the bits that were redundant, all the things that were flowery, and all the things he called bullshit qualifications. Where somebody, rather than saying what they mean, says, 'Well in certain cases, it's sometimes the argument that it may or not be' and by the time they have put all the qualifications in, they have not actually said anything. And Becker goes through and crosses all these things out, and he thinks he is doing a brilliant job, and the students are looking pained. And one of them says, 'Well, look, that is OK for you, you are a professor, you're Howard Becker, everybody takes you seriously. We have to do this to show that we are smart. If we write in a direct style like that, the people on our PhD panels will say that we are not scholarly.' And Becker says, 'You know, they were right', so the deal is to find a balance. So you cannot just write as if you were having a conversation, you do have to reference things. And referencing is not bullshit, referencing is to show that you have read stuff, you have understood what has gone before, that you are building on it. You are not showing off, you are using what is around.

So, it is finding those ways of balancing making the argument clear, against just being obtuse for the sake of it. Some people say my work is very clear. So I say at the beginning what the paper or the chapter is about, here's what the argument is, and then I say, 'Here's how I'm going to structure it. So there is going to be a section on that, a section on this, and when you get to the conclusion, I am going to go over it again.' Now some people say, 'I really like your writing, it is clear.' Other people say things like, 'I wish you'd take the volume down a little bit, because it's like you keep on hammering the same point just in case the reader hasn't got it.' And my argument is not that I imagine the reader did not get it the first time, I do not think I am saying the same thing ten times in a paper, I am setting out what the argument's going to be, and then I am taking you through it a stage at a time. But I do try to make it very transparent. One of the best tips in the Becker book is if you are writing in

educational social science, do not try and write a Sherlock Holmes mystery. So, do not keep the conclusion until the last page, because the vast majority of work in our field is not interesting enough to sustain people to the last page. If they do not know where you are going with this, they will stop reading. And stuff that really annoys me is if people start writing in an ironic or sarcastic tone, because you know what, it does not work. So if I read a page and I have to turn a page to find out whether they meant it or not, life's too short for that. So Becker, I keep returning to it because it was such an important book when I was writing my PhD, which was my apprenticeship: tell them at the beginning whodunit. Do not wait until the last page to say the butler did it. Say, 'My argument is that the butler did it, and he did it in the kitchen, with a pair of scissors, and he was in cahoots with the maid. Now, I'm going to show you exactly why he did it, and how it is that the others didn't realise he did it, and then I'm going to show you how we exposed him.' So the reader goes, 'Oh right, that's what it's about, here's where we're going to go, OK then, show me.' So that is what I am trying to do.

I think you show it to people. Show it to different people. There is always a risk in showing things, but if it is going to be published, it is going to be in the public domain forever. So it's a lot better to have a little group of folks who you will show drafts to, and eventually you build up a group of people, some of whom will be eminent scholars in the field, some of whom will know nothing about the field. If you are a sociologist of education, and you only show your writing to sociologists of education, you are only going to get a very slanted feedback. They will not notice areas that someone who is a classroom teacher, or even someone who does not work in education at all, will notice.

So, it is building up that little group of people that you trust, to show a draft to. And sometimes, particularly when you are starting out, you have to trust people with a draft, but sometimes they let you down. So if somebody comes back with 'well you have split an infinitive', then you don't show them your next draft because you are wasting your time. If somebody comes back with some intelligent comments, you show them the next draft and the next draft, and you build things up like that. But what you need to remember is, if you are going to show people a draft, you need to build in time for them to read it, for them to talk you through it, and then for you to make some changes. So there is no point in leaving it, if you have to have a chapter ready by Jan 1st, there is no point in starting to write it on 1st December. You have to have it finished weeks before the deadline. And even if you're not going to show it to someone, a good trick is write it, then leave it for two or three weeks. Because when you have just finished writing it, you know what it was you meant to say, so when you read it, it will seem fine. Put it on one side for two or three weeks, come back to it, you see all the typos, you see all the grammatical errors, and I mean I have done that and come across entire paragraphs that are just unnecessary. And if you wrote that paragraph last night at one-thirty in the morning, that paragraph took a lot out of you. And if you look at it the next day, there is no way you are going to delete that paragraph because it was hard work. You look at it in three weeks' time, you go 'Well, I don't need it, I will delete it.' So, time is a useful resource, just finishing something, and then leaving it for two or three weeks.

I: Do you think your writing says something about you?

DG: You're going to have to ask some people who read it. Because I think different readers would take different things from it. So, somebody would read it, and say this is an opinionated, arrogant person who does not understand that things are a lot more complicated than this. Other people might read it and say, 'This is a passionate engagement.' I hope that some people read it and say, 'Well this is really good scholarship, but it also is committed.' I think you can be committed to a set of ideas, but also be a good scholar. So I … if somebody says that my work is only passionate, I'd be really disappointed, because I don't want it to be only what I think, I want it to be what I think having read a lot and looked at the data and spent time doing things. I get angry when people do not take other people's work seriously. And that is not just my work, but if somebody just writes off somebody's study, because they have heard that it does not treat class very well.

Often, one of the traps people fall into is that they hear that a certain author, or a certain study, says this. And so they do not bother looking at the original. And often the original has a lot more to it, if you actually consulted the original you could use it, you could build on it, rather than saying that it is inferior, I am going to do something different. But going back to your question about what people take from the work, I hope the fact that it's clear – I hope it's clear, I hope it's committed, but I also hope that doesn't mean that people don't recognise that it is scholarship. So there was recently a paper in the *British Journal of Sociology of Education*, which says that 'Gillborn and Youdell, the *Rationing Education* book, on the basis of a single statistic, declare that these entire inequalities are created by their teachers.' And it gives a single page reference. Now that is bullshit, because that study was based on two years' ethnography in secondary schools. There is an entire chapter in the book about the way in which ability and intelligence have been constructed and there is another chapter talking about the whole kind of policy context that led up to the study. So the idea that, based on one statistic, Gillborn and Youdell make any claim, is absolute nonsense. And when people say stuff like that, all they are doing is identifying the fact that they are lazy and not seriously engaging with anything. So I hope I am not guilty of doing that to the people that I criticise. And it annoys me intensely when people do not take work seriously, when they just want to slot people into little pigeonholes.

I: How did you get into doing work on race?

DG: I come from a white working class background. And I knew very early on at school that I could survive school by making teachers laugh, or certain other tricks that they took to mean that I was working really hard or was clever. So at the age of seven, I knew that schooling was a performance. I knew there were people who were getting the wrong end of the stick about what other people could do. It was at secondary school when I started to recognise that all the black kids in the school were basically being treated like second-class citizens. They were all in the bottom streams, they were all in the bottom class, black kids dominated the sports teams, none of them were in any of the academic groups. And that was just wrong.

But it was only when I got to university and started looking at inequalities in education, and there was virtually nothing on race in our syllabus, it was all class and then gender. And we had a single lecture on race. So when I finished my degree I wanted to do some research, and it seemed blindingly obvious to me that what you needed to do was go in a school and look at how people talk and act about race.

Because as a pupil I was convinced that what happens between pupils and teachers is really important. But all the literature I was given at university was almost completely devoid of that. It was all statistics, it was people saying, 'Here's the statistics, what do they mean?' They were theorising from an armchair. So I said, 'Well, why doesn't somebody go in a school and do it?' And it was only when I started the research that I realised some people had gone into schools to do it, but they'd mainly done it in the States, and the stuff that had happened in this country really hadn't looked at race. So that is how I got into it. I mean, I look into other inequalities, but race is the thing that really drives me.

I: *How would you like to be remembered in terms of your writing?*

DG: I don't think I will be remembered. If you think about people who are remembered through their writing, you are talking about a very small number of names. So you're talking about Basil Bernstein, [Michel Foucault, Pierre Bourdieu], you're talking about those kind of world figures. If Stephen was hit by a train tomorrow, people would still be talking about Stephen Ball's work and reading his stuff in ten, 15, 20 years' time.

I hope I keep writing. And I would hope to attain the kind of level of standing, recognition where people are reading your stuff and seeing it outside of just an individual little study, or problem, and seeing it as a contribution to the development of a field. So that would be what I would hope, that the body of work was seen as having made a real contribution to taking forward an understanding about how race and racism operate in and through education.

I: *If you weren't in academia would you still write?*

DG: No. As I say I come from a working class background, where people do not write. I know there are exceptions, I know there are working class folk who write superb novels, and write poetry that moves you to tears, but they are like half a per cent. No. My career rests on two or three moments where if the wind had blown in a different direction I would have been a plumber. It wasn't even conceivable that I'd go to university 'till six months before I went, nobody in my family had ever been to university; I never even thought it was possible. So no, there is no way on earth I would have done any writing at all.

I: *What have you learnt about writing?*

DG: It gets easier the more you do it. So, my tips would be: do not be frightened of it, and plan it. So if you are writing, I don't care if it's a chapter, a thesis, a one thousand word article or an entire book, you sit down with a plan of what you're going to do, and then you start somewhere other than the beginning. Do not begin with the introduction, begin with the first bit that you are confident of. Write that section, write another section and write another section. When you have all that, write a conclusion, then go back and write an introduction. Because you cannot introduce it until you know what you are going to do and as you are writing, you are changing the ideas. As a qualitative researcher in particular, the more you play with the data on the page, once you see the data on the page, it makes you ask a new question, it makes you go back to the data constantly. So there is no point in writing the introduction, because you do not know where you are going to wind up until you have written it.

When you sit down to write something, at least have an idea what your point is. Do not sit down to write an account of some data, sit down to explain why something happened the way it did or to answer a question or to ask a particular question. But don't just sit down to produce five thousand words on the latest statistics on education: have a point.

I: *Any hints about writing for publication in general?*

DG: In general, there are very, very different styles. As an editor I see a lot of referees' comments, so the main reasons why people get rejected in my journal are that they haven't explained their methods properly, that they have completely ignored a relevant literature, that they're saying something that doesn't advance an area or an understanding of a topic.

You have to cover your methodological bases, have to show an awareness of the literature. It is really annoying when you read a paper that could really contribute to a field, but has been written as if no one has written anything on this before. You need the author to do more work than that, the author has to say, 'This is how it slots in, and this is where it takes us.' And doing a journal particularly on race and racism, the methods are important.

Because when I started the journal, I spoke to a lot of people, very eminent scholars on race in different countries, and the overwhelming message was: you must have really high standards because the moment you publish something in the journal that isn't good, everything else in that journal will be tarred with that brush. So it was really difficult at the beginning, because the referees would virtually accept nothing. They wanted the journal to be so prestigious that almost nothing was good enough for them. So there was a process of working it through with the referees, saying: look, we have to strike a balance, we have to let people take some risks. It has to be scholarly; there are things that we are not going to accept, but we cannot have a clone of everything that has gone before. Methods are really important, because the reason it's worth doing our writing and publishing it in journals rather than publishing a novel, is that we're making a claim to evidence. Novels are probably more powerful in the long term in changing attitudes and opinions than scholarship, but I can't write novels, and I think you need both. You need something like, you know, *Beloved* [by Toni Morrison] and you need critical race theory. You put them together and you have a much rounder analysis. But the point about scholarship is that it's just that, it draws on evidence, it's not just somebody's opinion, and it marshals evidence. And that means your use of the literature and your bit about your methods isn't there just to placate your supervisor, it's there because it's really important to convince people that you know

what you're doing, and your evidence stands up to scrutiny.

The way that I write is very much in isolation. I mean physically, emotionally. I have a little room at home with all my books in and the computer, and I just go in the room and work away at it. And it only comes out when I have a pretty good draft, I don't show people working notes. So, the people that would see the working draft of something are actually looking at a honed piece of work. Some colleagues have shown me their work and there are bits of it where there is a section that will say 'add something on ...'. Well, no, I wouldn't dream of showing someone something until everything's in there, otherwise I don't think they can judge it.

But it's very lonely, so I think it's about trying to find support mechanisms. I mean when I've done the session for staff development on writing for refereed journals, it is astonishing how many people just don't have any of this inside information. And it's not published anywhere, so you hope that people's supervisors and line managers share it with them. Tip: contact the editor. Run your abstract by them. Treat them as a human being. Some editors won't reply. I mean, I know an editor who says, 'I'm too busy to look at people's abstracts, if they want my time they have to send a paper in.' Well, if an editor's like that I wouldn't send them my work, because it took too long to write, it's too precious to me to send to someone who's going to treat it like that.

For me writing feels indulgent. I think there's a range of factors behind it, one is this class thing, that writing, it's a bit airy fairy isn't it? 'He writes books, my god…it's not proper work, is it?' And there's still an element of that in the Academy: 'Oh well, he wrote a book, but this person taught three classes.' Well yeah, they're both work, and actually it would be good if you were both doing bits of both. One isn't more important than the other; you need to find a way of balancing. But you have to be sure with yourself that your writing isn't an indulgence. So although you feel guilty not going into work, and you feel guilty shutting the door when you ought to be downstairs with the kids, or you ought to be downstairs with your partner but you're actually going to go upstairs and lock the door and be upstairs with the word processor, you're not being self-indulgent, you are doing something that's important and has to be taken seriously. And in that way, it is actually harder. If you are teaching a class, it looks like work, you're doing it away from home, there's a timetable, and you know when it's done. Whereas writing, there's two hundred other things that you have to ignore, the stack of ironing, you have to ignore the fact that the garden looks a mess and, if you can, you have to ignore the fact that the dog's destroying the front door because it hasn't been for a walk recently, and get on, because what you're doing is work.

Lucy Green

I: *How long have you've been at the Institute and what is your role now?*

LG: I think this is my sixteenth year and I'm now Professor of Music Education. In my time here I've taught on the PGCE, MA, BEd, Diploma, Primary Music and I've had lots of research students. Mostly at the moment I teach on the MA and supervise research students. I'm no longer the MA course leader. I'm heavily involved in research at the moment, out in schools. I've been spending a lot of time in classrooms the last couple of years, which has been lots of fun.

I: *You said you were pleased to be interviewed?*

LG: I love talking about writing and actually people

very rarely ask. So it's a nice opportunity to talk about something that I absolutely love doing. We talk about writing with our students. But we don't very often talk about it just for pleasure or to each other, so it is nice. This book – it's a nice idea.

I: *Why do you think we don't talk to each other about writing?*

LG: I don't know. It's never occurred to me until just now.

I: *Because we talk about lots of other aspects of our work.*

LG: Yes. I suppose for most people writing is a very

private thing, isn't it? You do it by yourself. I mean, one of the things about being a writer, you have to be prepared to spend hours and hours on your own, in solitary confinement, without seeing anybody, speaking to anyone or having anything to do with other human beings. And of course what you're doing when you're writing is trying to communicate to others, but in order to make that communication you have to distance yourself from others. And so it is a very solitary thing to do in the first place. Maybe that's why we don't regard it as something you can just generally ask, 'Hi Bob, how's writing today?' You don't say that. You say, 'How was your class that you've just taken?'

I: That's very interesting. Maybe we'll come back to that when we focus on other issues. We're asking people to describe a piece of writing that they're most pleased with, something they regard as their best piece.

LG: Yes, and I have thought about that, and you probably won't find my answer very helpful because I can't choose one piece of writing. It's because I write different kinds of things – two kinds of writing: one theoretical and one much more focused on practice-based things. So out of the theoretical writing it's probably still my PhD, which I wrote between 1980 and 1984. It was very heavily theoretical. It wasn't published as my first book. In my first book I had to cut out a lot of the theory from the PhD because I couldn't find a publisher at the time who was interested in publishing a book on music which had Bourdieuian theory and sociology of knowledge. Because at that time it wasn't fashionable to cross fields. Now of course, more music education people are digging into Bourdieu. At the time I had to cut it out or I wouldn't get it published. Therefore it's not my first book that I feel warmly about, but it's the PhD. Because that's where I did all that reading. I really got heavily involved in Marxist philosophy and sociology of education and I still learn from that. I'm still harvesting those years of full-time study where you get the opportunity to really get inside a field. The theory that I developed in that piece of work is still my favourite theoretical piece of writing.

And the other favourite sort of writing that's more non-theoretical, more fun to read, accessible and written more for practitioners, would probably be my last book, which was on how popular musicians learn. That was a kind of dream to write, really, because there's no real theory in it, it's just fun and it was fun to write.

I: Are there any other reasons why you've chosen those two pieces?

LG: No, I suppose one is the first thing I wrote and the other is the latest. I've written other things since the book, but I suppose I tend to feel that my longer things, the longer things that you write, give you more scope to express what you're trying to say, so I would be more inclined to pick a book rather than an article. So that's an issue, it's because they're longer. It's just how I feel. It's a purely emotional response; it's just that I feel like that about those two pieces of writing. If you ask me what don't I like, I could come up with a much longer list of things I've written that I don't like.

I: Would you like to tell me what writing you're least pleased with?

LG: I am least pleased with some aspects of my first book. I feel I was too wound up in language and not thinking so much about communication. Having said that, it was a very carefully wrought theory, but it has got some communication problems really, and I suppose I feel, I actually feel quite embarrassed about some of my writing. I feel embarrassed about some of my theoretical writing in particular, and I don't, I don't completely know why. I think, I've often found that a lot of people don't understand the theory that I'm putting forward. That can be a mixture of disappointing, slightly irritating and in general I suppose I feel slightly embarrassed that people must think things about what I've done if they can't understand it. So, yes, I think I would say that the kind of writing that I've done that I like least of all would be the more heavy theoretical writing. But that's because of the difficult regions that it gets into, I suppose.

I: OK, fine. You've mentioned the solitariness of writing and how you don't talk about your writing very much because there don't seem to be the opportunities at work. But the next question is about what's helped your writing?

LG: Yes. Talking about writing with a more experienced writer, getting advice from others. I mean, for me, the main thing that's helped my writing has been my 25-year relationship with my husband, and that was there right at the start of doing my PhD.

He's a brilliant writer and also a musicologist. When I started my PhD he was two years into his, so he wasn't that much more experienced as a student but he was more experienced in the world, because I was only 23 and he was 30. He has taught me everything I know about writing and I say that quite sincerely, although he, if he was here, he would say I have taught him everything because we have a peer learning scenario. We've read all of each other's work and immensely closely and it's that kind of peer-to-peer feedback that is just so valuable, more valuable, I think, than any supervision that you can have. And of course the care and attention that you spend with someone who's a peer is very great. He taught me how to read really slowly and interrogate the meaning of every word and sentence in a difficult text. Before you can write you have to read, and then he taught me how to read my own text really, really slowly and interrogate everything that I was trying to say, and how to try to make sure that I understood every single thing that I was saying. And he also taught me how to index my own work, how to go through, sometimes sentence by sentence, making a plan of what I'm saying and to ensure that the plan, when it's presented as a plan or as an index, that it adds up and how you can move things, using your index, move chunks of text from one place to another to avoid repetition, internal contradiction, going round and round in circles. I use all these techniques with my PhD students now.

I: Where did he learn how to do that?

LG. He's always written. He used to write poetry when he was a teenager, and stories, and I suppose he's fairly self-taught really. I don't know where he did it. He taught himself and we bounced off each other doing it.

I: What do you think he's learned from you?

LG: It's about having an intellectual relationship with someone who's a mentor and if I'm his mentor, he's my mentor. We have, over the years, read so many books together, talked about so many ideas and so much music together and we can have a conversation now which sort of flies. We can just talk at a level of understanding which makes the conversation go.

I: Is conversation part of what helps you with your writing?

LG: Yes, it is. It's an extended conversation. And of course nowadays, after 25 years, he doesn't read everything that I write now. Occasionally I ask him to read something and he doesn't usually make very many comments, I suppose because I've graduated. [*Laughs*] Similarly if I read stuff that he writes now, I don't usually have that much to say, but in the past we used to use our writing as a spur for getting heavily into debates and conversation and I suppose that spurs you on. When I was at Sussex University, which is where I met him, we had a fantastic postgraduate reading group. There were some lecturers in the group and some PhD students – and actually that reading group is still going. Funnily enough, the reading group still meets in the basement flat where we used to live. Very strange coincidence. And that group taught me a lot about writing as well, because the reading that we did: very close, very slow reading together. It's a supportive group of people round you, I think, that you can share your writing with.

I: Have you done any collaborative writing with your husband?

LG: No. Probably end in divorce. [*Laughs*] No, we've never done that, no.

I: And have you written collaboratively with anybody else?

LG: I've got very limited experience of it. And it's something that I really feel I don't know whether I would be good at or not, because after all these years of writing by myself, I'm probably quite set in my ways. I might find it difficult to do any substantial collaborative writing. Having said that, the small amount of collaborative writing that I have done I've found very enjoyable.

I: *Now the next area is about how you keep writing as a major part of your life, given all of the things you've mentioned, all the roles you have, the teaching, the research, all your other responsibilities here.*

LG: Yes. And is one allowed to mention two children, you know! [*Laughs*]

I: *Absolutely.*

LG: Especially as a woman.

I: *Yes.*

LG: A male colleague, who I have great respect for, once said at the beginning of a writing workshop, when you're going to write – and I completely agree with this – you've just got to clear space, you've just got to get rid of everybody and you've got to have ten hours ahead of you. The thing is, as a mother with two children, you probably know what that's like, try finding ten hours ahead of you. I have tried finding ten hours and I can sometimes find ten hours, but they're never going to be clear because there's always someone coming in saying, 'Where's my socks?' and all that. And you know, after having been a full-time PhD student, no children then and I did find those stretches of time, I do find it extremely hard. And now, of course, with email and all the rest of it, I do find it very hard, but I still think that, and I know there are some colleagues who I think are just amazing, how they write for maybe two hours a day. If I was going to do that, I'd do it first thing in the morning. I do that anyway, I have to write first thing in the morning and if I'm writing an article or reading students' work or something like that, I do that for the first two hours of the day, because that's when my mind's clearer. But I know some people can actually write books by just doing two hours a day. I couldn't do that. I have to feel that I've got ten hours of putative free time, even if it's not actually real free

time and, preferably, you know, stretches sometimes of two or three days. Otherwise you just can't clear your head, can you, enough to do it. You spend the first half a day catching up to the point that you left it off last time, which might have been three weeks earlier. So that is a real issue, I think, for everybody in academia now.

How have I managed to keep writing a major part of my life? I've been a bit ruthless actually, at times, and to be perfectly honest … I mean I … sometimes I look back and think when I started work here I was pregnant with my first child and I had another child two years later and my second book came out five years after that. I never worked at the weekends, but I did send them both to a childminder till six o'clock every day and, you know, I feel sometimes maybe I put my book a little bit more to the front than I should have. But there's a certain – perhaps ruthless is the wrong word for it – but I think people who write are driven to writing, and in a sense it's something that you can't help. I can't help it.

I've written three books, which isn't very many compared to a lot of people, but every time I've written one I've sworn I'm not going to write another. And every time it just comes up in me. It happens and then I just find myself organising my life in such a way that I am clearing those slots.

I: *Yeah.*

LG: I just do it somehow. I do it on the Tube, I do it on the bus. I'm dreaming about it. I think about it a lot and I might be sitting on the Tube with my eyes closed, people think I'm having some time off, but I'm actually writing. [*Laughs*]

I: *Yes. Do you use a Dictaphone …*

LG: Yes …

I: *… or write notes, or do you just come and write down what you've been writing in your head?*

LG: Sometimes I rush to a piece of paper when I get home or to the computer. Very occasionally I use some sort of Dictaphone thing to put ideas down or I just scribble it on the nearest thing that I've got and then I shove all the pieces of paper into a file and I just make sure that I reread that file periodically.

I: Do you find you're writing in your head all of the time, or is it only when there's a big book or a major article or …

LG: It is at particular times, because when there's a big book coming, as there is at the moment – well I hope there is – it's no good me thinking about that book in certain ways at certain times. Like now, the book is coming, it's a kind of cloud in my head. The kinds of ideas that I have are vague and structural. I've got to know that they might be completely wacky, totally wrong. I can't have detailed thoughts now, but they, they're just sort of, I don't know how to describe it. It's kind of general structural, possibly wacky things that I just feel might be worth keeping. And then gradually as time goes by, the thoughts that I have will get more and more detailed and of course then I will get more and more obsessed by the whole thing and that's when it starts to eat up my life and it's, it can get very oppressive. And then I am thinking about it, all the time, and I've had to learn strategies to stop myself doing that when I'm with my family or with my friends, because it's not nice [*laughs*] 'Mum?' [*gruff voice*] 'What?'

I: What about satisfactions then?

LG: Satisfactions. Well, I think, for me writing is both an art and a craft and so the satisfactions that I derive from it relate to those two things. From the artistic side of it, I have the satisfaction of creativity and I think it's lovely to create something which you feel is in some sense a complete expression, always flawed of course, and always could be improved. But it's kind of the best that you can possibly do to express what you meant at this particular time. That's nice. And the craft side of it, you know, I get a lot of pleasure from crafting language, from sort of moving text around and trying to streamline an argument and just using words in the best way that I know how to, to try to say something to a particular readership that I have in mind. That's a craft which I think is very pleasurable when it's going well.

But of course there's all the downsides of both those

things, which is the despair, the feeling that everything you're doing is a complete waste of time, the times when it really has, in a sense, been a waste of time. I mean, the amount of writing that I've thrown away is just staggering and I mean sometimes … for example, my last book I wrote the first chapter, I must have spent I don't know how many hours and days I spent on it or how many dreams I had trying to work it out. But after many of these and 30 pages I just threw the whole thing into a dump file on my computer because I realised it's just not right. You know, that's painful, you have to be able to take painful decisions like that and it hurts and sometimes I think you do feel terribly lonely. Specially doing a PhD, many students feel, you can feel, because you get to know the work so well, you begin to think that it's completely obvious and that everybody in the world already knows what you've spent the last four years trying to work out and so you feel like an idiot as well and, yeah, and it's very taxing.

Something else I was thinking of to talk to you about which I've often thought of but never spoken to anyone is the nerves that you feel. Particularly, if it's day one and I'm going to plan even an article, not necessarily a book, an article, and it's an article that I haven't actually drafted in any form before, but this is particularly when it's really a blank slate, I go to my desk in the morning and I actually feel nervous, as if I was going to go on stage and sing a song or play the piano or give a lecture. I think, 'So ridiculous, Lucy, I mean nobody's going to read what you write in this room today'. That's part of the deal with myself, of course, and yet I actually feel dry in the mouth, my heart's beating a little bit fast. It's crazy and I don't understand it. I'd like to know if other writers have that feeling.

I: You still feel that …

LG: Yeah …

I: … even though you've written so much?

LG: Yes, if I'm going to write. Even thinking about it now is actually making my feet go slightly cold.

I: Really?

LG: Yes. It's really strange.

I: *What do you think that's all about?*

LG: I think it's about exposing yourself, isn't it, because, although when you're writing it's very private and one of the tricks that a lot of writers play, and I do, is, you know, to tell yourself, 'Nobody's ever going to read what you're writing', because if you thought they were, you'd cross it all out immediately.

I: *Yes. Is that what you are referring to when you say that's part of the deal?*

LG: Yes. I have to know that I can write complete rubbish onto the screen, because, you know, otherwise you would be so inhibited. Ultimately you know that you're writing something for publication, therefore people are going to read it and you don't know who they are or where they'll be and what they'll say about it or what they'll think about it and so you are exposing yourself. Even though you're sitting in your own room now you're deferring the public appearance, which will be only, not your face, but a black-and-white version of you. So I suppose that's what makes you nervous. It's also the extreme difficulty of the task, of course.

I: *Well, it'll be interesting talking to a number of different people …*

LG: It will.

I: *… and seeing what themes are emerging.*

LG: Yes, and whether everyone's got a completely different take on these questions or what people have in common, there'll probably be bits of both, won't there?

I: *Yes, and I think it'll be interesting for people who are less experienced writers to think, my goodness, you know, these prolific writers are still experiencing these feelings.*

LG: I think that's a lot of it, people think it's easy. I'm not that prolific, but I've written a fair amount of

stuff, so they think it just comes out. I just write an article before breakfast, no struggle. It's not like that and I find, OK, it's easier for me to write now than it used to be, of course, but the emotional struggle is the same. Or, if anything worse, probably. I mean the thing that I've just written, my inaugural, I've just written my inaugural lecture which has driven me potty. I mean that's one of the hardest things that I've ever had to write and I was just having absolute kittens about that. Not just about the delivery but the printed version as well.

I: *Yes. Why were you so nervous about that?*

LG: I think it's particularly exposing giving an inaugural lecture, it's kind of like you're being judged, aren't you? That you've been given this professorship so people are going to be weighing up, 'Well, does she deserve it?', you know, 'What's she done?' And I think, I felt with my inaugural lecture, this is basically my life's work's got to go into this ten thousand words or something. I felt that it's not appropriate to just talk about research that I have been doing at the moment, I thought it had to tie up strands of years of work. That was particularly challenging.

I: *You've talked a lot about your satisfactions and feelings, but perhaps you could say something about what you most enjoy.*

LG: I enjoy most the kind of writing that comes easy. [*Laughs*] And that's when I'm interrogating data. That's the easiest type of writing. If I've got the data and it's nice data and I've done the spadework in collecting it and I've done the basic analysis and I've done it well, then it should write itself, really. And when that happens that's just really fun, because it can flow quite nicely.

I: *When you say 'it writes itself', what do you mean?*

LG: That something that I think of only in relation to when I'm writing around data. So I wouldn't say a theory wrote itself. But if I've got some data and I've analysed it well then in a sense – I'm probably only repeating myself rather than explaining myself, but perhaps in the repetition a better explanation will come – in a sense, if you've categorised the data in certain ways then you start explaining what is in the categories and why you've categorised it like this. The explanation will run out of the data because it's already there in the data. It's all in your head because you've already written it when you analysed the data, do you know what I mean? So it's just in your head, it's just a matter of getting it out onto the paper and it … if the data's properly analysed, it should just all come nicely. It's like a pack of cards that you stack up correctly in such a way that when you flick the first one they'll all go exactly how you wanted it.

I: *Yeah. So from the analysis you've already had to think about the themes.*

LG: Yes, you're articulating your own unconscious processes, aren't you?

I: *Yeah, that's interesting – it's very good to have that described, I think. Because for, again for less experienced writers …*

LG: Yes. I mean obviously in academic work we're trying to do something which approximates to an accurate or a fair description or critical appraisal of the world, so this is where creativity stops and some sort of attempt at something called 'truth' begins, and that's one of the hard things about academic writing, I think. So you can't just allow a complete reiterative process between your subconscious thoughts and your data, because if your subconscious thoughts are all geared around the idea that you want to prove a hypothesis, you know, then that wouldn't work at all. So what I said there is all in the understanding that there is a striving towards critical and accurate appraisal of what you're doing, against some sort of attempt at objectivity. So those are the tensions, which are very hard to handle.

I: *Which leads us nicely to the next question, about what your writing says about you.*

LG: I thought about that and I have absolutely no idea.

I: *But it's interesting, in the two areas that you talked*

about just before, which was to do with your inaugural and not just describing the work, the research that you're on, but making sense of all of your experiences that have led you to this stage …

LG: Oh, yes, I see what you mean. Well, I think one thing I can say, this might not exactly answer your question, but it might be relevant in some ways to your question, that everything I've written has always come out of a personal experience. Very often a personal experience which goes back to childhood. You know, those things that happen in childhood, or in your teenage years, where you start to think about something. You know, why is the world like that, or why is it like this? So everything, I mean the big themes in my writing, concern the split between popular music and classical music, gender in music and the role of girls and boys in classical and popular music, and how people learn in music. Now why it's always music, I suppose, is because music became a big thing for my life. I was learning classical piano, I was listening to various types of rock music, you know, the late 1960s, early 1970s, and all these questions were just part of my own childhood and adolescent years. And I think the reason why I've always gone down the sociological route, I've often thought about that, was because I was born and brought up in India and came to live in this country, and if you are uprooted from one country and taken into another as a nine-year-old child, as I was, it starts you asking questions about society and why people behave in completely different ways in different places and the way that music is a completely different thing. For example, in India where I lived and where we had no radio, no television, no record players, never heard music, come back here and there were the Beatles and the Rolling Stones and, you know, all those things. I could trace every single thing that I've ever written back down to a personal experience.

I: *That's fascinating.*

LG: Yes, that had a major effect on my life. And I think, you know, when I moved from India where I had loads of friends and that was my country and that was the land where I belonged and everything in my world, my little world there, was familiar to me. I came here and had no friends, I hated this country, I found it an awful place, and my big solace was the piano.

I: *Right.*

LG: And so I think that music filled a space there for me, learning music filled a space and, you know, it all became entangled up, this whole thing about musical meaning and what kinds of meanings music takes on for different social groups, different social categories, different societies.

I: *That's fascinating. You mentioned earlier about how you go about writing. Is there anything else you want to say about that?*

LG: I have to start first thing, it's no good trying to just go straight to your desk but that's what I do try to do. I have to have a fresh mind, it's no good, if I try doing an email first thing, that's it. I won't be doing focused writing for the rest of that day. Even one email destroys the kind of illusion that you have to get yourself into, of creativity. And so I don't open my emails first thing. I often work at home for a couple of hours, or even preparing a lecture, because that to me, lecturing is a type of writing. You speak usually in fairly normal language but even preparing a lecture, I have to do that first thing in the morning. So clearing space, the techniques, you know, I was talking about, like indexing and making, working with your text, making sure you understand everything that you've written and stuff, I probably answered most of it.

I: *I think so, yeah, perhaps we could move on to what you have learned about the process of writing.*

LG: I think one thing I would like to say, because I learned a lot from this myself, was something I came across in a book on writing blocks, because I had a very bad writing block at one time.

I: *Really?*

LG: Six weeks, during my PhD. Six weeks of sitting crying at my desk and no words coming. And I read a

book on writing blocks. One thing was advice from Graham Greene, who is a novelist that I admire a lot, and he said if, when you're writing, you have something that you really like, a sentence or maybe a paragraph that you're really, really fond of, cut it out. And I have so many times taken that piece of advice. And on the occasions when I've liked something so much and I've thought, 'I'm still going to keep it there, I'm not taking the advice', I always feel embarrassed by that thing afterwards and wish that I had, you know. And I don't know what it is about it, but it's to do with self-indulgence and if you've got something, a turn of phrase that you really like and it's a bit out of the ordinary, it's actually probably more likely that you're just doing it to please yourself and you're not thinking about communication. And it is better to cut out all that kind of stuff and just think about what are you saying and who are saying it to, and try to say it straight. The pieces of writing that I like least of all are the ones where I feel I've been less concerned to communicate to a readership and I've been more in love with my own words. Although I said my PhD is my favourite it's also, in that respect, my least favourite. And so is my first book, my least favourite piece of writing.

I: *Anything about writing for publication, then, that might be different?*

LG: The only thing I want to add is the importance of having the particular journal or anthology you're writing for in mind, or the publisher if it's a book, and the readership. So if you're writing for a journal it's really, really important to read the journal first. It comes back to that same thing about reading as being part of writing. It's very important to go and read some back issues of the journal, think about the readership, what kinds of things are those people looking for in an article, and think about the communication to that particular readership.

I: *So it sounds like you would be a writer if you weren't here at the Institute or involved in academic life. How would you know that you would be a writer?*

LG: I thought about that question, and the reason I'd

know is that I once, when I was Head of Music in a school immediately before I worked here and at that time, you know, there were very few jobs in music education and I didn't see that I necessarily had a future as a university lecturer, even though I had a PhD and a book out, and I found myself writing a book. It's the only book I've ever started and not finished. It was a book on the history of the voice, the singing voice, starting in Tudor times. It was going to be a social history of the voice and the way it's developed and the way it's used in different musics, and I actually was surprised – a couple of years ago I found all the notes that I'd written – I'd actually made quite a lot of notes towards that book. And I was writing it for absolutely no reason because I was working in a school. Then I got the job here and packed it in because it didn't fit. I turned my attention to more educational things. So I suppose it's for that reason that I know I would write even if I wasn't here.

And the other thing is that, I know everybody says this, but I do really wish that I could write a novel. And sometimes I think if I'd written three novels that were successful in the field of novels as my academic books have been in the field of music education, you know, I mean, I'd certainly be getting more royalties off them anyway than I am. And I'm absolutely fascinated by the process of novel-writing. I'd love to. I have actually started writing a novel. It's been an open file on my computer for about three years now and it's about one thousand words long, so I'm not getting very far with it. But I do think if I hadn't been an academic then I might have possibly explored that realm. And I wish that I could transfer the skill easily, but I can't. I just find it's a completely different way of writing, I don't know how they do it, it mystifies me and I'd love to have time, it would take a lot of learning and a lot of time to learn how to do that.

I: Well, it's interesting you said that, because I was wondering if it's possible using any of the art or the skill that you've talked about earlier and transferring …

LG: I think there must be transferable skills. But at the heart of the thing, it's different, isn't it? The whole thing about communication and what is the essence of what you're doing is going to be so different that I think it might be a bit more like transferring the skills of playing the trumpet to the skills of playing the violin, rather than playing the piano to playing the organ. There are transferable skills but they, they're going to be surface-level skills rather than the deep skills.

I: But if you had spent all of this time writing novels instead of writing academic work …

LG: Yes, I would have learned how to do it. You know, what a shame really. [*Laughs*] I could be having much more fun if I was a novelist. I wouldn't have to do all this admin. Go to meetings. Or the RAE.

Judy Ireson

I: *We just wanted a little background here: how long have you been at the Institute, what is your role and the key responsibilities of that role?*

JI: I've been a member of the School of Psychology and Human Development since 1989, when I joined as a lecturer, and before that I was attached to the Institute on a research project, I was a researcher. I'm now Professor of Psychology in Education. My responsibilities: for the whole of the time that I've been here since 1989 I've had teaching responsibilities connected with the Diploma and the Masters course in Psychology in Education. Currently I'm Deputy Head of School, that's my main responsibility. And, of course, I do have research students too.

I: *So tell me about the piece of writing that you feel most pleased with.*

JI: Well, I can't answer that actually quite that way. No, because what I thought was I couldn't pick one particular piece. I thought I was quite pleased with a couple of journal articles. One was an empirical study which I wrote up, the other was a review of research, and there was also a book chapter that I was quite pleased with. And so I found it difficult to pick one of those, but I suppose with each of them I felt that the piece had come together and it worked in bringing together ideas and evidence. As you know, most of my research, in fact all my research, is empirical.

So for me it's a question of linking empirical work and theory, and I think in all of those I felt that that worked. They all contributed something new, and I felt happy that the structure worked for that particular piece and also the style was accessible. I felt that I'd worked hard to make clear for specialist readers and not-quite-so specialist readers ... what I was about.

I: Your readers were teachers and peers?

JI: Yes, that's right. Yes – the book chapter was written for a wider audience. That was part of a book which was written for psychologists, students and educators. When I say educators I am including school managers and teachers in schools as well as educators in universities.

I: Now is there anything you weren't quite so happy with and why was that?

JI: Oh yes, yes. When I look back, I had a real struggle with my first attempt at writing up some qualitative research. This is going back quite a long way now. Up until then ... my first degree was in psychology, my PhD was a traditional format in psychology, so it was a series of experiments which involved statistical analysis and a very scientific way of writing. This is what I'd been taught to do. And when I first did some qualitative research I found that quite hard to switch genre into a different way of reporting, a different way of writing. So I think that switch was difficult and also, I remember very clearly, I wrote this article for an educational journal and I received some very unhelpful feedback [*laughs*] which simply commented negatively on the style of writing and didn't make any positive suggestions about how I might improve it. I think I'm right in saying that they suggested combining two articles into one and then, when I did, they went back on that decision. I mean it was all very difficult, so that was hard.

I: And so – what has helped your writing?

JI: Well, I think one thing that helped me was when I was a researcher and working on a project – it was a large project and we wrote some very long reports – and the project director wasn't working hands-on on the project, but came across from time to time and we

wrote reports and fed back. And, I think for his own purposes mainly, he would annotate in the margins the main points from each part of the report. So each paragraph, or every few paragraphs perhaps, would have some sort of notes for him – tracking through what you were saying through the report, and I found that a very useful technique myself.

I think it was to himself, to sort of track through what was being said and what the argument was. But it was making that explicit for me as a writer, how this was being interpreted for him as a reader. So I found that very useful, because it helped me see the structure of my writing more clearly, where it kept to the point, where it went off on a tangent and that sort of thing. And where there were gaps. So that was useful.

Writing with other people, well, I've done quite a bit of that and that's helpful because you do need to discuss the structure and the argument, the sort of evidence you're going to use, the kind of ideas you want to get across and so forth. So that's helpful.

I've also found that commenting on other people's writing helps me. Because I do a lot of marking now, of course, reviewing journal articles, marking students' work. And you can see where things are going wrong and what works in their writing and that makes it perhaps more explicit for you as a writer.

The other thing, I think, is that several years ago I was reading up some of the literature on text comprehension, because I was teaching it as part of one of the modules I was teaching for the Masters course, and some of the work I came across there was useful, particularly work on text coherence. And how much easier it was for students in school to understand textbooks that were coherent as opposed to textbooks that were not coherent, and so that made me think, 'Well, yes, if I want to make my writing clear for people, then building in coherence, making sure I am coherent in my writing'.

I: Those were particular authors who wrote on text coherence?

JI: Yes, researchers researching text coherence. Because what they did was they would compare students' understanding of texts in textbooks which they considered were more coherent and less coherent.

I: *Now, would you say writing was a major part of your life or …*

JI: It is now.

I: *So how have you managed to keep it so, with all these other commitments?*

JI: Well, I have to say I've found it very difficult. And at times it hasn't been a major part of life. I've found it, at times, extremely difficult to find the time to write. And when there are a lot of other demands around, I think getting started is particularly difficult. Once you're on a roll, then it's sort of easier to keep it going. And I think at times I really needed to have a block of time set aside without interruptions, to be able to write.

I: *You block out time?*

JI: I've tried to do that. I think I've got more successful at doing that – over time. I do see writing now as a much more major part of my work. So, I mean there are lots of things included in that, I mean it's not only writing for publication, but it's also putting in research grant applications, that's another kind of writing I suppose.

So now I do plan writing time into my diary. I try to set aside a day a week for writing. I don't always succeed, depends, you know, there are times in the term when it's impossible.

I: *Is it one of the first things to go, do you think? Your own time for writing?*

JI: It certainly has been in the past. Yes.

I: *You're protecting it a bit more now?*

JI: I'm trying. I am better at protecting it now than I was, I think, yes. And sometimes other things have to wait.

I: *Is that because you like doing the writing, or is it because you feel some kind of obligation to get these articles out?*

JI: There's certainly an obligation to get the articles out, yes, definitely. As I am an empirical researcher, the fact that I have got data sitting there that, yes, I've reported it perhaps in an end-of-grant award report, briefly, but I want to get it out to a wider audience and it's sitting there, you know, waiting to be written up. I think it's that sense of, it's there and it's waiting to be done. I also enjoy writing; it can be very satisfying.

The satisfactions are partly a sense of bringing together ideas, connecting ideas together, synthesising. One of the pieces I wrote fairly recently was really a literature review, but it was a completely new area where in this country there hasn't been any research before my own research, so I was reviewing the literature in the area and connecting up a number of themes. And I found that very interesting, because it took me out into a new field, which I haven't really looked at in-depth before. So a sense of moving on and developing, opening up a new area, that was. It's a creative process, which makes it satisfying.

Perhaps developing a contribution to theory, and you feel, yes, I've actually got a new idea here and something to say about it.

Frustrations, well, yes, they abound [*laughs*] yeah, you can hit blocks, everybody hits blocks, or times when you think, 'This is not coming together. I can't see how to make sense of all of this, it's just not working out the way I wanted it' and having to rethink the structure or rethink the framework, go back almost to a much earlier stage in the writing. I find it very frustrating sometimes, because you want to get on, get it done. And there is this pressure, you know, that you must publish. So you want that one done and out of the way and off to the wherever it's got to go, the publisher or the journal editor or whatever.

I'm a bit of a fiddler at the end. I'll sometimes hold on to it at the end a little bit longer than I should and tinker with it. So I now sort of say, 'No, you've got to stop.'

I: *What kinds of writing do you most enjoy?*

JI: Well, I'm assuming that we're talking about academic writing, because that's what my writing is at the moment. I don't write novels in my spare time or plays or anything like that, so, apart from the odd letter at length, I don't do much other writing nowadays. So, yes, I do enjoy writing a journal article if I feel I've got something, some good data there to present. I also quite like writing for a wider audience, trying to get ideas across to a wider readership than just my close colleagues in psychology and academic educational psychology. And that can be very challenging.

I: Yes. For whom, then?

JI: Well, it is within education; it's for teachers and other educators. Although I have written a few pieces occasionally for newspapers or, say, *Society Today* or *The Education Journal*. Or putting together a press release, which is trying to get our ideas across.

I: Quite a variety. So is variety one of the things you quite like?

JI: Yes, yes, I think I do, yes.

I: Can you add anything to the question – what does your writing say about you?

JI: Well, I thought about that and I think that's quite a difficult question really. I mean, I suppose when I'm thinking about academic writing it's saying something about me in my professional role. I mean, I am a psychologist at heart, but I am interested in thinking about the individual in a wider social, educational, cultural context. And I suppose that does come across, and how the wider context of school, as an institution, or the way people think about teaching and learning, actually impacts on individuals' learning and development. So I guess that probably does come across, broadly speaking, in my writing. In a way I'm working at boundaries. I suppose I work at the boundary of psychology and education and that, if you've read Engstrom's work on activity theory, is 'a challenging place to be'. It's difficult, it's sometimes dangerous, you can be attacked from both sides. But I think it's worth being there and it's a space for me to understand better.

I: You quite like the danger?

JI: Yes, sometimes, and at times, no. At times it can be demoralising actually. [*Laughs*]

I: Being attacked from both sides?

JI: Yes, but I think with experience I've got stronger, so I'm not quite so worried about it any more. But earlier on in my career that was pretty tough.

I: How do you go about writing?

JI: Well, I do most of my extended writing at home. I find it difficult to write in the office, apart from tinkering. Tidying up, editing and, you know, doing little bits and pieces I can do in the office, but I find it really distracting being here, so I work at home. I make a space at home now, actually have my own desk, my own computer, my books all around me – it's a room I like. I know I can work in there. It looks out over the garden, which is lovely. So it's quite rural really. So there are trees I can gaze out at and birds to look at when I'm thinking. So that's where I do most writing, but I do quite a bit in other places, like on the train.

I draw up timetables for myself for the next six to 12 months and slot in, especially when I think I'm terribly busy, I'll sit down and say, 'Right, what have I really got to do in the next six to 12 months' and, you know, what writing, what grant applications, what teaching, etc. So I try to set myself targets of when I'm going to finish a piece of writing because at least it makes me feel more calm about what I've got to do and how I'm going to fit it all in.

I: Do you have a way of structuring your journal articles?

JI: Yes, well, journal articles in psychology have a very clear structure, it's a very standard structure. Once you've got used to it, it really makes life quite straightforward, because you know exactly what you've got to do, you know, that's quite helpful, I think. So I use that, particularly when I'm writing up some quantitative research. So that's fine. Literature review, well, that stuff has got a different structure – it's more thematic, identifying core themes, topics covered, conceptual issues, methodological issues.

I: Do you ever keep a few things going at once?

JI: Depends what you mean by 'at once'. I have written a book as well and I haven't been able to write that all in one go without anything else having to be done in-between, so maybe I would like to try and concentrate on a chapter and get that pretty much done before writing something else. But not always. I think it depends: if they're closely linked, that can be useful because one can feed off the other, but if they're on different topics then that can be really quite disruptive because you've got to get yourself back into a topic when you start writing again. So it's nice if you can stay with one topic and finish it before moving on to the next.

I: What have you learned about the process of writing?

JI: I think thinking about the structure first is really important. So I try to think about that structure and where this journal article is going to go, which sort of journal it's going to go to, for example. Or for a book, obviously you've got to do a lot of work putting together the proposal, so you've got a good idea what's going to go in each chapter when you start, but then you have to think about the structure within each chapter and how that's going to look.

Very early on in my writing I think I was too much led by 'the current idea' and I would follow it, and so I would go off at tangents and end up somewhere that wasn't very good to be. So I've realised that I need to build a structure and try and take control of that structure rather than letting the writing kind of move me, lead me on. But there is a balance, because obviously as you write you maybe get some new ideas, so that makes you sometimes change things around.

It's difficult to remember how things have developed. I mean, I know that when I first started writing I found it very difficult. I wrote very slowly and I think that's because of this scientific structure and writing in the third person and you had to do it in psychology, and I did science before that. You know, I thought this was how you had to write, and I found it quite hard to move from that to something which was more fluid.

I: And with yourself in there?

JI: Well, maybe, but you don't really put a lot of yourself in there when writing scientific work. I mean, you don't write in the first person. It's not so much in the passive tense as it used to be, but it is putting yourself in the background, because you're trying to show objectivity. This is what scientific writing is about, it's being objective about your data, objective about your procedures and what you've done and about what other people have found.

I: How about getting published?

JI: If I'm thinking about a publication, a journal article and I'm not quite sure where to send it, I might talk to a few people. I'd find out who's editing the journal, who's on the editorial board, and look at some of the recent editions of the journal just because journals do change direction, a bit, according to the editor. So I would perhaps think of maybe a couple or three, and I would go to the library and look at their recent editions. Be careful about reading their advice for authors, because obviously that's there to guide you and it makes sense to follow their advice. Most journals in educational psychology require you to follow a particular style, the APA [American Psychological Association] style, and so you have to do that. Normally they will tell you how long, what word length, the kinds of articles that they're interested in publishing in their journal. They're quite specific about referencing style and that sort of thing. So in that sense they're clear.

But when it comes to the actual content, I mentioned the problem at the beginning of working at the boundary, so sometimes it can be difficult to find a journal which is happy to accept your work, because if you're at a boundary and they say, 'Well, it's not an area that we're really publishing in, or we're not interested in.' I haven't actually had that happen to me, but it is a question of looking at the scope of the journal, so what kinds of articles are they publishing here, what's the range?

I: If you weren't at the Institute or another academic institution, do you think you would still write?

JI: That's an interesting question. I haven't really thought about that one. But ... I might. I might. I am very much in a mode of writing – what's in my head at the moment, what, you know, research projects are on the go at the moment, so I'd find it quite difficult to think of doing any other kind of writing. I couldn't see myself writing a novel. I have spoken to colleagues, one colleague who just retired and was writing science fiction books. I'm not sure that I would do that. I guess I might do something, but I don't know what it would be.

Gunther Kress

I: *Thank you for agreeing to be interviewed. Could you please say how long you've been at the Institute and what your roles are.*

GK: I have been at the Institute longer than I have been at any other job in my life. I've been here since 1991, so I suppose that's 15 years now.

I: *And your roles in that time?*

GK: I have been an academic, and had two administrative jobs, one as Head of the Group, and one as Head of School.

I: *The next question on the sheet is: please tell me what you regard as the best piece of writing you have* done, *but there might, of course, be several best pieces. Which are the pieces you are most pleased with, and why are you pleased with them?*

GK: Yes, I was thinking about that then on the way to the loo, and back, and actually I'd been thinking about that before. It's like having friends, and you might have a number of friends, all of whom are equally dear to you but for different reasons. So some of the things I've written I'm pleased with because they've made a particular point in relation to what one wanted to explain and have an account of. And other things may be means of writing which express different kinds of things. So I haven't actually got a best piece from that perspective.

I: *Have you got a piece you're least pleased with, or several pieces of writing which you haven't been happy with, or is that less the case now you're well established?*

GK: I don't think it's to do with being established … well, maybe being established means that you get asked – as you will know – to write things, and sometimes therefore you're writing things which, in a sense, you've written before or you're kind of repeating yourself and you're aware that you're doing something because it's an expectation that you should do it, and it isn't something new. For me, that is maybe what comes out of that question that I would like there to be some change or something new in the things I write.

I: *There's not a question about this on the sheet, but would you mind saying whether or not you write in any language other than English? I think that would interest readers. Do you write in German?*

GK: Only personal things, not academic. I have tried, and the people who received it found it hilarious. In other words, again as you will very well know, academic writing is a much specialised form of writing, and I haven't learned that in writing …

I: *What are the differences, do you think, between German and English academic writing? What do they find hilarious?*

GK: Well, in part they find hilarious that my German is, I suppose in any case, frozen in time, a sort of Rip Van Winkle effect of having left the country at the age of 16, in a particular social place, and in any case languages do change over a period of 30, 40 years. So it's partly that. But maybe at a general level very much the same as in English, maybe forms of German generality and abstraction and that kind of theme, then, of course, German has its own textural forms and generic structures and syntactic structures, which are significantly different to those of the English language. But I think it is about levels of abstractness.

I: *What has helped your writing? How have you learned to do it? I mean, was it getting advice from others, say friends, or certain key individuals at certain stages in your career?*

GK: I think for me writing is inseparable from thinking and from other kinds of work. I couldn't think of writing separately from a whole much wider social environment. So what helped me in writing was moving through a place, specifically the University of East Anglia, a long time ago, where other people were writing, so it was a normal thing to do, it wasn't unusual. So that thing of making it exceptional or unusual wasn't an issue. The normality made it seem possible. But then, specifically, having friends and colleagues with whom I was working who had confidence in the kinds of things I was thinking, and therefore having the confidence to put those things, which otherwise had been private and unusual and maybe strange and certainly not to be paraded in public, putting them down on paper as in publishing. It's that, it was about a confidence in the community that allowed me then the confidence that people get from feedback, from people who I thought much of, who were friends and colleagues. That allowed me to take bearings, putting my thoughts on paper and publishing them. It was that really. So it's not writing as a mechanical or separate or decontextualised task or process.

I: *And what about the reviews, say, of journal articles you've written; have they helped or have you found that on the whole they don't help? And what about reviews of books? Do you take much notice of them? I mean, some people say they never read reviews of their books.*

GK: I think, again, I would go back to social environment. And in this case, the discipline within which you're writing as a social environment, and your position within the social environment. Are you content to be carried along in the mainstream of the discipline or are you – like I was – sort of marginal to it, and then sort of outside. The social position you have within the community in which you're writing I think has a lot to do with it. So I had a lot of difficulty in getting things that I was really interested in accepted, by the reviewers, before the thing actually got reviewed, from the proposal sent to publishers, most coming back with scathing reviews, so dealing with that at a personal level. And steeling yourself against that sort of thing, and retaining the confidence, saying, 'This is what they say, yet I think there is something in there.'

I: *There's a focus within linguistics which I think you've referred to as linguistic linguistics ...*

GK: It was very much mainstream linguistics at that time, which was I suppose dominated by versions of Chomsky and transformational grammar. And, as I say, and thought of socio-linguistics too, and responses said this is outrageous, and should not even be admitted into the company of polite people. (*Laughs*)

I: *It's good that you kept on writing.*

GK: Yes, this is what I mean about the environment: how do you see yourself? Do you see yourself as one of – the metaphor of course is being apprenticed to, and if you're apprenticed to, you accept whatever the conventions and the rules are of the trade and profession into which you're apprenticed. Or whether you're seeing yourself somewhat differently, as interested in but somewhat marginal. I think it's the social position that is for me prior to the activity of writing, which is not to say that the writing itself doesn't have real effects.

I: *I don't know what you think of the next question on this sheet: how have you managed to keep writing a major part of your life? I think, from what you have said, that it is – and I know you manage to keep hours that many people don't. You're very self-disciplined, aren't you, when it comes to your writing?*

GK: Well, I don't make a distinction between the private and the public in ways that maybe one should, or maybe other people can. I write because it's something that I find is about me. I don't regard academic writing as, in principle, different to fiction writing. It is about a means of saying who you are, and locating yourself in the world, and representing yourself in the world. Which, of course, can be done in many different ways, in sport or in all sorts of social activities. So my way of representing myself in the world has been through writing. So that it's been an essential part of me, so I don't see it as a kind of ... I find it still strange when some of my colleagues will say, 'I haven't got time for it.' I sort of think that's separation of the public and the private. And what sort of identity it is that regards this as not me, and this is me. So partly it's been simply a part of my life, and it's been a crucial part of my life in the sense that it's been a means of saying who I am. And then when I've had jobs when institutionally there's been huge demands on my time, I've simply extended my working day, or my working week, to make time for what I regarded as central in my life.

I: *This touches on a theme that is in other interviews. I mean, people who publish a lot do see writing as very much part of themselves. Another question: where you write, is that important to you? Can you write anywhere, for example, if you're abroad, can you write, or do you like to have a particular space or place? Some novelists say that writers need this or that. Virginia Woolf, for example.*

GK: I certainly had a very strange experience, maybe now 20 years ago, when I had study leave that I fully intended to use for writing, but I had moved away from my normal place of abode, and found that this location made it impossible for me to write. And then I spoke to a colleague who had gone from Australia to Italy in order to write, and found that he couldn't put a word down on the page. So it's for me, again, that commitedness with a whole social environment, and that dislocation, so ... More recently I think I've invented for myself a kind of imagined space, which I can produce, not wherever I am actually, but I can, given a little bit of time, put myself in that imagined place, but it is a specific space in which I can ... yeah, I need space and I need an imagined space. And the environment needs to be comfortable for writing. I don't for, instance, write in this office, ever.

I: *You're too aware of other pressures.*

GK: Yes.

I: *And then what kind of satisfaction do you get from*

writing? Is it particular kinds of feeling, or do you go through phases? In the early days, did you find writing very painful in the early stages, but is that less the case now? And do you spend a great deal of time thinking about what you are going to write?

GK: Well as I say, for me the notion of writing separate from other activities is inconceivable. So writing certainly is inseparable from thinking, which is inseparable from talking, hence the company of like-minded people, or maybe not like-minded, but interested people, who could be people in the class where you're teaching or could be your friends or could be at a conference ... talking, thinking, writing for me form a kind of inseparable whole. I mean, it might be temporary, I might be dislocated for brief periods, so that for me is essential. And in so far as I like talking, I like thinking, writing itself hasn't been separate, and the other thing I have to say is that because I see this as a social thing, I see it as continuous with talking and thinking. I have striven, I can say, since the mid-Seventies, which is now a good time ago, to make my writing much more like my talking, and not to have that distinction between the written mode, in its more pronounced forms, and the spoken mode. But rather, I suppose, to be conversational.

I: I remember a seminar where you showed an early piece of writing, within linguistics, and contrasted it with a recent piece, and there was a marked difference.

GK: And that's also to do with who you imagine that you're talking with.

I: Yes, the question of audience. Are you conscious of audience when you write, or is it something you've more or less internalised? I suppose if you're asked to do something for a particular journal you do, to a certain extent, think about the audience?

GK: Well, people accuse me of being not a proper academic writer. And so, it seems, to be a proper academic writer is to locate yourself within the disciplinary debate, and it requires several syntactic and textural forms, but it also requires conventions of referencing and acknowledgement, in nodding in all sorts of directions. Which, to me, isn't the conversational mode. So I don't write academically. And I'm now in the very lucky position that might cease tomorrow ... I mean, these things are never to be taken for granted ... I'm in the lucky position where people are nevertheless willing to accept that. So I imagine the kind of person, or kinds of persons, with whom I might be talking.

I: Yes, that's a more interesting kind of academic writing, isn't it, where you're imagining ...

GK: ... I'm imagining that I'm talking with the people. I never think about, let's say, the formal standing, but where I'm imagining a kind of shared interest and a certain intensity of interest.

I: What kinds or genres of writing do you most enjoy? And do you write fiction? You have written books for teachers, Linguistic Processes in Sociocultural Practice *(1989) comes to mind. Do you think in terms of different genres or is that not really how you think about writing?*

GK: I would like to be able to write those things which are called properly fictional dramas. But, at the same time, I do think that what I do is fiction writing. In the sense that I think good fiction changes, projects different worlds or changes one's perception of the world or extends horizons or reconfigures one's point of view. And that can be done in many very different genres and not, of course, only in writing but in other forms of representation. So yes, I would like to be able to write in novelistic or narrative forms, and I've tried it and I can't. Occasionally what I do, I insert tiny little bits into my academic writing. And when I do tiny little ...

Break in recording

I: ... you've tried to write fiction, but ...

GK: It kind of feels like thin gruel, but occasionally in things which I've written which are academic writing, I've tried little bits of autobiographical stuff. And to my sense, it works reasonably well, but it's very short sketches, and the difficulty would be extending that, and the problem of finding larger types of structure.

I: *What about images, drawings? Do you draw, do you paint?*

GK: No, I don't draw, I don't paint, I'm a very limited person in terms of forms of representation.

I: *But you've written about images, so you've had to select images and place them in relation to writing. You have discussed books that have images as well as writing.*

GK: I'm interested in how people make themselves in their world, and so the various forms that we engage with and through which we kind of get a sense of who we are. I actually don't make, for instance … well, I'll say because I can't do it, there's no distinction for me between academic writing and fiction, but if I could write fiction then I might not make that kind of statement. I don't make a distinction between what is aesthetically valued and aesthetically not valued, banal representations, I find them in some way equally interesting. Which also I think appals lots of people. I would say that I find them as means or forms or representation, interesting, and for me the aesthetic is a separate question and maybe comes two or three steps after that. So it is how humans represent themselves, and how human representations are taken in by me, that's what interests me first. But no, I don't paint, and I don't draw, and … in the earlier part of my life I was able to play a musical instrument, but …

I: *You don't any more?*

GK: No.

I: *The next question could be interpreted in many ways. It is: what does your writing say about you or what do you hope it says about you?*

GK: I suppose that the refusal … well not the refusal actually, the thing I sort of take as assumed is that – and I suppose that is my theory of representation if you can call it that – we represent ourselves in our representations. And so, that's the first thing. Therefore any representation of somebody is a representation of their person. An assumption that humans are equally valuable, that one human being is as valuable as another human being, and therefore an attempt to understand what humans are about, through their representations. That's … what was your question?

I: *What do you think your writing says about you?*

GK: It says about me that I want to understand or assert the dignity of humans, that's what it says about me, that's how I would like to see myself: as a human being in relation to others. What it says about me is that the ordinary is what life is about really, and that's really not a lot …

I: *How do you go about writing? For example: do you make notes; do you do it all on screen; do you do all of it by hand; do you set aside a certain number of hours a day, if you can; do you prefer to work at certain times of the day, or do you have to because of other pressures?*

GK: Well, how I go about writing, I go back to the things that we were thinking about before, that I see it as part of the whole social environment in which I am. So, how I go about writing, for instance … much of my writing happens after I've talked a lot. So, a talk at a conference or talking with students in a normal teaching session or with somebody who's doing a PhD. A lot of talking and working out ideas and testing ideas and seeing how they're received. So going about writing is embedded in that. It comes out of a lot of interaction, then the formal process – I would say, yes, I then sort of jot down notes. In terms of what I think this thing is meant to be or for whom it is meant to be, organising it in relation to a sense of what I want to say, and what this audience might want to hear, or might be useful for this audience. Jotting down notes, ordering the notes, I have a very kind of mechanistic approach to that. I would see it very much like a problem, say, of fitting two bits of pipes together … as you may know, I had a period in my life when I was an ordinary tradesperson and you have steps in which you do … I see that part of writing as actually not mysterious, not mystical, you sort of put your things together, then you order them, then ... If I did a writing course, I would want to say, actually, if you're a tailor, this is how you do it; if you're a plumber, this is how you do it; if you're a writer, this is how you do it ... there's no great mystery about it. The mystery comes at the point where I cannot write extended pieces of things in certain passages, and mystery comes when I read something which I find, in some way, really I suppose, maybe sort of profoundly moving, whatever that may be, and how does that happen, that's where the mystery lies.

I: I remember you said once that as an apprentice you had to study – was it a fur collar? – in great detail, and you felt that had been translated into an interest in texts and how they work.

GK: Yes, the relation between the theoretical and the practical. I had a medieval training within my trade. I think that continues from medieval guilds of training, when you were taught certain things, but then you were asked to stand back and look at this is how he had done it, this is how she had done it, what is the difference? So the practice in reflection that is for me ... but also the detailed engagement with the material stuff. That's why I think I like detailed engagement with stuff.

I: Gunther, I think you have actually already answered the next question, which is: what have you learned about the process of writing? Talking about how you actually go about writing, you said you had detailed notes. To continue that question, if you're doing a paper, do you begin at the beginning and do a draft of the whole, and then go back and edit, or do you start with the bits you find most difficult, or do you leave the easiest till later, and is the composing done on screen once you've got all your notes?

GK: Well, it depends very much on what I'm writing. If somebody says, 'Can you do a chapter for a book?', and I'm in any case now four weeks behind the deadline, I would kind of put my notes down, and put them in order and really, in the most mechanistic way, I'd start at one and go through. If it's a book, I will

do the same actually for the book, but I might start with a chapter which I find easiest to write. So it depends on what it is that I'm writing. But the second part of your question, I've forgotten ...

I: I asked if you compose on screen?

GK: Well, that's interesting, because for a long time, I was really not yet confident to write on the screen. My first writing I did, I was on an old-fashioned ordinary typewriter, and that really had an effect on how I wrote. Then for some reason I moved away from that and wrote by hand, that had a real effect on how I wrote, and then I moved to the screen, that's having a real effect, so I think that the technology that you use ... both ... and in all sorts of ways. Affectively, I think, the tangibility, the sensoriness of paper, and the instrument with which you're writing. The fact that you can re-order sheets of paper in a completely different way to re-ordering ... I'm finding ordering on the screen extremely difficult, and I haven't often got time to print it out and do the double kind of thing, so I think that is really important. I like the fact that the screen is portable, and I can take it with me, and therefore create the moments where I can write, whereas with the writing on paper, used to be at a desk, with a lamp that produced a continual light, and certain types of space. I think there's a lot to be thought about and understood about the whole environment – sensuous environment as much as intellectual.

I: Yes, I know people who are into computers and ICT, and yet say that they like to write with pen and paper, because it captures the rhythm of their thinking.

GK: I can understand that completely.

I: What have you learned about writing for publication, and what advice would you give to young academics starting to write for publication? What have you learned ... is there any generalisation you can make or is it all ...?

GK: Well, apart from the difficulty of getting going, I suppose maybe the most important thing might remain producing an environment which is conducive to that person for writing, an environment of confidence. Confidence not about their writing initially, but about them and who they are and what they're thinking, and then making writing not mysterious, not extraordinary, not unusual, but it is one other thing that you do. You're going to go off and give a talk and that's perfectly all right, and then you go and write that down and that's perfectly … the normality of it, that's what I would say. Then, of course, there is now a completely different social climate around academic writing, which I find difficult for myself, although I'm protected by having a certain standing. And I also realise that people of a generation or two generations younger than I am, don't find it unusual, and that's a difficult thing for me to realise, it's a usual environment for them. But the constraints which are being put on writing … and I think one would have to ask them whether they find the fact that the Research Assessment Exercise expects certain forms of written production is felt as limiting for them, or maybe it is normal for them? Maybe they feel it is no different from my earlier experiences where somebody said, 'This is too bizarre to put into polite company.' Maybe these things are always there but differently, I realise that.

I: *Some seminars were arranged with a writer from outside the IOE to help staff respond to RAE pressures. He gave a very strategic kind of advice: think about your message, but also the market. He said, 'Go and look at journals in which you might publish, look at how long the articles are, how many references, what kind of titles and whether or not they use verbs, etc.' I know some people there found the seminar very useful, especially if they were wanting to produce a journal paper from something they'd already written, say a PhD. But others said they could not work in that way.*

GK: I've read some of the reports about those sessions, and maybe that's not you, in individual cases. You will always have had to think of a market, but maybe the notion of the market has become so naturalised that you weren't aware of it, and that you had become apprenticed into a particular mode of action and hadn't realised what you had. The idea of demystifying the process, I find completely OK. What I do think, for me would need to remain is a kind of inner energy, which comes from a certain kind of commitment: this is what I do want to say. This is important, for whatever reason. If that's missing – and that goes back to the thing about having enough time for writing – I would then … for me that's a sign that there isn't that energy. But how you make use of that energy and then realise it and entext it, I would want to go along with de-mystifying it. Whether every sentence is planned is another thing, because what I actually do think about the process of writing, is that all processes of an extended kind produce their own [generative terms of affects]. And if it is absolutely planned, then you kind of planned out the possibility of that.

I: *Next question. I think I know what you'll say to this question … do you think you would still write if you were not at the Institute? Yes, because you think it's a part of yourself. Am I right?*

GK: Well, if I was at a different academic institution, then the answer is, of course I would. But if I wasn't at an academic institution, then everything I said about social environment would mean that I might find it extremely difficult. In other words, if the social environment is such that you can't have that, then I would find that difficult. What I've been thinking about is whether there ought to be generational differences in writing, and if you're not a member of an academic institution, whether you write things that respond, or correspond, to a different phase in your life, including your social life.

I: *Finally, is there anything that you would like to add?*

GK: Not really. I think, as I say, I don't see writing as separate from the rest of one's life, and I hope that continues. I suppose I'm optimistic, things like RAE and constraints of that kind, probably have always been there but in a different form, and it's the newness of the form that makes it seem unusual and therefore problematic. And, of course, some constraints really are deleterious, but I think humans won't change over the short time.

I: *It is said of Doris Lessing that if she didn't write, she would just fall apart. And there are people like that, aren't there? They have to write, it's so much a way of shaping their lives …*

GK: The only thing that I feel, is writing is how you and I, or I'll just confine it to myself, writing is a major means by which I represent myself in the world, including to myself. And then I think for me it would be important to understand how other people do that. People who don't write still represent themselves in the world, including to themselves, and finding means for acknowledging that, and not assuming because they don't write, they don't have a representation. It might be playing darts …

I: *And it might be through teaching?*

GK: It might be that – 17-year-olds, 14-year-olds who go smashing up bottles or breaking newly planted trees, need the means of representing themselves in the world. So I think there's a real need to understand that we need to be able to represent ourselves in the world in some way, and from that understanding, seeing how we can make that possible. Could that be the way forward for most people? And writing isn't going to be the only means, or even the means for most people.

I: *Well, thank you very much. It's been a very interesting interview.*

Diana Leonard

I: *Thank you for agreeing to be interviewed. How long have you been at the Institute, and what are, or have been, your roles?*

DL: I think I came to the Institute in something like '76. So I came as a lecturer, senior lecturer, reader and professor, and I headed the Gender Centre; I was in sociology. Then I moved to curriculum studies, and now I'm in CLC [Culture, Language and Communication]. You're only going to use bits of the tape anyway, I'm sure.

I: *Yes, a biography and perhaps a photograph, and then we have to look for themes. I think the gender issue is probably going to be important.*

DL: If you want to focus on that, that's fine.

I: *If you want to ignore some of these questions …*

DL: No, no.

I: *What's the best piece of writing that you've done, or best pieces perhaps, the ones that really pleased you? Could you also say why you were pleased with them?*

DL: I think I enjoyed writing *A Woman's Guide to Doctoral Studies* (2001); even though it's all secondary data, it's nice to try to write for a general audience, even if you have fights with the publisher about referencing. In fact, there's very few references in that book, and it does make it read quite smoothly, and there's a lot in there, and, yeah, I'm pleased with it. It hasn't sold particularly well, because you shouldn't put 'woman' into the title, because then you lose half your potential readership and, in fact, you lose three-quarters of the women who don't identify themselves as women, or don't see that gender's got anything to do with their progress through. But I do think – to a degree – there is such constipation in academic writing because we do reference things so fiercely. They made me take them out, and I put them into a chapter saying there is evidence for Chapter 1, the following were used in Chapter 2, and then I lost that chapter altogether. So that was a good exercise.

I: If you were looking at writing that fits the conventional notion of academic writing …

DL: I think all the books I've written have … I'm still happy with them. That's the one about familial exploitation with Christine Delphy (1992). I've enjoyed translating, I'm not a sophisticated translator, I just, I knew how to translate into English because I knew what the debates were in English, and I've translated three books, I think.

I: From which language?

DL: French into English.

I: Do you read quite a lot of French?

DL: Almost none. I mean, I used to work quite a lot with a French colleague so I was going to France three or four times, so I read more then. But it's bizarre, isn't it, we never have occasion to pick up a French journal and read it. I don't even know where I would go to find journals in French or German. I'm doing a literature review for the HEA [Higher Education Academy] at the moment, and we said we'd look at French and German literature; we're the only literature review out of five that's going out of the English language. So anyway, that's a second, a kind of side, issue.

I: Perhaps you could say something about translation as it is an aspect of publication that is likely to interest readers – what do you enjoy about it? What are the

specific difficulties or issues that come up for you when translating?

DL: I think if I was a more sophisticated person in the translation field, I might get more tied up in it. I just feel you have to make it comprehensible to the audience that you know is reading it, so I blithely break sentences up, and try to choose words which … because often the proper translation doesn't fit it into the debates, because people wouldn't read it because they wouldn't see it as relevant. But it seems a very constructive thing to do, because you're actually producing a … and people in France do say that publishing in French is equivalent to not publishing at all, in certain, well, in feminist debates certainly. Academic work, you always end up somewhat dissatisfied with academic work, I suspect you kind of think it's good when you finish it, but then you … either it's got a lot empirical stuff in it and you look back and think I should have theorised: if I'd taken this theoretical angle I would have seen this kind of stuff, or you can see the shortcomings of it when you revisit. But mostly I have to say, when I reread stuff I've written, I'm impressed by myself!

I: A 'Did I really write that?' response?

DL: Yes; you couldn't do it again. You're always so influenced by the things that you've read recently, in the way that you write stuff up, that you couldn't do … and you have to be on top of the literature so … I've just done something about the debates on co-education, and a lot of people said, 'That's a really excellent piece.' Again, it's a secondary thing so maybe I should spend my future not doing original research, but actually it's the same process of synthesis as you find in translation, as you find in analysing data, as you find in going through and kind of arranging the secondary data. It's that process of synthesis and the emergence of …

I: Meanings, and issues …

DL: … and insights, new insights into the field, that's what's interesting in all of them, I think. What pleases me least about them …

I: Well, about any writing you have done, or what do you find most difficult to write or …

DL: … all the difficult things that you got nine-tenths of the way to finish, and you're never quite sure why you don't just pull them out and do them. I think you have to be under such extraordinary compulsion to finish something. So maybe if you've got a deadline for an edited collection, I think that's why I write mainly… well, I write mainly for edited collections, which I realise now I'm doing the literature review. I know the RAE doesn't value them, so they don't really pick them up, they pick up books, but above all they pick up academic articles. And I don't necessarily find academic articles the best way of publishing. I mean, who reads them except other academics? At least with books, or chapters in books, you stand a chance of getting interested others.

I: And do you think you're perhaps freer, too, with a book? Is it that with an article you've got to try and mould it to a particular journal? I'm just thinking of the writer who came to talk to staff about publishing. He writes popular science, he does a lot of newspaper work and has to meet deadlines, and he was saying, oh you academics you're so egocentric, you think, 'I've got this wonderful article, and I'll just send it to a few journals.' So he was telling people to think of the market, think about your message, to spend three weeks on what your message is going to be. His approach obviously comes out of science; he was a research scientist at UCL … you know, map out the paper in detail – the rationale, the why, and the what and the how. He told us to go and study journals: do titles have verbs, how many sections, references? Some people found that useful, some people just felt too constrained by that way of going about writing.

DL: Partly if you're asked to write a chapter in a book, somebody's done the thinking already, they know there's a market, they know the niche they want you to fill. They ask you, and then you debate about the abstract that you produce, and then you write it. What I do to get the argument to come out, and the point of it, is to always to give it as a paper. Because there's nothing like producing a set of overheads, or PowerPoint presentations, for making you realise you

can't go off onto that digression or that really you need to move that forward earlier on. That frankly, the article that … what you spent half the paper doing isn't really what it's about at all, you're trying to argue something different at the end. So you're going to have to mention the first part because that might be your evidence, but you're going to have to cut it down to about a quarter. But then I don't publish in academic journals very much.

I: What sort of papers or things do you publish?

DL: I publish solicited articles in books. I produce conference papers and articles out of research projects, partly because that's a requirement of the research project, but also that's how people come to know that you're interested in that topic. But then you go on being asked to write about that topic way after the actual project and, in a way, that's when your ideas become clearer. In the write-ups for recent projects that I've done, the academic articles … which were actually all in special issues of journals … so there isn't clear cut decisions, they were kind of … they were the prod that made me analyse, but they're full of quite relatively raw empirical stuff. And it's only when I subsequently go through and read a colleague's article that I realise that, you know, it's always that conjoining of the data you've, the stuff you've got which you got from one perspective. I mean I've been doing that stuff on alumni and the introduction of research skills and employment skills in the doctorate. But then I've been reading some of the people who've been writing about vocational education, and what they're saying about how you teach the specific employment-related skills, and what has been found to work and not to work in vocational education, and you realise that that's exactly what's being pushed on the doctorate. So then you kind of think, 'Ah! There's at least a good article there, about saying that people are doing things for the best of motives, but they're actually, according to the evidence from another field, not going to succeed.' So things kind of run around. And I found really difficult whilst I was teaching and doing admin, I found two things very difficult. One was to be as involved as I needed to be in qualitative research projects, because the timing is completely different, but also to do as much writing as I would like. Because writing, again, doesn't kind of fit in with … you have to be some species of hermit, and really panicked, and able to take a period out to do some writing, it has to be obsessive. And you need, I need to time limit that because otherwise it's a very boring life. You could really, really write, I can really, really write for three, four days, maybe a week, maybe two, but after that I think, 'There's more to life than this.'

I: *Another academic I interviewed said he can write anywhere – he carries the place in his head. So if he's in Egypt and there's nothing on in the evening and he can't talk Arabic to the people there and their English is limited, he can write.*

DL: Oh, that's a perfect place, I've written in Pakistan.

I: *Whereas another academic I interviewed said that for him writing comes out of talking, out of the social environment. Like others he knows, he found that he could not write when away from his usual writing place – he needed the familiar place, the people, the social environment. Virginia Woolf referred to the woman writer's need of a room of her own. Is this perhaps the moment to talk about gender issues as you see them. Something to do perhaps with status, with domestic circumstances, with …*

DL: Well, I don't think women ever get the 'waiting on' as the creative genius that various men do. Waited on by their spouses and partners, waited on by secretaries and other people. We're just seen as heartless bitches if we try to put things … and certainly little periods that I put aside, the week after Christmas I thought I would get some writing done, and then my partner and daughter and two small children arrived. I managed to get some filing done, because that was about the attention span that was possible, you know, pick up the piece of paper, decide where to put it, and then you got distracted. And I don't know, maybe some guys would have [*pause*] would have wanted to be as involved with them. I don't think they would necessarily have felt the same social pressures, I mean I was happy and I wouldn't want to have not done it, because that's part of femininity, that I do enjoy doing that kind of thing. But it was a period that was a bit of a goner. I think if

I've got my laptop with me, and I'd take some papers and a limited amount of support reading with me, then that's a very good way of doing a bit of writing, because it clears all the … I mean I don't have a lot of domestic distractions because I live on my own at the moment, but …

[Break in recording to check battery]

I: *OK, we can go on.*

DL: I mean in the past, that was the problem. I think that the gender dimension is, well, it's multiple. But one is being too prepared to say, 'Yes, I'll do various things', which isn't only women because certain of my male colleagues are very obliging. But more of my male colleagues than my female colleagues say 'no', firmly, and absent themselves. So there's that, plus the servicing. But because I live on my own, I find the need to get out of the house and socialise with people. And somehow I find teaching and administration … I mean the thing is now I'm older so I haven't got the domestic responsibilities except I have got grandchildren that do take up quite a bit of time and attention. But I don't have the energy that I had before, so if I come into the Institute and do several hours of teaching, I'm fairly wiped, I need to go home and have a cup of tea and a sit down before I get back. And it's the 'before I get back' that's the trick, because really you need to … I mean the trick I've learned about writing is to leave something from the day before on the desk all ready to start the next day, so you go back … because I could spend all morning mithering around in my study, organising, doing and chasing, so if I say, 'Today I'm going to write the websites for the two current things', which is what I did this morning, then I need to have found everything and set it all out the day before. But even just directing projects ends you up in endless amounts of admin, which is not the same as actually doing the project. Writing the websites for three different places where I felt we ought to be advertising what my two ongoing projects are, it takes time. I'm also engaged in writing a long piece, which is a kind of progress report, because we want to have some input from an advisory committee, but I have to … it's useful because it will be the report, but I have to … right at the end I've just changed the tenses, but I do want their specific input on specific problems. So there's a hell of a lot of writing that we do and have to do, which isn't kind of creative writing. Maybe at the end we can convert it into an academic article about the processes of doing it, or maybe it just about counts because it's an introduction to a report in which we will say what we found about the nature of the field. But there's always so much admin-y stuff to be going on with, you can really lose all your creative writing time doing bits and bobs, even if you're not doing a lot of teaching. And if you're doing teaching, then the teaching always takes precedence over everything else because you have to be there at nine o'clock on a given day, and then you're really exhausted in the evening. I think these things …

I: And do you think that, on the whole, women tend to …

DL: We do more teaching, more pastoral stuff.

I: Do they put the students before their time for writing?

DL: They do. And a lot of pastoral work always ends up … I mean, obviously because of running a gender centre and being known to be sympathetic towards gender, a lot of gender problems arrive. They take a long time to sort out, and terrible things do happen to women. And most of one's colleagues, and particularly one's male colleagues, don't have a clue how to handle them, so they do pass them on. So we always say that women are employed to do the same jobs as men, and then various other things on top of them. And that's certainly one of them. It's making space. I mean I know – and I recommend to everybody – the thing about writing at the beginning of each day. But somehow if you haven't read the stuff you're going to have to give back to students in the afternoon, for very good reasons, the day before, then you're going to spend the morning doing that.

I: If what you teach is going to sound fresh, you need to have thought about it before you go in and do it.

DL: And you can't do that very long in advance, I can't anyway, because I've forgotten what I did. My

teaching is always newly constructed. Anyway, I've retired in order to write, to have more time to do it.

I: Well, I hope you are getting it, or will get it. Shall we go on to the next question: what has helped your writing? Do you feel that over the years you've learned to do it better? What helped – were there points in your career, or somebody or something that helped a lot? A more experienced writer, getting advice from others, reviews?

DL: I'm sure it's positive feedback on the writing that you do, and people saying they're interested. I guess the general pressure within universities that you should be writing has helped, because when I first started if you produced a couple of articles every two or three years, you stood out. Did I learn from others?

I: Collaborative writing?

DL: I certainly like collaborative writing. Though you have to have the right collaborator, I can't bear people who rewrite everything for no apparent reason, and I do try not to do that stuff. Though I go over my own stuff again and again, so if you're writing with someone it's difficult not to keep making slight emendations, because that's part of the polishing and the focusing process. I think doing translations helped a lot.

I: In that it made you think about the language and the writing, and how one expresses ideas, and synthesises things, as you said?

DL: Yes, and the specific words. Because so much of writing is about seeking the right words.

I: Le mot juste?

DL: Yes, *le mot juste* indeed. It makes you more aware of how English works better with shorter sentences. And I think that generally writing that is more, I don't know, I'm sure there's a technical phrase for it, but kind of where you have the subject, the verb and the object, rather than where you start at the back end and turn it around and have your subordinate clauses in front so that people are left guessing, I don't … I find that confusing and I have to work harder at it. And I think that a lot of mandarin academic speak is like that. It was the women's movement that made me start writing, and the colleagues, well, the friends that I had within that. It's interesting, how we do learn how to write. I'm not even sure …

I: We learn how to get published perhaps?

DL: No, I think it's about learning to get your point across, and having a point that you want to get across, that focuses your mind on writing. And that's why I couldn't be bothered with the marketing into various … I mean, to be arrogant, I've never had any problem in placing the stuff that I've written. And I've always put a finger up to being told by the RAE that I have to worry about the quality of the journal, because frankly I don't read many of the quality journals, so I assume that other people don't. I suppose you learn an awful lot from sub-editing your students, everybody else's stuff, and you learn a lot from being sent endless proposals and articles to referee. You see what other people are doing wrong. That's what Becker says, isn't it, in his *Writing for Social Sciences*, or whatever it's called. It's that process of editing other people, and having other people edit you, that teaches you how to get your point across, and to write in an interesting … I always think that. … the other thing that's a painful but very good exercise is when you've written your article and it's seven and a half thousand words and it's got to be cut back to six, to realise how much better it almost always is after you've cut out, what would that be, a quarter of … maybe it's not, my mathematics isn't very good, but 20 per cent of it. Because I do tend to go off at tangents, and to have kind of bulbous phrases, and overuse parentheses and things like that, and getting rid of them always does improve it. And cutting out a whole load of footnotes and references. I do think the referencing by academics is … especially as the older you get the more references you can just supply without even thinking about it, and the more you tend to put them all in.

I: Well, a colleague says people say he's not an academic writer, he doesn't use enough references, he doesn't place himself in the field, not explicitly anyway.

DL: I think I go the other way, and I think it's trying to demonstrate that I have read the stuff even if I'm not necessarily agreeing with it.

I: And because of your interest in women's studies, have you deliberately tried to adopt a particular kind of style that differs from 'conventional academic writing'?

DL: I think that use of the first person and the almost requirement to give an account of why the particular topic is of interest to you and how you came to it and why you want to develop: I find that really important and liberating, in fact. Because kind of disguising that, which is how I regard conventional academic writing, where the subject descends from the sky, and where the researcher isn't present in interaction with the subjects of the topics … I mean I don't have a particularly post-structural bent to my writing, but as a structuralist or quite an empirical writer, I think it's really important to say why you're interested in it and where you came from. And that always is the valuable opening that gets you started on …

I: Jane Miller has written about 'the autobiography of the question'. It can help students …

DL: It doesn't have to be the very first thing, but it has to be in there somewhere. Because the object is still the topic and the findings – it's not me. And you can start by saying it's a really important topic because, but then a few paragraphs later you can say why you got interested in it, and why you took the particular line. The kind of coming clean about the shortcomings of the methodology, which there always are, and the limitations on the data, all that kind of stuff, I find that really, really important. It's often what I write first, even if it isn't what appears first. I think what I've learned most about writing is the process of editing.

I: I think we may have covered how you have managed to keep writing a major part of your life, particularly as a woman, and what kind of satisfactions you get from it, as well as what kind of writing you most enjoy. We haven't talked about what your writing says about you or how you go about it.

DL: I mean, I see writing as an engagement in a debate. And to that extent I'm a bit constrained by writing via having been trained to write academically. Because if you really want to contribute to the debate, you'd be publishing nowadays in the mass media and not in academic journals. And I suppose that's why I'm happy and will probably carry on writing monographs, once I'm freed from these constraints, I can write more. I don't regard *A Woman's Guide* as a textbook, I regard it more as a survey of available evidence that we have about what helps people. It is a bit of a 'how to do it' book, but it has a much broader contextualisation than most textbooks, which are very narrow. And that reflects the sociological background, I suspect.

I: So obviously you intend to go on writing, and you find it satisfying.

DL: But the writing's always been the most … well, the research and the writing, the two go hand in hand, you can't research without writing. But you don't really analyse or see, I mean, the stuff always emerges in the process of the writing. Certainly with the Terry Threadgold, Brian Street stuff about the emergent nature of ideas, when you're writing. And I suppose that overlaps a bit with the Gunther approach, of why do people use the particular – I mean being in this School makes me realise why you choose the particular words you choose … I think to begin with I thought that was just the question of choosing the right word to get the ideas across, but now I see it as much about producing the right emotions or concerns or – I don't know – politics or passions in your reader.

I: The men I interviewed feel writing should be so much a part of people's selves, of their thinking, of how they are in the world, that they would want to do it.

DL: Yes. I mean, we do teach a kind of, well we don't teach it, the RAE produced such routinised … I mean, not everybody wants to be engaged in that thing, not everybody wants to write to get their ideas across. Some people want to teach to get their ideas across. I'm so tired of teaching, I mean, I'm aware that you do get your ideas across by teaching but it's an exhausting

activity, whereas … well writing's tiring as well, and you kind of look up and you've been at it for five hours, and you think, 'Goodness'. But it's less ephemeral. I suppose that's the trouble with teaching. It's very tiring, but it's a performance for 25 people, and maybe it changes their lives but you don't always know it. Somehow if you write, you have a product at the end.

I: What do you think your writing says about you? The question could mean several things.

DL: I produce a lot fewer short journalistic-y writing pieces, and that says that I'm no longer part of an active political movement, and I live in a society where I think many people have given up in politics, because they don't feel that what they're going to do says very much. And the sort of writing that I do says that I'm now part of a much more academic community, which does try to go on producing evidence, and arguing particular cases …

But I'm part of groups and seminar series who are very interested in what each other is doing. And where we think we've got some really important answers, but unfortunately they're not the practice-based evidence that people are looking for, that politicians are looking for, neither institutionally or local community or local authority, and certainly not nationally. I just suppose I'm hoping that a new millennium will come when it feels like it's worth … a part of me thinks, 'Maybe, Diana, what you should do is reskill, and learn to write as a journalist, because the media is where there is influential writing.' But just as I feel I couldn't bear to learn another language – and I feel really bad that I'm doing a lot in Pakistan and haven't learned any Urdu and don't intend to – I also feel journalistic writing is a skill that I don't have.

I: But you could probably do it.

DL: Maybe one of the things we should be doing since we're always being told by the … I mean, the ESRC [Economic and Social Research Council] makes various efforts to get us to disseminate, and I have been on things with … doing TV and doing radio stuff, but it's not enough. I'm always aware we don't do enough of project management, and that ties into the writing as well, because the project management ought to involve writing as you go along. And now that I am more engaged with my researchers, we are giving more papers, and that writing as we go along is getting done in ways it wasn't in various of my other ones. But maybe we ought to do much more stuff about dissemination, and not just journalistic-y stuff, but we don't have time. I mean, journalists frequently phone me up, and sometimes I phone them back, and they will take ages and they pick your brains – and they don't give you credit.

I: And maybe say something you didn't say anyway.

DL: Absolutely. But what we have by way … I mean I'm very fond of Helen Green and she will help you with press releases, but you then have to have two or three clear days in which if the journalists do phone you, you're available for doing things or I could pitch things to *Woman's Hour* and they might well take them on, but again it's all time, and you have to be very well planned and structured. And I don't feel that my time at the Institute has been very well planned and structured. And I don't know, maybe men are better at doing that, I don't … at planning and sticking to it.

I: Or at putting other things aside or sticking to a daily plan: I'm going to work from five till seven, then nine in the evening till midnight …

DL: Well, I need sleep, and I like sleep, and bed is a major pleasure, maybe that's a serious failing. But certainly some of the guys I know who write a lot are quite hermit-like.

I: How do you go about writing? Do you write some things by hand?

DL: Never.

I: So you do it on screen?

DL: Well occasionally I take … my writing is barely legible and my students complain about that, so I even have to type student comments. I wish I'd learned to touch type, I wish, I wish, I *wish* I'd learned to touch

type. I sometimes take notes by hand, and then type them up. But that's partly just because I don't want to lug my laptop, that's only on occasions where I can't use my laptop. No, it's so much better to have them virtually there, then you can just move stuff around.

I: Is there anything else you want to add?

DL: Well, I would say that although I would write if I wasn't here, it is important to have the attachment to here. You do need a location to function in as an academic, and the email's very useful, the library card is very useful, the IT support is very useful, all of those are really important. I don't work in the Institute at all, well write in the Institute, you understand what I mean – that's an interesting slippage – but I think it's important, and I do think that perhaps there's a special role there for emeritus, emeriti people who want to keep on writing, and I think they do a lot of useful stuff, and also may be freer to speak up, because they write in their own capacity…. Obviously you always write in your personal capacity, and there's always disagreement – civilised, moderated, well-argued disagreements is what I think academics are supposed to be about.

I: Now you're very well established, but do you think it's important to have that affiliation – to have a chapter in a book and that says 'Diana Leonard, Institute of Education'? … The affiliation, do you think it's important?

DL: No, I think it's just practical. After all, one can always say one's had it, if one's had it. To begin with it's important, and that's why we struggled in the women's movement to get a foothold in the university, because the university was the producer of validated, status-full knowledge. But of course now we're in a different knowledge economy. And the universities don't have anything like the …

I: They're not listened to …

DL: There's a word which has left me.

Barbara MacGilchrist

I: *How long have you been at the Institute? What's your current role? And perhaps tell us the chief responsibilities of that role?*

BM: I've been here nearly 16 years. I'm Deputy Director and my main responsibility is for the quality of all the academic work across the Institute, with a particular emphasis on quality assurance and enhancement in all that we do.

I: *Would you like to tell me about some writing you've been really pleased with?*

BM: Well, I thought about this and I think the best piece of writing that I've done is the second edition of *The Intelligent School* (2004), 'TIS 2,' as my

colleagues and I call it.

I: *And that's because …*

BM: I've chosen that because it was a huge learning journey with two excellent co-authors. It actually took longer to write than the first edition and represented a significant development in our original concept about the intelligent school. I'm also pleased about it because it's been very well received by practitioners and by academics, and we've had some very good reviews, which is really encouraging.

In the first edition we weren't going to call the book *The Intelligent School*. Our first idea was to bring together four almost discrete areas of research – school improvement, school effectiveness, teaching and learning – and to pull together all the research literature in those four areas. And that was our initial aim for the book. Having done that and got lots of examples from schools of the sorts of things that they were doing, we actually sat down and realised that a school is greater than the sum of the parts and we began to identify a number of characteristics of schools that, collectively, we believed were very successful schools, in the broadest use of that definition, and we came up with the concept of the intelligent school. Second edition, not only were we much more rigorous – and perhaps more controversial – about challenging current policy and practice, but we also really thought through the concept of the intelligent school and defined that much more clearly than we'd done in the first one.

I: What has helped your writing?

BM: I like shared writing. I also like writing on my own. But I like shared writing where it's very productive. I've had one or two occasions where I've written with other people and that's not proved to be as satisfactory as I thought it was going to be. But on this occasion – and it's why we came back together again – it was such a learning journey that it was a joy. So although it was difficult finding enough hours in the day to fit it in, we got so stimulated every time we met and the ideas were sparking off one another, and we had a work schedule that we stuck to and couldn't let one another down. So we carved up the book and each of us wrote specific chapters and then commented on it. I found that was really helpful.

Writing with others … I mean, especially my first book, *Planning Matters* (1995), because I wrote that with three others, one of which was Peter Mortimore who was so experienced and so supportive; that was the kind of encouragement that I needed, writing with genuinely motivated colleagues. And that comes back to writing with Jane Reed and Kate Myers, and more recently, I've just had a book published last year, where I wrote with a headteacher and we wrote up a project that I was involved with, with her school and four others. And that was a very refreshing experience and she, she thinks differently from me and the two of us complemented one another remarkably well. So that was good. She thinks visually. And that comes

through in her writing whereas my style's very different to that. And it was very refreshing, because I've never written with somebody who quite looks at life through that particular lens. So that was good.

Other things that have helped me with my writing, I would say, are having mentors. And I've had four mentors that I can identify in my career. And it goes back to way before I joined the academic world. My first mentor was someone called Chris Athey who was my tutor when I trained to be a teacher. We're still good friends and she made me believe that I could write academic essays. Her feedback was wonderful. And she would just put a little question mark or just make a little comment and that would send me off on a whole range of thinking. So she opened the door for me. Then I had two excellent tutors when I did my Masters degree, Joan Tambourini and James Willig, and they were wonderful at, again, enabling me to write. And there was one thing that I never forgot, because only at the eleventh hour did they start looking at surface features. Up until then it had been helping me to develop my ideas and to get those ideas down on paper.

And then at the eleventh hour, when I thought I'd finished my dissertation, they told me to go away and I had to retype it, because they said I had an Achilles heel, which was doing split infinitives. So I was somewhat miffed, but I went away and I did it. What I didn't know was that I was in for a distinction. And what I didn't know was, quite often in the academic world, it can be things like split infinitives and spelling errors that actually can make the difference. Then my third mentor was Peter Mortimore for the reasons I've already given. And then my fourth mentor was Denis Lawton, who was my PhD supervisor, who is a wonderful teacher. Absolutely wonderful teacher. And doing that PhD was a watershed for me and got me into *serious* academic writing.

So I believe you learn to write by writing, by having thoughtful, appropriate feedback. And to me it was the quality of the feedback and not trying to impose their ideas on me, but encouraging me to think and to not be satisfied. I was always going away, soon as I'd had a tutorial or a discussion with any of the people I've mentioned, my brain was off, starting thinking about new ideas. Tearing up what I'd already written and starting again.

I: Is there anything you're not so happy with?

BM: I think one of the things that I did find was spending absolutely ages putting together a major research bid. It was really challenging. And the very first research bid I put in was actually to the ESRC and I got it accepted. I did it jointly with Peter Mortimore and we had it accepted first time which, as I understood it, then was not necessarily a usual occurrence.

I spent ages putting together that [other, later] major research bid. It involved vast amounts of time and energy and we didn't even get past the first hurdle. So that was my first experience of rejection. Well, I guess you just have to swallow hard and then pick yourself up and try, try, try again.

I: How have you managed to keep writing a major part of your life?

BM: I don't know that I'd say it's a major part of my life per se. It's been a major part at times. And it's at those times, like when we were rewriting *The Intelligent School*, with a publisher getting very frustrated and saying, 'You're only doing a revised version' when, in fact, we wrote another book, really, that we stuck with it. I mean, that's where if you're doing joint writing I think it's quite helpful. I only write when I think I've got something to say.

So when I do write, I'm normally very motivated. I'm not just writing because I think I'd better write another article. I'm writing because I think I've got something to say.

I: We touched on one of the satisfactions of writing: approval by the research community …

BM: Yes, and by practitioners.

I: And by practitioners.

BM: That's very important.

I: Yes, of course. So anything else you'd like to say on the feelings that writing stirs up?

BM: Well, I suppose finishing an article, a chapter or a book, whilst I find it very satisfying … but I actually rarely go back and read. Once I've written that, I've finished and the pen goes down. And I often don't go back to reread. Only if I'm going to give a talk do I go back and I might take the odd extract. But I rarely ever completely read an article or a chapter or certainly a book that I've written. It's very satisfying when it gets accepted for publication. There's always a sense of satisfaction when it's finally published. Although, as I say, there are kind of frustrations.

I find I have very mixed emotions when I'm writing. Sometimes I get very frustrated, because I've sat down and I've given up a whole Sunday, and at the end of the day I've written two lines, which is enormously frustrating. And the other extreme can be great, you know, exhilaration when you've been concentrating very hard and suddenly you find that new ideas … you've actually been able to capture them on paper.

And I find that ideas come to me very quickly and I've got to be quick at getting them down on paper. And that sense of satisfaction when the ideas and the pen flow together. Which doesn't always happen.

I: I note that you've written in the past – INSET materials and different types of things. Which would you say you enjoy most?

BM: To be honest, I like writing books. I never thought I would, but I do. Having said that, I did write a book in my first year of teaching and it's still sitting in my loft. I sent it to one publisher and got rejected and, at that time, I didn't realise that you've got to keep at it. But when you write a book, the whole output is you, or you and your colleagues, rather than you being asked to do a small part of an unknown whole. So, you know, you're asked to write a chapter and you write this chapter, you've no idea what people have written before you or what they're going to write after you and then suddenly, if you're lucky, the book gets published and there's your chapter sitting in amongst the rest. Whereas creating a book, it's in your hands, if you like. Any book I've written I've no idea quite what it's going to look like at the end till I get there. But at least I feel that you've got a degree of control over it.

And it's not an unknown. It's you. I mean you take a greater risk, of course, because it's you or you and your colleagues in the firing line for getting poor reviews and knocked down, whereas if you're just one part of a bigger book or, you know, one article in a journal, OK.

I: What does your writing say about you?

BM: Oh dear, [*laughs*] I thought about this. I'd like to think that it says I can express my ideas clearly, that I'm not afraid to challenge and to speak out, and that the way I write is accessible to the audience for whom the writing is intended. That's the practitioners, for me. They're my main audience. Because I want to make a difference out there. That's what motivates me to write, is wanting to make a difference for children and teachers.

I: And how do you go about writing?

BM: I only write when I think I've got something to say, and that's the idea of the moment. And then I stick with it until I've finished it.

Writing for me is a learning journey. I very rarely know what the final message or outcome will be. I know the general themes that I want to write about, but I never know at the beginning exactly how it's going to pan out. I'm often pitching into the unknown. Now *The Intelligent School* first edition was a very good example of that.

The publisher was somewhat surprised when we came up with the title at the end [*laughs*] because it wasn't the title we put in at the beginning.

Once I've decided to write something, as I say, I stick with it. It's on my mind all the time, and this comes back to your earlier question about how do you manage to fit it in. 'Cause I do travel quite a long way in to work, for example. So I have a lot of thinking time coming in and out of work. So it's on my mind. I have a notebook by my bed, in my pocket. Some of the most creative ideas I have are when I'm out walking with the dog.

I don't know whether I'm prepared to admit this, but I do actually sometimes take a tape recorder with me when I'm out with the dog because as soon as ideas start to flow, I have to capture them, otherwise I've lost it by the time I get back.

I write and read a lot on the train each day, so as to keep the ideas developing. When I did my PhD I always kept it on the front burner.

I handwrite almost always as I like to see the text in front of me so as I can play around with it. I don't use the computer.

I like to be able to cross-reference, I like to be able to use Post-its, I like to be able to chop up the text, move it about, and yet I can't use the computer screen 'cause I can only see one piece, one wedge of text. Whereas when I've got it spread over the dining room table, with Post-its and etc. etc.

I: And physically move it about?

BM: Physically moving it about, yep. I'm a bit of a perfectionist, which is a nuisance. So I'm forever rereading and refining as I go, which can sometimes get in the way of the flow of ideas, but that's the way it goes.

I: So what have you learned about the process of writing?

BM: It's a varied passage. I find that writing comes in bursts. For me, the first couple of sentences are often the hardest, i.e. getting started. I think I've thrown more, screwed-up more pieces of paper and thrown them in the bin at the outset. I like using quotes and being very thorough and careful over references, and that to me is important. And I find it very pleasing. I like, I like analysing research and drawing together different themes coming out of the research literature and I like quoting and referencing, to do that. I always have to do a lot of reading around the subject, and there are times when I have to tell myself to stop: no more reading, get on with the writing. And that can be quite difficult.

Getting the title sorted for an article or a chapter or a book, indeed, is very important to me because I try and encapsulate in the title the central theme of the article or the chapter. And quite often I ask a question because I'm usually trying to provide an answer to a thought or an idea. I mean, for example, for my professorial lecture I asked: 'Has school improvement passed its sell-by date?'

And I like to come up with a title that actually hopefully catches the eye and encourages the reader to read on. 'Improving self-improvement?' was the title of a journal article I wrote.

I: So would you come to that question after you'd written something?

BM: No …

I: You would start with it?

BM: On the whole, that question would be my major idea. Having asked the question 'Has school-improvement passed its sell-by date?' … actually how that professorial lecture panned out I'd no idea until I'd finished the journey, but I knew that there was an issue there that I wanted to address.

I like to develop. I like to move myself on in terms of my own learning as I'm writing. I know some people know exactly the beginning, middle and end and they've sketched it all out. I never do that. I struggle with the first two sentences. I've spent a long time thinking about the title. Sometimes the title gets changed, but usually for articles. For the book it was quite a long time … I mean our first book we discussed for a long time the title. We knew it was about school development, but eventually called it *Planning Matters*. Like *School Matters* [as Peter Mortimore did]. And you say, you say, 'Yes, of course, why didn't we think about that earlier?' [*Laughs*] I think the title is terribly important, actually.

I: What have you learned about writing for publication?

BM: Well, you need to be clear who the audience is. That's very important, because that will determine the style, etc. You need to be quite clear what the particular journal or publisher expects – and which journal or publisher it's best to target – for the sorts of things that you want to write about. So deciding whether or not you're wanting to write an article that really is going to be in a peer-reviewed, prestigious international academic journal or whether actually what you want to say is much more going to be geared towards practitioners and therefore you'd be better going for a well-known but accessible professional publisher …

In the case of books, I think developing a very good relationship with one publisher I found to be very, very helpful. Because once they've got confidence in you and you've got confidence in them you're much more likely (a) to have any book proposal you put to them get accepted, or (b) from my experience, get the publisher coming back and asking you. For instance, we were invited to do the second edition of *The Intelligent School*.

I: An invitation like that is very satisfying too?

BM: Very satisfying. Very satisfying. And delivering on time and in the format expected. I am amazed by some drafts of articles that academics have written that have been sent to me by, you know, the editorial board of a journal to review and comment on, how poor they are. And they just haven't paid attention, so immediately that puts me off. So I think delivering on time and in the format expected. Standing your ground, I think, is very important. We had a considerable discussion and dialogue with the publisher about the cover of one of our books. Because we felt very strongly about it, and we came to a very amicable conclusion to that discussion. And from my point of view it was worth standing our ground because the cover that was being suggested did not portray the core concept of the book. So it went against our integrity as authors.

Having someone to act as a critical friend I think is very important. That's why shared writing that goes well, you can be a critical friend to one another, for example. As well as … when we wrote *The Intelligent School* we critiqued one another's work but we also went out to other colleagues and asked them to critique what we'd written. So we had a double benefit there, if you like. And I think, as a result, that noticeably improved our writing for publication.

I: So you've always been someone that doesn't really mind giving out your work to people?

BM: No, no, I don't mind, but I do like to put it out in a reasonable state. I do like to test out – particularly if I'm commenting on an area that I don't have a huge amount of expertise in but I know that … that aspect, that concept, that idea or whatever it is, that piece of research, is really important to my argument. But I want to check out that I've interpreted that research OK. So in that instance we just give an extract to someone, to actually the originator of that research, for example. I can think of several times when I did that in *The Intelligent School*, and tested that out. Say, 'Have I captured this?' And obviously to acknowledge that personal communication you have had in any writing that you do for publication, which is very important.

And I think choosing carefully if you want to invite someone, for instance, to write a foreword to the book, choosing someone who you know will actually read the manuscript and try and do their best to, you know, capture the essence of the book.

I think probably the only other thing would be is that publishers, particularly for books, they like an abstract that they can use, say, on the back cover. And I think working very closely with the publisher on the wording of that abstract, to again be sure that the essence of the book is captured.

I: If you weren't in this institution or any academic institution, would you still write?

BM: Probably not. It depends what the writing is. I write for all sorts of purposes at home, but they're not academic purposes.

I don't envisage that once I've retired I will continue writing for academic purposes. But that doesn't mean to say that I won't write for a range of other purposes. Because I actually like putting pen to paper.

I'm planning a long trip overseas and I'm already writing a great deal [*laughs*] in preparation for that long trip overseas.

I can see myself writing a lot of recipes, when I retire [*laughs*] 'cause I've got to improve my culinary repertoire.

I: Is there anything we've not talked about that should be in a book about writers at the IoE?

BM: I feel I've been very lucky as I've had some excellent support as a writer. I never imagined I would write the books and articles that I've written and I … as I said to you, I did actually write a book in my, it wasn't my first, it was my second year as a teacher,

but I never actually thought that I would do the sort of writing that, you know, I've been engaged in over the last sort of 16 years. And I've really enjoyed it. Great sense of satisfaction.

Pam Meecham

I: *First of all, some biographical details about how long you have been here and what jobs you have, what roles you've had?*

PM: I came to the Institute in 2000 so I was 50. I came from John Moores University in Liverpool and made the transition from the north back to the south where I was born. I was appointed as Research Tutor to what was then the Art and Design Department and subsequently have become the Research Tutor for the School of Arts and Humanities. I teach mostly Museum Studies and lead the Museums and Galleries and Education MA. My research students are almost entirely drawn from people working in the museum and gallery sector, many of them teachers or artists or administrators.

I: *Great. The first question we are asking is whether people can choose some piece of writing they are really pleased with, something they are proud of, something they can pick off the shelf and say: 'This is something that I really like.' Have you been able to do that?*

PM: Yeah. That's quite tricky. Initially I lent towards something quite educational, something that fitted into the kind of Institute remit, but then I realised those pieces of work weren't always the pieces that I was most proud of and actually, because advocacy for the visual arts is probably my greatest strength, I have chosen a piece of writing that reflects this. The piece that I am currently most proud of is a very short one that I wrote two years ago about the non-instrumental in an instrumental culture. So for me it was really important on two levels. First, it wasn't written for payment, it was written because somebody asked me to do it. It's also only about three or four thousand words whereas normally I would be writing something much longer. Two years ago there was a piece of conceptual art in Trafalgar Square by a Japanese artist called On Kawara. It's called 'Reading One Million Years'. Its appearance on the Square coincided with the first anniversary of the Iraq War and this quiet, insistently consistent piece of work that has been going on since 1969 was placed in Trafalgar Square for seven days, 24 hours a day. Two performance artists read in rotation with others 'One Million Years' forwards and backwards, just naming chronological dates from a large book. There was no real performance aspect to it, these weren't celebrities, these were very quiet, unremarkable-looking performance artists reading quietly in this extraordinary space that is becoming a kind of corporate space. I was concerned about what was happening to visual culture and the re-emergence of On Kawara's project that, as I said, has been going on since the 1960s, reminded me of the radicalism of that period and how exciting art was at that time. The performance artists were in a bullet-proof glass box in Trafalgar Square quietly reading. It brought together the things that I feel quite passionate about – visual culture, politics, the way in which we operate in the world – but also encompassed the Zen-like quality of quiet that can be achieved in a very busy world.

Bringing all that together into an article required an understanding of the history of conceptual art, a rethinking of the transformation of Trafalgar Square and a view of where these things fit in our so-called postmodern culture. So it was actually quite a challenge. But for no other reason than absolute pleasure I stayed and watched part of the performance and felt quietly reassured by On Kawara's artwork. So I tried to pull together quite a lot of strands – public policy on the arts, the corporatisation of our culture – and in writing it felt that I had managed to combine a lot of the things that I really cared about. The lack of instrumentality in On Kawara's work mirrored in some ways the reason for writing it, which was entirely for pleasure and to provide access through a publication for other

people because this particular performance could only be seen in Trafalgar Square.

I don't know if the article's entirely successful. I think it could probably have done with being longer, but having to write a smaller piece is actually quite useful sometimes because it made me condense many of my ideas. I also was working with an editor, Karen Raney, that I trust and who is extremely good. She is supporting without being didactic and her suggestions are nearly always absolutely right. I trust her judgement in terms of what she says and I enjoy working with her too, but I think there was something about that piece, that appeared in *engage*, a visual arts journal, that probably brought together all the things that are really important to me. I think the passing of time and our lives are encapsulated in the kind of work that conceptual artists are involved in, but equally there is a need for advocacy for that kind of work.

I: Can you just say what you hope to achieve by writing that piece and what you hope the reader would take away from reading it?

PM: I think the conceptual art projects of the 1960s have had a fairly difficult time in much of postmodern culture because postmodern culture and the arts have tended quite often to consist of slick one-liners and much that is ephemeral. The strength of On Kawara's project is consistency and tenacity: working on a project, over a long period, quietly and insistently without drama, in a very Zen kind of way. For most people it wasn't possible to see that piece and I wanted it to reach a wider international audience, so writing about it enabled that. But, I also wanted to draw together the strands of what's happening with 'World Squares for All' in Trafalgar Square and the politics of the sculptures for the fourth plinth and the kind of corporatisation and internationalism that is changing a place that is traditionally a repository of national values. I also wanted to draw parallels with the Iraq War. So I felt there needed to be a wider audience for that particular piece, which is what I'd hoped to achieve, but also to try to draw out its underlying strength, which is easily overlooked in a very noisy world.

I: Perhaps you could now identify something that you are less pleased with – something of a contrast?

PM: I think probably my very early pieces of writing, where I mistook being clever for really good pieces of writing and I tried to use too many long words. My sentences were over-long with too many clauses and too many ideas. It took me time to learn that writing is a craft, a skill that needs to be learned. There is nothing innate about writing, there is no gift and so it has to be worked at. My early fumblings and ramblings seem terribly complicated. I have tried to work towards a simpler way of writing, but also a way of condensing many ideas more successfully so that the reader doesn't have to do so much. My earlier pieces were just too long and too difficult for the reader and too demanding. Now I'm impatient with writers who needlessly demand too much of me because we live in a very busy world where reading and writing time is often snatched.

I: So who helped you with your writing?

PM: Well, I came to writing very late. I went to art college at 16 and so my early experiences were of visual art and practical activity rather than writing. My second subject at teacher training college was outdoor education and so if I wasn't painting, drawing or print-making, I was walking up mountains or canoeing and not engaged in the kind of stuff that writers were preoccupied with. By the time I was 40 I became more involved in written academic work and started to change my focus. I think I started to read more difficult and complicated texts in a period when art and culture became highly theorised. I became increasingly interested in art history and theory and I also felt I had something to say. That was the first thing. Art education, particularly at school level, also needed advocacy. There were very few people coming out of art education who were writing. There also were very few journals that published art education articles. I felt that art education needed people to talk about it and write about it, but there weren't very many people to work with. I also worked across fields – education and art history – and so I often worked with a younger art historian, Julie Sheldon, from Liverpool John Moores. We worked well together and I found that working

with another person that I trusted was a huge help, partly because my flights of fancy were quickly brought into sharp relief by her sensible approach. She is also willing to press the delete key and doesn't worry about losing whole pages whereas I think I used to be a little precious about my writing. So working with somebody who I have confidence in, but who also had a much better writing style than I did, helped. I learned from that. I contributed to her writing in terms of the depth of my knowledge of the field so we worked symbiotically in that sense.

I: How did you write collaboratively? What particular model?

PM: We've written two books together and previous to that we have written chapters in books. We are now writing two further books, one on American art and the other on museum histories. While the books are alphabetically, Meecham and Sheldon, they are absolutely 50–50 in terms of contribution. We jointly devise our projects working out general content and chapter headings. We then write half the chapters each and so have sole academic responsibility for our own work, but we do share ideas and edit together, making our styles more consistent. Julie will tell me if I am being pompous and I will look out for quirky things in her writing that perhaps are easily overlooked when concentrating on content. We also collaborate in the sense of the research. Knowing that one is writing on performance art … for instance, if we come across an extraordinarily good example we'll share that and see whether it fits. We also discuss theoretical concerns. There is a kind of research collaboration that takes place.

I: How do you keep writing as a major part of your life with all the teaching that you do and being a Research Tutor?

PM: I've made writing and research central to my teaching. I have recently been on study leave looking at the Australian War Memorial, which is actually a museum, looking at the dioramas (or picture models as they were called) that were created for the First World War – mostly around the Gallipoli and Northern France campaigns. The dioramas are an extraordinarily interesting area of study; historically set below the radar of art history, they are also interesting in terms of learning so I have actually been using the research at the Institute in my teaching for a museum learning course.

Both the books I have done with Julie also come out of teaching. The initial eight chapters were piloted as lectures and seminars with primary and secondary teachers at Tate Liverpool. I use the material that I am writing about with students and will ask their advice about what works and what doesn't. Even something that seems quite oblique, for instance the international reception of American art in the Fifties, which is the other area I am working on, will feed into one of my PhD student's work. So I don't really separate out my teaching from my writing or from my research. It all has to mingle, otherwise I can't fit it in. I would love to write a book on botanical history for instance, but I can't see quite how I can fit that into my teaching so it will have to wait.

I: Great.

PM: I think because I was a mother at another period of my life and because I always worked full time, once the children were two or three, I always had to multi-task when it came to writing. I have always had to work on trains, 'planes, at bus stations, a doctor's surgery – anywhere where I could find ten or 15 minutes. It isn't ideal. The notion of sitting quietly down in a study endlessly writing for days just hasn't been my experience.

I: Because you fitted the writing in around bringing up your children?

PM: And initially with a full-time job as a busy head of department in a Liverpool comprehensive. So reading and writing has always had to be integrated into my professional life. But that's helped because students are hugely helpful. They often come up with things I just haven't thought of and can critique from a distance. I have actually removed things that just didn't work and followed up suggestions.

I: Under their guidance. You are using them as consultants?

PM: Absolutely, yes.

I: That's great. So what about the satisfaction of writing?

PM: I still find it a frustrating, difficult process. I have to find a little bit of space somewhere to think it through first and to think, 'What is it that I want to write? Do I have anything to say? Is it worth embarking on this?' And then, at the end, looking to see if I have actually helped in any way at all. I think partly being a teacher, I always feel that my work should be accessible and should support other people in what it is they are trying to understand. Writing about contemporary art is really complicated and difficult and many people find it challenging. But if people feel at the end of something I have written that they have understood, then yes, of course, I feel much better about that. But there is also an archivist in me, the academic sleuth: I enjoy finding an obscure piece of knowledge.

I did some interesting work in the Czech Republic on the fallen monuments of the communist regime and I took lots of photographs of statues of Lenin, Czech communist leaders and various other political casualties post-1989, stored in an aircraft hangar near the Polish border. I got tremendous satisfaction from my photographs appearing in a publication (and an art exhibition in Germany and Liverpool) together with an explanation of the fall of this particular regime. This piece of work was particularly satisfying because it combined travel, politics, writing and art practice. The experience of going out to look at these monolithic, huge, socialist realist statues, of Lenin in particular (who now has a little tag around his ankle to remind everybody who he is), was quite extraordinary. When I finished that piece about the politics of the removal of monuments from the streets and memory and the importance of memory in the formation of identities, I did get a tremendous sense of pleasure seeing my photographs supporting my writing but also displayed in their own right.

I: So it doesn't get any easier?

PM: No! Well, a bit maybe. I read my work with more care now. I think initially I was so concerned about the process and so in awe of writers and writing that I was afraid to read my own writing. Many of the things that I wrote were not edited well enough because I didn't want to be confronted with my own work. I used to have the same problem (I think many artists do) when my work was up on the wall in an exhibition: seeing my writing felt like the same thing. Now I am much more ruthless and willing to be critical, but I also read with more care.

I: What's the fear about?

PM: Erroneously, I think I had a conception of the writer as someone special. I don't feel like that now. I feel that anybody can write. It's a craft to be learned, it's a skill to be acquired and once I had removed the aura from the writing and demystified the whole process, I realised it was a craft that I had to keep working at. But also writing for different audiences requires a different kind of writing and that was quite difficult to do initially. Now I think more carefully before I write. But, I am no longer afraid of this imaginary, mythical writer. I don't feel a piece of writing is part of my ego. I don't feel it is an expression of myself.

I: I suppose writers might be in awe of artists?

PM: Yes, while I worry about the disenchantment of the world, and I wouldn't like to see a complete overturning of any set of specialness in our world, I do think that there are a number of myths that needed to be removed and myths around artists and around writers are not helpful. I think, in both cases, if I have a contribution to make, it's that what people do is special, but not more than anyone else. I don't like the aura of mystification that has been attached to those two particular processes and it took me a long time to get over the hurdle. I also felt that in spite of there being so many good women writers – particularly in the field of art history and art education – it was a male preserve. It seemed like quite a hurdle for a woman, particularly coming into writing late and from a visual arts background, it was quite a transition to make, but I did come to it through education rather than any innate talent.

I: What kind of writing do you most enjoy?

PM: I like a solid problem that needs to be interrogated, I suppose. The dioramas that I was talking about earlier struck me the first time I visited Australia because they're very old-fashioned technology. These are models of battles, not the sort of thing you would expect to be particularly interested in. What I noticed about the many visitors was that they paid attention to the models in a way that they didn't look at the paintings, they didn't look at the photographs. The models held their attention, so I wanted to find out why. That set up all sorts of historic problems too about how those kinds of models were constructed, who did them, why, when. So it involves a lot of historic research as well as contemporary work around learning. I like that combination of drawing together learning engagements, visual culture and the historical aspects. I like those kind of problems. I often look for something that's compelling for some reason and then try to work out what it is that's compelling. I might approach it from a philosophical point of view, which I'm very interested in, but always with an historic basis. It seems rather an old-fashioned way to think, but I still think history is important. I still like to uncover the historic reception and production of something and then try to draw that into contemporary relevance. I try to do that across a range of interests.

I: So what does your writing say about you?

PM: I don't think writing is about self-expression. I don't think it's really so much about me as about a learning process. It might say a little about the kind of areas that I am interested in and anybody who reads my writing can see that the motive is always the historical aspect in much that I do, but I don't know how much it's about me. I think it's very often about my audience, about who I am writing for. At least that's what I try to do. I am reluctant to say that it's about me – I think my garden's more about me than my writing.

I: Could you connect what you said at the beginning and what you feel the writing of that article might say about you?

PM: I think that the visual arts, visual culture, have played a really important part in my life since I was a child. You know, I had that moment of epiphany, I think it's called, when I first saw a drawing of a woman in an art book in my school. The moment when visual art suddenly became for an unknown, inexplicable reason extremely important as a part of my life and I think if there is a thread through all of my writing it is a keen interest in visual culture. I do write about politics sometimes and regeneration and the role of visual culture in regeneration, but visual culture is always there and the historic is important as well. I guess those things stem from my childhood, a passion for history and a passion for visual culture.

I: *Politics?*

PM: Yes, there is in my writing and teaching a commitment to what could be called 'cultural democracy'. Even as a child I was wary of the cultural elitism that went with many forms of visual culture. By the age of 16 I was well aware of the pitfalls of working inside museums and galleries; however, I am also convinced of the issues of cultural access and inclusion. At the same time, because I think cultural democracy is really important, a lot of the work I do is not just advocacy for the arts, but to situate the arts in broader networks of culture so it is not seen as an elitist activity.

I: *Thank you. Now to move on to more about the writing process – how do you go about it?*

PM: Randomly I'm afraid to say. I would like to say I had a structure. I would like to say I was methodical and I'd like to say I was consistent, but I am none of those things. My writing is much more a stream of consciousness, partly because I write while I'm gardening, cooking and doing a lot of other things. The computer will be on and I'll dash back to it and write something down. I'll often start with an idea or, if I'm working on a book, a particular chapter that's formulated around an idea, so 'monuments' would be one. Then I will work fairly randomly to bring it all together and only at the end really put it into a structure. I am not advocating that as the norm because I think everybody works differently, but it

works for me doing it that way. I find writing to a very fixed structure frustrating and limiting. I do have a fairly scattergun approach, but then I'm very willing to press the delete key if something just doesn't fit.

I: *What have you've learned about writing for publication or about relationships with publishers?*

PM: I think probably one of the most interesting things that the first publisher I ever worked with said was, 'You write as you lecture, you have to stop doing that, you must learn to write as a writer.' I didn't really understand quite what she meant at first and so I went back to read the chapter I was working on more carefully and of course I was writing as a lecturer, assuming a complicity on the part of my audience, which was a mistake. I was assuming that my audience were looking at slides and assuming a shared knowledge. One of the most interesting things about working with very good publishers has been that they've made me read the sentences as a reader, not as a writer. That has meant changing the way I write for my audience – and it might sound like a subtle distinction, but it is a really important distinction because many of us lecture first and write second and so our instinct is to lecture, so publishers have made me aware of that. I also think they've made me aware that the form that the words take influences the way they are received. That also comes out of visual culture – that the form a painting takes actually makes a difference to how it's received: so a nude isn't just a nude, it depends how that nude is painted. So I'm much more aware that the form of writing, the way in which you write, affects what it is you've got to say or how it will be received. So publishers made me very aware of that.

I: *Do you feel that writing is such a part of you that you would do it wherever you were, whatever job you had?*

PM: Yes, if I had something to say. I think currently there's a great deal to say about arts policy, about learning in museums, about visual culture in general, and I still feel I have a lot more to offer, more to research so I would still write. I can't imagine not writing, but I am not a diarist, I don't feel compelled to blog or to write down my every thought. I don't feel like that about it, but I can't imagine not having a book in the background quietly murmuring away. Writing for me is about research because I research in archives, museums, galleries, in visual culture generally. That means travel and looking and spending time with other people who also write and talk about the visual arts and I can't imagine that disappearing. That is part of who I am or who I've become over the past 50 or so years. So, no, I wouldn't give up writing because that would mean giving up visual culture.

I: *Anything else that you'd like to add?*

PM: I think writing with other people is something that's complicated and difficult and I have written with people who were not generous because they were very much more experienced than I was. They also took an approach to writing that was very much about ego instead of what's important to say. Finding somebody to work with effectively, I think is probably one of the most important things in my writing life. I feel confident about writing on my own now, but I also love writing with other people. I like the shared experience of writing. I like what others can bring to my writing and what I can bring to theirs. But I think you need to find someone that you can trust and will support you and teach you as well as learn from you. And I think that's probably the most important thing about learning to write, even if you come to writing as late as I have done.

I: *Right. Thank you very much – absolutely fascinating.*

Heidi Safia Mirza

I: *Heidi, thank you so much for agreeing to be interviewed. Can you just say something briefly about what you will do when you join us, your job title and your responsibilities?*

HSM: I'm going to be the Professor of Equalities Studies in Education and I'm very honoured to get the title. I will start in October. I understand it's the first time someone has been appointed to this Chair, so it's a new initiative. It includes setting up a Centre for Equalities and Human Rights in Education, which is very challenging. It has generated a lot of excitement and I understand that expectations are very high from my new colleagues, which is rather nerve-wracking!

I: *Absolutely. But you've done similar work elsewhere, though.*

HSM: I've been Professor of Racial Equalities Studies at Middlesex University for the last five years, which I've really enjoyed but it was very challenging too. After September 11th there's been a lot of racial tension and global upheaval. We have Islamophobia and a backlash against multiculturalism, not to mention the xenophobia against asylum seekers and refugees. At the same time there has been a lot of positive talk about diversity with new equalities legislation here and in Europe, and we have the Human Rights Act and the Race Relations Amendment Act. At the Institute I'm hoping to take what I have learnt and focus more on educational issues as a way to challenge racism, whether it's in the classroom or in the workplace. So this job is a great opportunity for me to do important research that makes a difference.

I: Great, thank you. I'd really like to start by asking you if you can tell me something about your best piece of writing or some of your best pieces of writing: those which you're most pleased with.

HSM: It's such a difficult question. I have been thinking long and hard about this. In my writing life, which has spanned the last 25 years, different things have influenced me at different times and I can be proud of something the moment I write it, then I move on to another piece and then I'm proud of that. So in different eras and different times I feel differently about my work. Sometimes I look back on a piece of work and I say, 'What was I thinking?' So writing is about progression, it's a process. I think one of the big mistakes we make in writing is to think what we are writing at the time is final and it's got to be perfect. Perfection, I think, is the biggest enemy of a writer.

Because writing is a journey of self-growth I would have to say my favourite piece is my first book, *Young, Female and Black* which I wrote in 1992. I have an emotional attachment to it. It was my PhD thesis and it's become a best-selling book with Routledge. I am amazed it did so well because it was a small-scale ethnography of young Caribbean girls. I am myself from the Caribbean, but grew up and went to school in London and so I wanted to write about these experiences and the interplay between career choices and educational structures. So in a way this book was about my own life, it was a process of exploring the practices of racism and exclusion which I saw around me. I suppose it was a cathartic thing to see it in print. At the time it was very exciting for me. So that is a favourite piece of work.

I: So it stemmed from your PhD, and is perhaps autobiographical?

HSM: Yes, it was autobiographical to some extent, and I think that's something that's underpinned a lot of my work. The thing with academic writing is it can be like a mask. You can use academic theory and academic conventions to articulate, in a very objective and distanced way, something that you've experienced yourself, but you're not really naming or implicating yourself in it.

When you write I do believe your personal experience is driving it, but you are using academic language and nuances. I always tell my students they should write what they feel about a subject, put themselves in the text and then go back and make it 'academic'. It makes it better and more meaningful to them. I do think that sometimes we leave out the personal or we ignore that in our writing and we should bring it to the fore.

I: It would appear that race and gender dominate your work?

HSM: Yes, there's a connection between that very first piece of work, that cathartic outpouring if you like, and the next book which I edited, which was *Black British Feminism* (1997). I think it was a very powerful piece of work because it brought together women of colour who were writing and doing brilliant work, but in isolated little 'pockets' in different universities in the UK.

Independently we were writing on similar themes. Some were just finishing their PhDs, some were already established. Black British feminism opened up a moment of possibilities and brought us together to make such a powerful statement. It created a new subject area based on our collaborative writing. It was such an energetic and vibrant time. I'm very proud of this.

I remember after finishing the book I went on holiday and I saw my mum in Trinidad. She was giving me a massage because I was so stressed, and I said to her, 'Mummy, if I died now I would be so happy, I think I've done what I need to do. I've done my opus!' I felt the book would leave a mark. And she reminded me of that the other day because I was feeling a bit low about something I was writing. With writing we do go in peaks and troughs.

We do so easily forget our achievements, because in academia you're pushed forward, to do more and more and there's such little praise or chance for reflection on what you have done. You always have to do something else, be onto the next project, and you forget the value of what you've done. It's only when someone comes up to you or emails you and says, 'I read that, thank you, it made me think differently', that you realise well, actually, your work is valuable. But we do work in our little pockets. It's the isolation that's so difficult.

I: What are the pros and cons of collaborative writing?

HSM: Working in collaboration, I would say, can be the best of times and the worst of times. Collaborative working really makes you think differently. I've written, of course, with Dave Gillborn (2000) here at the Institute, but I've written mainly with women, such as Diane Reay (1997). What's challenging is to write so that it's seamless. We take responsibilities for different areas, but then we interweave so that the style seems seamless, and that's very hard to do, it takes time.

Then there are always problems of ownership and that's where collaborative work can come unstuck: who owns this or that? So if you work in a very deep feminist way of saying, 'Let's really pool our ideas and writing styles together', then who owns it? And in academia, let's face it, it's very competitive, first authors matter and ownership matters, and it becomes difficult as people are at different phases in their careers. So I would say always, always have good ground rules that everybody understands and agrees to and talk about it openly.

I think what's really nice about working with others is that you don't get writer's block! Let's be honest, it can be really difficult, but when you've got that synergy of working together, you feel excited about what you're doing and so the passion comes through. So I would say collaborative work is creative, but it can be a minefield as well.

I: When you talk about 'creative', do you find that through your co-writers you view your writing in a different way?

HSM: Well, of course, other people bring their own theoretical understandings so you can see something differently from their particular point of view. So yes,

I think collaborative work has proven very useful for doing research work. When you're on a large team and you are working together on a huge national project like I did with SCRE [Scottish Council for Research in Education], and you've got researchers going up and down the country collecting data, how you pool it all together is crucial. You do learn a lot about good organisation and good leadership in those contexts. It's important that somebody has oversight over the style and presentation and knitting it together. Though, when you are finished, the sense of satisfaction is very different from when you have written something yourself.

I: Earlier you mentioned about the difficulty of choosing your 'best' writing and you alluded to having other pieces of work where you feel it was not your best. Do you want to say anything about your least favourite and why that might be?

HSM: Ten years ago I was nominated to give the Lister Lecture at the BA [British Association for the Advancement of Science] Festival of Science – it's a huge annual jamboree. The Lister Lecture's very prestigious, it's awarded to an up-and-coming academic, and I wrote a very angry lecture. It was on racist pseudo-science and IQ. I looked at popularist right-wing academic arguments such as the bell curve which linked race to low IQ. I was so angry about the stuff I was reading at the time and the revitalisation of Social Darwinism through the new genetics discourse. I look back on that essay now and I think how angry I was. I don't feel that any more and I guess what I'm saying is at different phases of writing you're at different places in your life, and it's always an unfinished process.

I feel similarly about *Young, Female and Black*. While it is my favourite because of its status in my life, and it was my starting point, when I look back at the writing style and the simplicity of my arguments, I could crawl under a table and cringe! I can see that the style is clumsy and I would now use different theoretical approaches to the same work; in fact, I am thinking of doing *Young, Female and Black* 20 years on.

I'd really love to do that because I think things have changed so enormously for young black women growing up in Britain now. I would take a different approach to the theory and methodology, which has developed. In terms of the writing and the style, I would say that it really does make me cringe! Especially when I know people are still buying and using it.

I: What's that 'cringe' about?

HSM: I feel I've moved on so much since I wrote this, but I still get A-level students emailing me, saying, 'I'm using this book for my project can you help me?' They see it as valuable, even though I am cringing. When you write you are putting something 'out there' and it has meaning to others but it has a different meaning to you. Writing is so personal: what matters to you is how you feel about it, not how others feel about it.

I think when you're writing you've got to learn to let go. One of my affirmations is 'trust and let go'. Whenever I'm nervous, whenever I'm not sure, I say, 'Just trust and let go' and let whatever I'm doing or saying float out into the ether. In your writing and your talking you have to trust people will read and hear and find their own value in it.

1: I like that, 'trust and let go'. Would you say that writing is a major part of your life?

HSM: Yes, it's obsessive, it dominates my thinking, I wake up in the night worried about an idea I've been working on and if it's not good enough. It's very difficult. You're always testing yourself, and it's lonely, and it's hard. Last summer there was a sculpture on Hampstead Heath, it was a massive table and the chair. It was enormous! It was the size of a house. It illustrated the loneliness of the writer and it did, because that's how big your table and chair feel to you, as big as a house! It does dominate you. Once you're in academia, and you're always being pushed for the next piece and the next one and the next one, and you're held up to scrutiny by your peers, you can become obsessed with the writing. So you can't easily 'trust and let go'. It's a process of just learning that you have to. Using deadlines is how I let go!

I: Just staying on this theme of writing being a major part of your life: if you weren't in academia would you still write?

HSM: Oh yes. I really like playing with writing styles. I did this in my inaugural lecture last year at Middlesex University. The theme was love and hate in the context of educational desire. It took a year to think it through and about three months to write and, in fact, talking to other people who did their inaugural, that's very much the pattern. It's the most petrifying thing you can go through because it's about your life's work and not only are you up for peer review and scrutiny, it has to be meaningful to friends and family. And yet it's the most cathartic and therapeutic thing you can do, so the lecture – it's my third favourite piece. I feel like I'm on 'Desert Island Discs'!

The lecture was almost like a rap poem, it had a rap beat, and it was divided up into seven stories or verses. I feel very strongly in my writing that I should be able to communicate and that it's accessible. You have to break down some of the academic language and concepts as it is a public audience where I knew some people, like my mum and my friends, have not got degrees and have never been to a university. This is a totally unknown world to them and I wanted them to feel comfortable with what I was saying, and not feel excluded. We do that a lot in academia, exclude. In fact, the more excluding you are, the more you're valued!

The idea of the lecture was to tell a personal story about my own life and how I've come to do the work I'm doing and explore the emotions and passion that's driven me. I do feel so strongly about social justice issues. What I was able to do in that lecture with the writing style was feel confident that I'd reached a point, after all these years of writing, to write as if I'm talking to you, and not hide behind the mask of over-articulations and over-theorising. It took a long time to write and I'm very proud of that piece, because it made people cry and it made them laugh – it brought out emotions in people.

Part of my process of writing includes getting inspiration. So I went to the Jazz Café to see Ruby Turner singing. I love Ruby Turner because she's got that gospel power in her voice. I watched her perform, because giving a lecture is a performance, and I saw the way she worked the audience and I thought, 'Yes! I want to do that in my lecture!'

My grandfather was a minister in the Caribbean church and I wanted to be able to emulate giving a sermon, but not preaching to people, of course! I wanted to bring out emotions in people. It was very difficult, but I think I achieved it on the day and it was great, I really enjoyed it.

Writing this lecture allowed me to enjoy the process of writing. I'd love to write novels. Novels that have all this emotional power in it. In fact, I've just come back from Trinidad where I did some research for a novel that I would like to write. You see I can't get the academia out of me, I'm still doing loads of research! Somebody said to me, 'But if you're writing a novel, just write it!' I said, 'No, no, no! I have to get the facts right!' [*Laughs*]

I did go to a writing workshop, it was a week away and it's with the Arvon Foundation. They do script writing, poetry workshops, short stories, whatever. Many famous writers have contributed financially to this trust for writers. It was just amazing. We stayed in Hebden Bridge in Yorkshire in the house where Ted Hughes and Sylvia Plath lived. They get well-known novelists to come and work with you. They give you exercises, like giving you postcards and say, 'There's a picture, just write what you feel', and it's so different than academic writing. 'Write what you feel'! We never do that in academic writing! I started writing in a very stiff way, and other people who'd been doing it for years, writing for women's magazines or for Radio 4, they were just flowing away. I was like 'everything had to have a political purpose', until one of the workshop leaders, who was a very famous novelist, he said to me, 'Why don't you just relax?' [*laughs*] 'Why don't you just not be so serious?' And it was an epiphany, one of those moments where you just go, 'He's so right!' But I realised I have to unlearn academic conventions if I want to … no, when I write my novel!

I: When or where did this desire to write come from?

HSM: I think my desire to write has come from the need to have 'voice', to find a voice, to get to my own truth, whatever that is! I think that driving force has

driven me, even though technically I'm not a very good writer. I wasn't very good at English when I was at school in Trinidad. I was really terrible, and when I came to England I had such a strong Trinidadian accent the school wrote me off! I was 16 so I was quite old and I found spelling really difficult. I found schooling here very difficult and I still can't spell very well! Thank god for spell checks!

I tend to write back to front, I write almost an illegible draft, only I can understand it! And then I go back and fill in the gaps and it's something I've always had to do because I'm not actually a very good writer, or at least I don't think of myself as a very good writer. No teacher ever told me I was a good writer! I read other people's work and I think, 'Wow! That's so fabulous! I wish I could write like that.' And then other people tell me they read mine and they say, 'Wow! I wish I could write like that!' So everyone's always looking to someone else.

I: So what should be the starting point for the less experienced writer?

HSM: I think your starting point is knowing that you've got something to say. What I've learned from my education, coming from Trinidad and going to school in Brixton, is that our confidence is schooled out of us, so we come to believe we don't have anything to say.

So much of the teaching I had was about erasing who you are, instead of a teacher actually saying, 'You've written an essay. Well done!', even if it's not technically brilliant. When I worked at Middlesex and at South Bank I had many students, very often black women, who did not have a traditional education. They think they have to live up to a notion of academic writing, be something they're not, because they have learnt their experiences don't matter. They think to themselves, 'My life is of no value, I need to learn something to make me better.' It's part of our educational mindset, we've always got to be better, what we have isn't good enough. But we are good enough!

For my inaugural I was so terrified and I thought, 'Oh, I'll be exposed, people will see me as not good enough.' I went to a life coaching session and we had to decide, if we are up against a challenge, what would we do, how would we tackle it? How would we rephrase a negative thing like, 'Oh I'm petrified and I'm not good enough'? And I said to myself, 'I've got something to say.' That's my positive affirmation to the negative one 'I'll be found out, I'm not good enough.' So I now say to myself, 'I have something to say.' And even if it's not what someone wants to hear, I still have something to say.

Even if you're working in a large team and the research isn't about your personal life, it's a so-called objective study, you still have important experiences and perspectives to include. You're the filter that is writing the work, you're the eyes that are seeing the data, so however you construct it, you are engaging in a creative process. It's not an objective process, it's a personal and subjective process.

I've learned from examining PhDs that judging academic writing is so subjective. There are a few objective criteria, of course, such as the structure and the form of the piece of work. That is always there and once you learn the craft then you can play with it, which I'm very privileged now to be able to do. It's like famous painters, isn't it? Picasso was a very good classical painter and then he went on to abstract work because he knew the foundations. It's the same with writing, you have to get those foundations and then you can experiment. It's all about confidence really; confidence is the biggest block and the biggest help! And I guess I need to be inspired too. I think the key is confidence, inspiration, passion, good leadership if you're working on teams, and just feeling positive about what you're doing.

Recently I was teaching on the writing of Frantz Fanon. He was a black philosopher and psychiatrist in the Fifties and he wrote a very famous book called *Black Skin, White Masks*. He also wrote another book called *The Wretched of the Earth*. These were seminal postcolonial texts. And in the seminar we were deconstructing the text when one of the students said, 'You know what's so amazing about this book? It's a stream of consciousness. He doesn't care who his audience is, he's just got something to say and he says it.' And it's a book of anger and of passion and it's still one of the most powerful books on race all these years on. I learnt something then: that writing for an audience can be a barrier, because you're thinking of your peers or whatever, and you

forget that you're also writing for yourself. In a way that is an important tip, I would say explore what *you* think.

If I'm writing a paper, I'll just hammer it out. I'll do lots of reading, I get lots of inspiration, I'll get a sense of where I'm going. Then I write. It might be two or three thousand words which I just pour out onto the paper, but when I go back and tidy it up I'm editing it and sorting it, fitting in the references, fitting in the data, fitting in the context. So I don't start with a blank piece of paper, it's too terrifying. So the stream of consciousness is my framework, and then I work back to front and fill in all the bits. It's just the way I have worked, it may not work for others. You may think I'm totally nuts, but it helps me to build my confidence about what I have to say.

I: Any other tips?

HSM: Well, when I was doing my PhD I was a single mum. I had a three-year-old daughter when I started my PhD and all through I did childminding, among other things. I always had children around so I never had the luxury of locking myself away. When my daughter was very little I used to write through the night when she slept. I would take her to the little nursery school or, as time went on, to school and I'd sleep while she was there. So my writing has always fitted around childcare [*laughs*] and so nothing would disturb me now. The TV could be on in the background, and noises here and there, and, if I'm really concentrating, nothing bugs me. I'm not precious about having writing space. It just has to fit in with life. I tend to like to write at night and work through the night and hear the birds in the morning at five, when it's so quiet and still. I like a long run on something and I feel calm. I can work for five or six hours at a stretch through the night and then I feel happy with myself, it's kind of a deep satisfaction really. But I don't have any rules.

I: How do you juggle work responsibilities with writing? How do you find time?

HSM: It's becoming increasingly difficult, I have to say. When I first started out as a young lecturer I had loads of teaching in unfamiliar areas, which required a great deal of swotting up. So that didn't give you much time for your own work, but somehow I just had the energy. Now I don't have all those kind of teaching things to do, but I do have a lot of admin responsibilities. Now it's running departments or running research centres, getting budgets in and going to committee meetings. Things like that just start making me frustrated and angry because I can't get down to the real business of writing.

To write you have to switch off and move into another mode. I used to work through the night, but now I have to work through the weekends as well to get that run. So I find that I use more of my own time, which does make me feel resentful because I use my holidays. I might go away for a week or two, but actually I'm using my own leave, my own time, my night time, my family time, because of what I call the increasing bureaucratisation in higher education. I think most of the meetings we have are a waste. We could make the same decisions in five minutes instead of an hour of chewing the cud, but nevertheless we have to go through the process and *when I think about the RAE!*

For the RAE you need to have a minimum of four pieces of work in good academic journals – I mean who decided this nonsense? I have no idea! You know some years you have good years, some years you have bad years. Sometimes you have a fabulous idea that everyone wants to publish in many journals. The other year, you're cruising along, you know? Sometimes you work on a very good research project and sometimes, politics being what they are, they don't want to publish it. This has happened to me, when the research findings are too difficult for the mainstream to accept. The RAE is like making up a rule to measure quality, but it doesn't measure reality!

It's ironic that the RAE comes along at the same time as the increasing bureaucratisation of higher education has come along, so it has squeezed our time. Which makes me feel like my time in academia has a bottom and a top. I don't want to stay under this kind of pressure where I'm working harder now than when I first started. The irony is that I should be having more time to think, but actually I have less time to think now.

I: So, where is your work-life balance?

HSM: I won't lie to say that it's easy to get a work-life balance. Because a project will have a deadline, and you'll just have to achieve what you have to achieve by that time, it doesn't matter if the rest of your family is going on annual leave, you have to do it. So I won't lie and say that it's great on that score, but on the other side I would say that the satisfaction of writing something is so great and being part of a research team chipping away at new horizons and saying, 'This is another way to look at something', is so deeply satisfying.

I can't think of any other professions where you could really get that from, and that's what makes us stay, but the RAE is killing our inspiration and I feel very strongly about that.

I: Are you arguing that the RAE hinders one's creativity?

HSM: It does, it makes you panic, and I used to write because I felt passionate about things and now I find I'm writing because I'm panicking. I'm playing the game.

And the question is: 'Does it make one's scholarship any better?' It's made me panic and made me push more out there, which takes up good creative time, when I could be actually saying, 'I want to think about this data differently.' I'm not doing that, I'm just pushing it out to get the right number of hits with journals, and I think it's a shame.

I: Do you think there's an issue here about being a woman and writing and being a success in academia?

HSM: Yes, I think it's a huge issue, and if you look at the career structure of any institution in higher ed. you'll see that, yes, there are lots of women, but where are they in the hierarchy? A few at the top! It is still very much a man's world. You just have to look at the career structure and criteria for promotion. And so there are definite gender issues about our productivity and how much we can do and the choices that we have to make. Because as women we do say, 'Listen, forget this, I'm going to spend more time with my family' or your parents are getting older and you have to spend more time doing caring – caring issues are huge. Life is complex for women.

I would say that what I've done is not juggle so much as worked damn hard! That's what I do, to the point where it's affected my personality, it affects who you are, it affects your friendships. I'm always working and my friends say, 'But Heidi, we never see you', and I always feel so embarrassed and I give the same excuse, 'I'm so busy', and you know what, I really *am* busy! And so, I feel like I'm not juggling as much as intensely working. You have to be a very good organiser.

I love cooking things in the evening when I get in because it relaxes me and it stops me thinking about whatever project or paper or thing I need to work on. It's the chopping of the onions, it helps me to relax. [*Laughs*] I also like salsa dancing, which I did last night, and I try to fit things into my life that are pleasurable because I find that academic writing is so intense that you lose your laughter. So I love to go to comedy clubs. I also do swimming, running and yoga!

I: Does your writing say anything about you?

HSM: You have to ask someone else that question. I feel it's hard to ask *me* that question! [*Laughs*]

I think writing is very egocentric. My daughter loves literature and we were looking at something on Evelyn Waugh the other day and I was struck by the self-centredness of some writers. You have to be quite single-minded to be successful.

I: Well, what would you like your writing to say about you?

HSM: I love communicating with people, I love people, and I want my writing to be accessible and inspirational. There's a poster the ATSS [Association for the Teaching of the Social Sciences] have made of me with a photograph and a quote of mine. It is such an honour as it is in every school in the Sixth Form common room. And it says: 'Sociology is about your life and my life, we all have something to say, our voices must be heard.'

So it goes back to that 'if you've got something to say' … so I'm pleased I'm doing this interview. I want to encourage people to talk and write about their experiences. Maybe it's because I teach a lot of ethnic minority students and I would like my writing to give them the confidence to say, 'Yes, if she can write that so can *I*.'

For example, if they are doing an essay on identity and the embodiment of difference using Bourdieu or Butler, they are actually talking about their lives, their experience, so it's about facilitating them to make that connection between theory and practice in their writing. I want my writing to make what seems inaccessible and make it accessible. Because nothing is difficult, nothing is hard, we obfuscate things, we make them unreachable but actually I think it's all within our grasp. I would like my writing to be about the search for truth in our own lives.

My most recent book, which is a jointly authored book called *Tackling Roots of Racism* (2005), has sold a thousand copies in three months which, for an academic book on racism, is pretty good. It's because it's so accessible. Schools are using it, courses are using it, and it's chatty. We start with everyday social problems and then we look back and ask: 'What are the roots of racism that lie at the heart of the problem and how can we solve it?' We look at the theories and facts behind these everyday phenomena. I think it's touched a chord with people, and it's been selling like hotcakes. It's on a second print run, after six months.

I: That's fantastic. So is there any particular type of writing you enjoy more than others?

HSM: I really liked writing my inaugural. And I want to write more like that, which is more as if I'm talking to people. Of course, I know a lot of other black women that have written like that. There is Patricia Williams, an African American law professor who did the BBC Reith Lectures. She wrote about her experiences of racism from inside out, and she received a lot of criticism. And then there's other people like bell hooks, an African American cultural critic, who writes using a stream of consciousness based on her experiences. She always says she's not considered to be a real academic, and she talks about it with pain in her voice, saying, 'Why is this not acceptable? Why is my life as a black woman not theory?' I know that there's snobbery about what is real knowledge, but I think it's important that we do write like that sometimes – it is a different kind of truth.

I: How do you find a publisher who will publish what you want to write about?

HSM: Well, it's very interesting because I'm writing another book at the moment, which is a collection of essays. I was speaking to the publishers and I said, 'Oh, I'm going to be sending you this proposal', and she didn't ask me the title, she didn't ask me about the content, she just said, 'What's the market?' [*Laughs*] That was the first question, 'What's the market?!' My daughter's working in publishing now, it's all about sales! In order for books to sell well they have to reach a wide audience, particularly an American audience, because that's a huge market. So it's about being pragmatic about that, but I think, at the end of the day, a good book is a good book. They say 'cream rises', so it's got to be solid, theoretical, but entertaining, then it will sell well.

I: Is that all?!

HSM: [*Laughs*] I know the RAE is driving us in terms of these heavy academic peer reviewed articles in refereed journals, which few people read, but in the publishing world of books it's about the market and you've got to know what courses would buy your books, so the criteria for the publishing world are different than the academic world.

I: So you've got to really bring yourself up to speed on what they're looking for out there?

HSM: In the specialist field that I work in, which is about the inter-sectionality of race and gender in education, my peers are small in number! And peer review means you're competing with a select number of colleagues in similar fields. For all kinds of reasons they may not like your work. It may be a subjective disagreement or an objective judgment based on historical differences of opinion or on methodology

or something. And the same goes for when you submit a bid for research grants. Somebody else very close to it is saying, 'Oh, that's a good idea', but won't support it. So peer review is fundamentally flawed. It's against equal opportunities. It is based on academic networks and clubs and if you have a good reputation or not. It's not based on merit. But it's our main measure of quality in academia.

And when you get rejected or *if* you get rejected from a journal, it isn't always just because it isn't good enough, it could be for a whole variety of factors, because it goes to two or three people who've given a subjective opinion. I've had things rejected by a journal, I've sent it to another journal and they say it's fabulous! But it's been ripped apart by another one! It's just about who reads it and where they're coming from. So, it's very difficult terrain.

I: Heidi, can you say something about how you discipline yourself and start writing? Where and how do you start?

HSM: I learned a technique from my supervisor when I was doing my PhD. The typical scenario would be me appearing in his room, with tears in my eyes, saying 'I haven't done it' and 'It's not good enough' and 'You don't want to see it really because …'. And he would snatch my scraps of paper out of my hand and say, 'Give it to me, let me read it anyway', which broke down my perfectionist barrier. He used to give me headings, almost like an essay question. They were, in effect, chapter headings and he'll say, 'Go away and give me a short five thousand words or three thousand words on this title.' It broke it down and it became do-able psychologically.

I do workshops with my students who are about to embark on their Masters dissertations or their PhDs and I use a version of his method. I tell them to choose a title, a sexy, racy title, for what they are doing. I tell them to visualise it on the bookshelf, so it's tangible and fun, and give it a cover. Then think of the chapter headings and the whole big project begins to gets its form.

Then we make each chapter into an essay question. So it has a bottom and a top and sides, and it really works. It's the same if you're on a research project and you've got lots of data and analysis to do. You need to ask yourself three good research questions that can frame the writing.

It's all about taking one step at a time. You break down huge chunks that seem insurmountable into small, little essays, so in the end, each chapter for your report is five thousand words. If you've got five chapters that's five five thousand word short essays. You tell yourself you can manage that! It's even better when you're doing a dissertation or a PhD or a book, because each essay is on the same topic so it's easier than having five essays on five different courses in a semester.

So it's a great technique, it's what I call 'baby steps'. Don't think about an insurmountable, huge piece of work of eighty thousand words!

I: Well that's a very good tip.

HSM: It's great to have the opportunity to reflect on my writing with you. This isn't something we often get a chance to do. Recently I got very ill, with breast cancer, and I guess for the first time I was aware of my own mortality and one of the things that gave me some solace was that whatever happens, when you write it's permanent. You leave it behind, it's something so powerful.

There are strong oral traditions in the Caribbean and among the First Nation people of America and Australia, and in African and Asian cultures too. I grew up in the Indo-Caribbean community and I've heard stories about my grandmother and stories about the history of our family which have been passed down from generation to generation, but we never write about it. I'm one of the first to write anything about that experience and I realise how powerful it is. The oral tradition is so important to our cultures, but writing it down leaves a different kind of mark which is valued in Western societies.

I do often reflect on the power of writing and the power of 'voice'. It embeds you culturally and politically in other spaces. Because of *Young, Female and Black*, people can say, 'Well, yes, I know what it's like to be a young black British woman growing up in a school in South London.' That's an important experience that white researchers might not know about or have access to, and it's important to tell that story. I think it is really important to tell our stories.

It's a way of bringing the oral tradition into the academic writing.

I: Heidi, it seems to me, based on what you've said, that writing is a discovery, an on-going learning process. It's never perfect!

HSM: Exactly, and it's both petrifying and pleasing! I think the one thing that I've learned – it's all about staying power! You need to see that project through, you need to get that PhD done. Somebody told me once, there are people who are finishers and then there are non-finishers. A finisher has to finish it because it gets under their skin and bugs them for the rest of their life. Non-finishers can move on with no regrets. So you have to decide which one you are if you are taking on the challenge of coming into writing.

I: Have you ever had a coach or mentor, writing mentor or anyone like that?

HSM: Your supervisor for the PhD is the nearest really.

I: But when you're writing as sole author, how and when do you seek the support of others?

HSM: I have a select group of feminist and critical friends and I send something to them and say, 'What do you think of this?' But I usually do that after I've honed it quite a lot, I don't do it early on. I tend to feel very nervous about sending it out too early, I've still got that perfectionist streak in me. I really want to control it for a bit longer; I don't want too much feedback too early.

I want to actually have it all down and then incorporate the ideas of others, but I do find criticism difficult, even if it's friendly criticism, especially after working so hard on something. And when I say working hard, I mean four or five drafts later – it's a lot of drafts! So, it becomes very precious to you and you don't want to let it go and when you have someone saying, 'Have you thought of this, or have you thought of that?', you get protective.

I think the whole writing process is one of control, you're controlling the words, you're controlling the ideas, and it is hard to let it go, especially if you're on a team.

I: Do you have any final thoughts?

HSM: Everyone can learn to write. I was not good at it at school. I taught myself how to write by looking at other's examples. When I did my PhD I went to the library and I read everyone's PhDs around my subject. I found out which was a good one and which was a bad one. During the Civil Rights in the Sixties they had a literacy programme called 'Learning by Doing'. In order to increase voter registration the black activists would roll out literacy classes and people who learned to write, to read, would then teach others.

I: Like an apprenticeship, perhaps?

HSM: Yes, it's like an apprenticeship. I know it's an old-fashioned notion. My Dad did this in Trinidad in the Forties. He learned from a more senior person in the community and then he'd become the teacher and would teach the younger ones. So I share that same heritage. If I read someone else's work and I'm inspired – I would try to identify what made it 'inspiring' and try to use that style in my own writing.

   We need to learn from others. I've done it organically, not consciously. It's been a brilliant journey.

I: Heidi, thank you for letting us hear your 'Desert Island Discs'!

Peter Moss

I: *So we thought we'd start on a biographical note: just tell me how long you've been here at the Institute, the role you play now and the kind of key responsibilities of that role.*

PM: OK, well I've been at the Institute since 1970, and I was at the Thomas Coram Research Unit at its birth, which was in 1973, and my role, I am Professor of Early Childhood Provision. And for the moment I am the Executive Head of Thomas Coram Research Unit, so I've a management role as well.

I: *I don't know whether you've chosen one piece of writing or more than one that you are pleased with …*

PM: Well, I think the piece of writing that's been most pleasing has been a book I wrote with two colleagues, one from Canada, one from Sweden, called *Beyond Quality in Early Childhood Education and Care, Post-modern Perspectives,* which was published in 1999. It's pleasing for a number of reasons, one of which is that it marked for me a completely new perspective on my field. I won't go into that in great detail, but it basically introduced me to a whole different paradigm of thought, which at the time was summed up as postmodern, but you could call post-structural, postmodern, post-foundational. So it was a book that was about to be aborted when we found this perspective, this framework which suddenly opened the whole thing up.

And what is also very gratifying, for an academic book, it's had a large impact. I think it's been reprinted in English six or seven times, it's going into second edition, it's been translated into six other languages, and is very widely cited around the world … which, for a book which some people would say is quite difficult, is very gratifying. But also it makes me think that it was a book that helped a lot of people to articulate concerns they had about the current discourse, and helped them to articulate alternative ways of thinking about early childhood. And it was very enjoyable to write and I learned a lot from doing that. I've gone on to write another book, and I did a series with my Swedish colleague (Gunilla Dahlberg) and that's been an extremely productive and important relationship.

I was there in Stockholm last week, as it happens, for the day, to talk about work that we're doing together. And these are people I like to be with, and I find the relationship opens my mind to new ideas and so on. And I just do like writing, working with other people.

I: So is there any writing you weren't too happy about?

PM: I've been trying to think about that. In retrospect, there's nothing I really go: 'Euch, that's appalling.' There are things that I look back on, I mean, there are the sort of reports of studies, which are sometimes rather tedious, gathering actual electronic dust somewhere and which, looking back on, you're not certain … I suppose the point about the book I've just mentioned is that I actually felt that I saw things differently after I wrote it. And one way in which I find I can incorporate new ideas is to write about them. So I was trying to understand really totally different ways of thinking. Having to write about it in a way that you hoped would be accessible to people also is quite a good way of having to get to grips with these things. So I suppose the other extreme is the stuff you do more out of duty. Although I have to say that I've been very fortunate in recent years, in that I've been able to write things, I mean there's been a number of books that have been more in that vein … being able to think through things.

It may be something to do with age, that you do get a bit more space when you're a bit further on. Not only because you're more senior, but you don't have

young children, and that's very liberating in terms of writing.

I: What has helped your writing? You've already mentioned collaborative work, being somewhat senior and having some more time. Anything else?

PM: There is a space issue. And you're avoiding writing the same old thing over and over again, you're kind of reinventing yourself a bit, which is interesting.

I suppose I look back to when I first started … I must be careful not to get too nostalgic. When I came here in 1970, I had the privilege of working under an exceptional person, Jack Tizzard, who was the first Director. On the one hand there was remarkably little expectation that you should publish anything, so I remember feeling excited that one year, in my first five years, I jointly authored an article [*laughs*] and it was: 'Wow!' But, on the other hand, Jack had a remarkably good writing style, I think he was a model of academic writing, and I think that it's quite important, when you're just starting out, to have friendly but firm criticism, not just about the academic content, but whether this is something anybody's going to want to read in the first place.

As you get more senior, I personally find it a bit harder to ask people to read my stuff. I always like to think I'm available to comment on other people's things, but I feel it's a bit of an imposition sometimes to ask them – everybody's so desperately busy. And in a way, you kind of feel, and it may not be right, that you ought to be able to stand on your own feet and get on with it. So I'm not certain if I couldn't do with some advice from others at this time, but at least if you write with other people it may help there.

I suppose I think (and this is quite unempirical) that it's very important to read good writers, and I don't just mean academic writers. So I personally, in my personal reading, I probably don't read enough academically, as I try and read other stuff. I read novels and things, and I think that rubs off as well simply because they're good things to read. So I think actually being a reader yourself is important.

I wouldn't say I was particularly good at writing some sorts of things, and I may be better at others. I think the sort of books I write are just academic-OK, I'm not certain though. And I do quite a lot of short articles – practitioner things – but I'm not certain I'm that good at necessarily doing things that are really sparky for a more general readership. Fortunately, there are other possibilities here (at TCRU) for getting that done, so there are many different types of writing for academics these days, and you're always likely to be better at some things than others.

I would also say that I think I've got quite good at editing other people's work, and again this is one aspect of writing (being an editor of writing) or editing books. I particularly find myself editing a lot of translated stuff. I edit a magazine called *Children in Europe*, which gets articles from all over Europe, usually translated from another language (because we tell authors to write in their native language) and that invariably requires a lot of work. So I think, as you develop, that becomes an important ability: to be able to take something and edit it so it's clearer.

I: Can we say how editing helps one's own writing? Can we actually pinpoint that?

PM: I don't know, whether your own writing helps editing, I'm sure it must do in the sense that again it's kind of artisan stuff. You think, 'Well that sentence doesn't look quite right; does it look better if I [do such and such]?'

Sometimes you get that with translation in particular, where the translation at one level is quite literal, but it doesn't read right, and you're puzzling, 'What's the matter with that, why doesn't it work?' So I think again it's a journey round the stuff, that you're having to work on the nuts and bolts of what makes a good sentence. And what do you really need to say there. What can you cut out?

In this magazine that I edit, which is a fairly popular one, we publish 1,200-word articles. Very often you get two, three thousand, because the authors seem to be incapable of writing to length. And then it's left to somebody else to sort out, which is a bit unfair.

What editing also makes you have to say is, 'What can I cut out of that which will not affect the basic premise?' And it's surprising how often you can, and that makes you think, 'How much superfluous stuff, how much overwriting am *I* doing, and therefore losing the narrative?' So I think editing is quite

important, I think you need to get up to a certain stage, but it's part of your development. If you start by practising, doing yourself, and then working on other people's, it's salutary.

I: Would you say writing is a major part of your life now?

PM: Yes, I'm always clacking away on the word processor, yes.

I: So how do you manage to keep that up?

PM: Well, I don't know, I work quite long hours, but I know everybody does. I do think that I'm at a stage of the life course when … I've got colleagues with two or three young children, and that's really difficult, I think actually it's a very difficult time because they know for their careers they've got to do that stuff.

I: So you don't have that pull now?

PM: Not now, but I remember at the time it was very demanding. So there is that about it. I also think that as you get a bit more senior, although there are other demands on your time, you also perhaps have got a little bit more freedom to say, 'Well I want to do this' and I don't have to report to somebody to tell them. But that varies at different times and places, and the different demands that are on you. What I think is very difficult to get, and I've just come from a committee meeting, is to be able to get space to read, think, discuss and write.

I: That's because of endless meetings and things?

PM: Well, endless short-term contracts, endless meetings, the whole way in which I think that we and other service industries have been increasingly squeezed to get more productivity out of us. The whole ethos means that everything has to be accounted and paid for and so forth. And actually the opportunity to go and just make space … writing is harder obviously when you can't get a run at it, when you're doing it in bits. And you think, 'I've got an hour on Friday, I can just about revise that article, phew.'

I: What kind of satisfactions do you get from writing? And you might also want to say something about the frustrations of the process.

PM: Well, for me, I think it's a way of constructing (that's sounds a bit pompous) but constructing new understandings. And in a way writing forces you to confront ideas. If I'm just sitting here, I can have a clever idea and I don't really have to test it. But when you're writing, you read it back and think, 'Really, I don't understand what I'm saying there' or 'That's incredibly banal', so it helps you to anchor, construct, develop an idea, a story, an account, and … I see this really as a creative art form. You're constructing something, be it an article or a book. And that is quite satisfying, because often, at the end, I think, 'I've no idea how I've got to be here.' Because I don't know how other people do it.

I think the technology for me has changed it. Because in the old days, when we had typewriters and secretaries, you had to sit down and work out exactly what you were going to say, and then say it. And then you could get away with a certain amount of changes, but actually word processors have fundamentally changed my way of working. I tend often to have a very broad idea of what I might want to say, and then it's a bit like working at a bit of sculpture: you chip away, you add a bit, you go back, you shift. So it's a different creative activity, or so I find it.

I find it much more liberating. I can remember the anxieties, especially being more junior, approaching secretaries. I think it has become that you have more control over the situation, more possibilities. So yeah, that is satisfying, I think.

It's quite nice just to be able to put yourself into something – and that is increasingly difficult, the 'person from Porlock' is always at the door. I mean literally – at home, I'm surprised how many people knock on the door when you're trying to work. So there are feelings of frustration sometimes: 'Will I ever get a run at it?'

I: You've written books, articles, and worked collaboratively. Any particular kind of writing you enjoy most?

PM: Well, I would have to say I've got the greatest satisfaction out of books I've been involved in writing recently, because they've allowed space (in a way that sometimes articles don't) for exploring and developing complex areas. And although obviously articles have to be part of your portfolio, as indeed do other things, I've got the most gratification out of that. And also a little sense that, although sales aren't massive, possibly they're read a bit more. Because you never quite know; there are so many journals and who actually reads articles you write in journals?

Journal writing can be a bit formulaic. Horses for courses. There are times when you've got an article worth saying, but I suppose in the last few years, I see myself as being more interested in theory and concepts, and then trying to relate examples of practice to that, and it's just taken more … the subject matter has taken more space.

So *Beyond Quality* was really an exercise in trying to understand what the problem was with quality as a concept, and that involved going into exploring the kind of paradigm that quality came out of, then looking at other paradigms, then following those through, to say, 'Well where would they lead you in how you approach evaluation?', if you take 'quality' as a language of evaluation which grows out of a particular paradigm and has certain values; it's not a neutral idea. And if you work with other values, other paradigms, you come out with a different evaluative tool, and that whole process is difficult to do. And subsequently after writing that book I've written a couple of articles which try to present the argument more concisely.

You have to write at length before you can write briefly. So now, having written the book, I can distil the argument more readily. It would be difficult to write an article with so many loose ends.

I: Is there anything that your writing says about you?

PM: I would love to be able to write fiction and to have that particular form of imaginative creativity. And I know I couldn't do it. So I suppose what writing says about me is that I have a certain capacity to organise, and present certain sorts of academic stories (which is what I think writing is.) I've known one or two people who've been novelists and academics, and it would be interesting to know how the two work together and also what the implication is. Because I think that could be very powerful.

So my writing says I'm a person who has certain limitations and certain strengths, as we all do.

I: How do you go about writing?

PM: Well, I almost never write in the office. And again, I try writing at home, try and write early in the morning because after about ten o'clock, it fizzles. The more I can get done in those first few hours, the better. But often it's a case of squeezing in bits and pieces. And often it's a case of blocking out a day here and a day there. The only time I've had a continuous period of time is when I took study leave and combined it with holiday. I think I went to Spain and spent the mornings sitting round the pool, and that was good.

I: So you can't write in your office?

PM: No, it's not conducive to writing, I don't think I ever write here. All this is about replying to emails, doing memos, which is rather worrying really. So use of time is an issue.

I realise I'm not a terribly structured person, although I need to feel in control of things. Sometimes I sit down with a paper and pen, and try and draw it all up, but then I think, 'To hell with this'… so I start with a rough idea in my mind of what the story is going to be, but then it is a question of working this up … especially writing with other people. The two books I've written with Gunilla, there have been real struggles – in the good sense. We've written chapters and they don't work, and we go back, and I say, 'Well, I'll have a go at this', and so forth, so it's very hard.

But I prefer this idea of seeing it as a creative activity, or creating a piece of writing. I think if you're presenting research results in a report, for example, then there's a formula. In the contract, it tells you what you've got to cover. Writing for an academic journal, there's a formula for that. It's when you're out into new territory, as with my most recent books, where you're not quite certain where the story's going, or how best to talk about it, that you have to be more creative.

I realise in the area that I've become quite interested in, because it's very much about the idea of provisionality rather than conclusion, one of the implications is – when you think you've just got something nailed down, somebody says, 'I really think we ought to explore so and so's perspective.' And my first reaction, being the kind of person who likes to be in control, is to say, 'Oh my god,' then often later I can say, 'Thank goodness we did.' So there's an interesting tension between freezing something and saying, 'OK, that's it, we go on to the next book and think about Derrida or whatever it is' and saying, 'Oh well, perhaps we do need to do a bit more.'

So that's how I work – at home, I try and work particularly in the mornings because I know the day begins to fizzle out from that point. I plan roughly, though less roughly if it's for what I would call formulaic writing.

I: What have you learned about the process of writing?

PM: One thing is you've got to trust your feeling about it. Because quite often, there have been occasions when I've said, 'This doesn't work. I can't see where this is going or what it's trying to do', so then I need to go back to square one. But on the other hand, with experience you get a sense when something is working. I think, unless you're complacent, and that's where other people reading things helps, there's often a sense that *now* I can see where this is going, I can see the story taking satisfying shape.

This happened with this book *Beyond Quality*, actually. The three of us, for two years beforehand, were trying to write a book following on from an edited volume, but then it's different to write a book than an edited volume. We met in Sweden, we met in England, we met in Canada, but it just didn't feel right, it just wasn't going anywhere, people wrote bits. And at a certain point my Swedish colleague said, 'We need to give this a theoretical frame, what about postmodernity?' And I said, 'What do you mean? Can you tell me in a nutshell?' And subsequently it really drew me in, and then it all began to fall into place, because the story became much, much clearer. But for two years it was formless, directionless …

I: Does that 'coming to know' happen periodically?

PM: Well, that case in particular, because I could see that I had a problem concerning this work: why was I uneasy about people talking about quality so much? And I'd been part of that discussion. That said, perhaps quality is relative, value-based, etc., but I couldn't work out how to get beyond that. And the way to get beyond that is to say, 'Well, if you want to work with those sorts of values, you have to have a different sort of concept, you can't make quality (which is a normative idea) into something that it isn't.' And you have to start from the idea that there are very different paradigms, mindsets, whatever, of looking at the world. So that suddenly led to a lot of energy over the last few years, because it's opened up this new world.

So I think also … you have to just do it, over time, the same piece of work, go back and worry about it. So you write a draft, and redraft, and redraft. So you spend a lot of time on it. I suppose it is also a good idea, although I find it quite difficult to ask people to do that, to get somebody else's view on it, but I think that is really important.

And, as I say, I do think this question of reading, and what you read, really influences you.

I: What have you learned about getting work published?

PM: Never write without a contract. I mean, really, it's a waste of time. Yes. But again that's an experience thing, especially for the more formulaic bits. There are obviously ways of writing for publication in journals, which you can't get round if you haven't got something to say. But if you do, then there's a way of writing. And I'm … which again comes with time … I'm in a reasonably fortunate situation that I can probably get published, always get a publisher. I've got a relationship with Routledge that I've been very happy about.

I have an editor. I personally find that what I expect from a publisher is to deal with the contracts, deal with the process of getting it published, nice if they consult you about the cover, and so on, and that doesn't always happen. But really – to get a publisher who reads what you've written, and says, 'Well I

really think that's very good, but you could do this or that', I've never had that. So don't expect very much from publishers.

But as an author, recognise that if you want your books to sell and be read, then you've got to be quite active. And I actually want my books to be read, so it's no good just sending it off and turning your back, you've got to think all the time about how you can promote this.

I've just read that in this country alone, a hundred thousand titles or more are published every year. And that's an awful lot, and your one or two, they're not going to sell by themselves.

I: If you were not at the Institute …would you still write?

PM: As you will have seen, I can't really imagine another life. I suspect not actually, because I don't feel I have the talents to be a writer of poetry or fiction.

But there are other things in life, people do seem to lead perfectly adequate lives without writing. And there's a slight danger, if you're in the academy, of thinking that's the only thing that makes life worth living, and it's not. Obviously.

Ann Oakley

I: *Thank you so much for agreeing to be interviewed today. Can I just ask you to say something about what you do at the Institute?*

AO: Well, I 'retired', so to speak, a year-and-a-half ago. That is, I gave up being Director of the Social Science Research Unit and I'm now re-employed on a part-time contract just to work on research, currently half time. So, I'm not in the office every day, but I still work quite hard, although I try and convince my colleagues that half-time is half of a 45-hour week and not half of an 80-hour week. Not easy.

I: *No, I'm sure. Can you tell me about the best piece of writing that you've done, or the one that you're most proud of, or pleased with.*

AO: I find this a difficult question, because it depends how you define 'best'.

I'm quite pleased with some of my fiction writing, and with parts of an autobiography I wrote some years ago. In terms of academic writing, I find it difficult, as it were, to disentangle the writing from the analysis. There's a book that I'm particularly proud of, which almost nobody has heard of.

I: *Please, tell me more.*

AO: It's called *Women Confined: Towards a sociology of childbirth* (1988), and I think that the analysis in that – the thinking processes that I hope come through in the writing – is one of my most important achievements, but I'm not sure that that counts as the 'best' writing, you see.

I: OK. And you were proud of it because …

AO: I think it was because it was so intellectually challenging to do.

I: Yes.

AO: But I'll give you a couple of other examples. I wrote a book, which was, again, based on research, in fact the same research – a book called *Becoming a Mother* (1979) – but I'm not sure whether it would be defined strictly speaking as an 'academic' book: many people who are not academic read it. The point about that book is that what I did in it was I put together a narrative of the process of becoming a mother which was essentially based on what women had said in interviews, and the connecting and introductory pieces that I wrote were actually much less important than the narratives. I remember having a struggle with the publisher, because I wanted my words to be in italics and the women's words to be in bold type, so the women's words, the interview data, made up the text of the book, and I was just playing a kind of facilitating role in relation to their stories. I was proud of that, and I think that it worked quite well, but the challenge for me was in not being too academic.

For me the point of working in a university and doing research is not about communicating with other academics. We all have to do that, it's part of our jobs, but that's not the point of it to me. The point of it to me is that one should communicate what one has learnt to a much wider public, because most of us are working on issues of great social importance, and if we can't see the value of communicating those messages back and if we can't actually manage to do it in terms of the wider audience, then I think we're actually failing.

So, I think in quite a lot of my writing, what I've tried to do is combine a kind of academic approach with a rather more popular one. But I've also learnt in the process of writing various things over many years that what gets through is simple text. It's a great fault of academia to suppose that the long paragraph and the long words and the technical words that need to

be defined are the best way to write. They're not the best way to write, not the right way to communicate. A lot of my work has involved working with healthcare practitioners of various kinds, including doctors, who, of course, specialise in jargon.

I: Yes.

AO: And you know, it's by working with them, and trying to write things with them, that I've learnt that their jargon is incomprehensible to me, but the jargon of academia and sociologists, perhaps particularly, is often also unintelligible and unnecessary. Communication isn't about using technical language. It's about saying things in such a way that whoever is hearing them or reading them is going to be able to know what you're on about. Writing clearly – plain language is important. Short sentences, short paragraphs.

I: So, how do you apply such principles when writing for the RAE, the Research Assessment Exercise? Where I'm assuming they want more than just short sentences and plain language.

AO: Well, I should have said that there are different forms of writing and there are different purposes for the different forms of writing, and one needs to be very clear about what kind of writing one's doing and, ideally, you need to be very clear about the type of audience and the format and so on, before you start.

So, in answer to your question, I can remember a particular point in my life when I thought, 'Well, I need some more papers in peer-reviewed journals', so I sat down and made a list of six or seven papers I needed to publish, and I identified the journals that I would submit them to, and then, of course it takes time, but a year-and-a-half later, I had them. There are certain places that only recognise the value of certain kinds of writings. I think it's quite perverse, actually, that a paper in a peer-reviewed education journal, for example, is worth more points in the RAE than a book that might be read by millions.

I: Yes, I suppose it could be viewed in that way.

AO: But, there we are, these are the constraints within which we operate, so this is the advice that I give to people who want advice about writing. 'Who are you writing this for?', 'Who are you trying to reach?', 'What is the purpose of writing?' If you're going for a journal, then work out what kind of journal you want. If you want a journal with a high impact factor, where you might have a ten per cent chance of getting published, that's one thing, but if you just want something in a peer-reviewed journal, then you might want to research other possibilities.

I: *Just before we move on. Do you want to say anything else about writings that you've been most pleased with?*

AO: Not the last book I did, which was a compendium of various of my writings, but the two before that. In those, I think that I managed to bring together the academic interest and style with something which, hopefully, appeals to a broader audience. My book called *Gender on Planet Earth* (2002) has got personal narratives in it, and it makes quite a lot of use of biographical material at various times, but also it's packed with science and statistics, though I hope in such a way that it addresses the important issues, so people get interested in the question and the issue and find the statistics and the facts and the theories just illuminating, rather than getting in the way.

The book before that was called *Experiments in Knowing* (2000). It's actually a very academic argument about the history of methodology in the social sciences, and about the gendering of qualitative and quantitative research.

I: *Can you say something now about what you think about the process of writing?*

AO: I would never describe writing as enjoyable. I don't think, on the whole, people write for fun. People write for two reasons, either because they have to for the RAE or, because they are driven, they are writers. I've always considered myself to be a writer, so that's a core part of my identity, and writing is something which, although I don't describe it as enjoyable, obviously yields for me far more

satisfaction than many other things that I have to do. But the doing of it isn't fun.

I have very different ways of writing according to what I'm writing, so if I'm writing a paper for a journal, I will identify the journal and get their instructions to authors, so that I'm following those from the beginning. If they want an abstract of one hundred and fifty words, I'm not going to bother to write an abstract of five hundred words; the footnotes go in the right format from the beginning. So I'll get that, and I'll do it straight onto the computer.

But if I'm writing fiction or something a bit more reflective, then I handwrite, because there is something about the action of the pen and the ink and the page, and the connection between the head and the arm and the hand which is important.

I think people write very differently when they write by hand from when they write onto a computer. The temptation, when you're writing on a machine, is always to go back and change what you've just written, and that's fine for some things, but it's an absolute disaster for other kinds of writing, because you need to get into the flow, you need to go with it.

I'm the kind of person who discovers what I think by writing. Other people know what they think, and have a problem about getting it into words. For me, the process of writing is also an analytic process; it's a thinking process. So the first draft of something and the last draft of something, whatever it is, may not bear much relationship to one another.

I: *And then …*

AO: And then, I turn myself into an editor, I have a different identity at that point – I'm not the writer, I'm an editor, and I find it's often useful to have a bit of time in-between writing it and editing it, so you approach it with fresh eyes and quite critically. Another thing it took me a long time to learn is very important, and that is that you mustn't hang onto sentences that you like just because you like them. If they're somehow in the way, then they've got to go, it doesn't matter how fine you think the piece of writing is, it just doesn't work, so chuck it.

I: *Some really useful tips there. Tell me, have you always wanted to write?*

AO: Oh, since I was about five or six.

I: *Oh, really?*

AO: Oh, yes. I was an only child and only children have to find their own amusements, so I used to write a lot and lived in very much an internal, imaginary world. Later, I was told by a teacher I had when I was 16 or 17 that if I wanted to write, I should not go and do an English degree. So, I went and did a politics, philosophy and economics degree with sociology thrown in.

And then, after that, I wrote a couple of novels, but was unable to find a publisher for them, so I decided to be an academic for a few years, which became 40 years, but I did get to write some novels at one point. So, yes, it's very core, writing, and you find that, I think, with a lot of people who write consistently throughout their lives. This is something that they feel that they are, and whether it's about the creative process or whether it's about communication, may differ.

I: *That's interesting, because one of the questions we're asking contributors to the book is: if you weren't in academia, would you still write? And clearly you would.*

AO: I would, yes. In fact, that's one reason I've decided to stop being Director of this Unit – to have more time for writing, although it hasn't quite worked out, but, yes, but I hope it will.

I: *And how do you combine work and home life with writing? Do you have to juggle a number of jobs in order to find the time? Is it a struggle?*

AO: Well, you're right, it is a struggle, and it's particularly a struggle to fit it in when you've got lots of other things going on. I suppose my most serious writing has always been done at home in a room with nobody else there, preferably with the door shut, with one of those signs on the outside that says, 'Only interrupt me if it's a matter of life or death!'

But it's still difficult to arrange. Sometimes, when my home is full of people who want my attention, I've gone to a library. I do find libraries are quite good

places to do writing, because, in theory, people can't find you there, and you can go and find a desk, like in Senate House Library, there are lots of little desks hidden away behind the bookshelves. If you find one of those, you've got no distractions, well, only from the books that are around you.

In order to get writing done, you have to see it as a priority and, for me, it has always been the case that, unless I'm engaged in some sort of writing project, I tend to feel quite depressed. I need to have something on the go, even though it is difficult to fit it in.

The novels that I've written while I've been employed full time have been written in the summer vacations – the first drafts have been written in the summer.

I: *Where does the holiday fit in?*

AO: It doesn't. But it's actually very therapeutic to be able to focus on one thing, so it hasn't been too big a problem. I'm now trying to organise regular holidays!

I: *You write about feminism and gender. Do you think there is more of a struggle for women in academia to find time to write than it might be for men?*

AO: Absolutely. I've had that, certainly, the double standard, whereby the man comes home and says he's got to work on something, that's fine. A woman comes home and says she's got to work on something – the children and the man will say: 'Ridiculous, you've got to cook our supper and do this, that and the other.' And I think that being the mother of small children is quite inimical to creativity in this field. Motherhood itself is creative, so this doesn't matter. It's very difficult. I found it possible to write 'narrow', academic things when my children were little, but very difficult to write anything more creative. But, you can't do everything. It is a big problem – the way men and women's time is seen, with women being perceived as these people who are permanently accessible to other people.

Of course, now I have it with grandchildren, who ask why I can't fetch them from school today. Oh, because I'm writing something. So, my six-year-old granddaughter said to me the other day: 'I think it's time you wrote a book for children. I want you to write a book for me.' 'What should it be about?' She said: 'Human beings.' And she's agreed to email me some themes.

I: Mmm. Do you have any writing that, on reflection, you haven't been so pleased with or where you feel that 'given my time again I would write it differently'?

AO: Well, I remember some papers which were a tremendous struggle to write and were very academic, and I don't think were particularly widely read and were done for one or another purpose. I can remember three papers I wrote with a statistician on a research project. I think some of the messages in these papers were actually quite important, but they got lost in the detail. I agreed to help him because he needed to get some publications, so that was a different motive for writing.

I: I want to pick up that point, about co-authoring. Can you tell me about what it's like to write with others?

AO: Yes, I enjoy working with other people. I enjoy doing research with them and I enjoy writing with them. One of the streams of research that I still work on is to do with health promotion and public health where we very much work as a team. We essentially do commissioned reviews, but at the same time, we're making methodological advances and contributing to debates in health policy.

Every time we've done one of these reviews, we sit down as a team and consider how we might turn it into publications. We identify the different issues: for instance, a review of children and healthy eating – is there something that we ought to write for parents? Is there something in there that we ought to write for people working in school health promotion? Is there something that we ought to write for methodologists doing systematic reviews, etc.?

We have a kind of formula, I suppose, for working out who's going to be the lead person on each paper and other people who've agreed to contribute. We set a timetable, we identify a journal and then the lead person takes the lead and carves up the work and we each do our bit and put it together. It's successful; it's not quick, but the trick is to agree a workable

timetable, so you don't say, 'We'll all do this by next Friday', you say 'In four months, we'll have a draft ready to submit' and that gives you enough time to go backwards and forwards.

I: Any disadvantages?

AO: There is the downside with writing with other people, which is you don't individually have control. So if people lapse and don't do what they've said, or if they write something which you feel is not well written, then that can be something that's quite difficult to handle. But researchers are often quite keen to learn to write and this experience of writing as a team can be a very good one for them, because they have the opportunity to learn from people who've been doing it a while. Sometimes, they say, 'I don't really understand why you've changed this' and I sit down with them and I go through it with them and I explain, not in a patronising way, I hope!

I: Have you ever had a mentor or a writing coach, somebody, almost like a significant other person who you have felt had influenced how you write?

AO: Not really – I wish I had done. I think I've had to learn some lessons the hard way. It would have been good if somebody had cut out some of the agony for me. I think I've learnt a lot from reading other people. I did actually once go on a creative writing course, and it was quite a savage experience. We were asked to write a description of something that had happened and then the person who ran the course went through it with a red pen. I found that quite awful, actually, and he wasn't a very successful writer, so I don't know, really, how useful it was.

I wouldn't call that a mentor experience. I haven't had that, not even at school: it's odd, that. As I said before, I think I've learnt a lot from having to work with people who write medical papers, because, although they use jargon and so on – they can be criticised on those grounds – they don't have this notion about these very long paragraphs and pages and pages of text. They've learnt to be concise, and that's in part, I think, because the word length requirements of the journals are often much shorter than for social science journals. You have to do it in one thousand five hundred words – you haven't got eight thousand words. That applies, also, to presenting things at conferences. If you go to medical conferences, you've got eight minutes or whatever, and if you can't say what you've found in eight minutes, then you probably don't know what it is. So, I think I've learnt the benefits of being concise.

I: Where do the themes in your writing come from? Is it part of your identity in terms of who you are?

AO: I suppose I've always had a fairly experimental approach to writing. Part of that comes from the fact that I quite easily get bored, so I want to do something new. Of course, it also comes from my involvement in feminism and the social sciences. The Seventies and Eighties were about the importance of subjectivity and issues to do with equality, personal narrative, the importance of biography in explaining what people do and in influencing it. That tells you something very important about the absurdity of these divisions between public and private and between fact and fiction and gives you a more fluid approach to what it is that you can write about and how you can write about it.

But, of course, it also means that sometimes, particularly early on, people writing in these new genres were not seen as doing proper academic work, and you had to be prepared to stand up for yourself. That kind of criticism happens much less now.

I: But standing up for yourself comes with confidence.

AO: Yes. You build that up over time. When I did the books I mentioned earlier, *Becoming a Mother* and *Women Confined*, I just knew this is how I wanted to do them, but I had no idea of what kind of reception they were going to get. Now I know that those books were important, and so that gives me confidence in my own judgement about how it is that things should be written. In that sense, you have to learn as you go; it isn't something that people can teach you.

People can teach you how to write in a tradition that already exists, they can teach you how to follow formulae and write something in a standard way, but if you want to do something rather differently, then you are actually taking a risk, and sometimes it doesn't come off.

I: And your experience of writing fiction as well as non-fiction?

AO: I've found the experience of writing fiction compared to writing fact quite interesting, because one thinks of fiction as a place where you can go where there aren't any rules, you can actually write anything, so you have this sort of total freedom, whereas if you're writing a research paper, you have to be truthful to the research data and you have to address that particular audience in the right kind of way. But, in practice, I've found that writing fiction does actually have all sorts of constraints of its own, particularly if you're writing a novel. You create characters, and they will then dictate to you what you have to write. So, you might have a view about what you want the characters to do, but actually, they won't do it, so you can't write that bit, or you write it and it doesn't work and you have to rewrite it, and it then has to be truthful to the characters you've created who are your creation, but, nonetheless, they're setting down rules of their own. So, it isn't a place where there's total freedom. There's very much a framework.

Conversely, I've often felt – you know, there's nothing stranger than life itself – some of the interviews that I've done in the past have just been extraordinary; if this were a novel, no-one would believe it. There are a couple of places where I've used bits of interviews for dialogue in novels. Nobody's spotted it, because there are parts of those interviews, the stories people were telling me, which sounded just like fiction. One thinks that fiction is extraordinary and 'fact' writing, academic writing, is ordinary, but it's much more complicated than that.

I: How was this combined work received by other academics?

AO: I've always done both. My first book, called *Sex, Gender and Society* (1972) was commissioned by a journal that no longer exists called *New Society*. I wrote it in six weeks and it's academic, it's got lots of references at the back, I did a lot of research for it, but it's written in a very popular style, and it was sold as a popular book. What's interesting about that is that it was a commissioned piece of work and I did it in the middle of my PhD work.

The book is credited in the Oxford English Dictionary with introducing the concept of 'gender' into the English language and I've found a lot of social science texts actually say that as well. Now, I had absolutely no sense of that at the time. What I knew was that I couldn't find what I wanted, and this seemed to me the right way to organise the material and the right kind of concept. Therefore, I wrote about the distinction between sex and gender being very crucial, but I was backing a hunch, and I don't know that the reviews at the time actually picked this up.

With a lot of writing, the reception it gets immediately is quite different from the way it's received ten or 15 years on, which is, of course, one of the nice things about writing, because it creates something which, hopefully, is going to last.

I: How do you create that 'something which will last'?

AO: It's easier in research than if you have a teaching job, because part of research has always been to write. You have to write the research up and, usually, you have to write it up not just for the funding body, but it's a requirement that you write for publication, so it's an important part of the job. It's also part of the job that people don't allow enough time for.

There's a big problem about research funding here: funders, on the whole, are unwilling to pay for researchers' time in taking the material and writing it up in various ways. You can submit a paper, which is then rejected; then you have to redo it, resubmit it. You might get sets of referees' comments six months on, and the paper has to be rewritten then, and it still might not be accepted. It's a long process, and it's quite painful, and I've often said it's easier to write a book. It is in some ways, because you don't have to go through this kind of process.

Contract researchers have been complaining about this for many years, and I don't think it's any easier now. It depends. I hope that places like the Social Science Research Unit actually do recognise this and try to provide help and support for people who have to write and want to write, but we can't do very much about the fundamental funding structure here, which is that people are paid to go out and collect data and cobble something together at the last minute for the funding body, but not actually to turn the data into an interesting and accessible paper or two.

I: And then on top of that we have the RAE. Do you find that it has hindered or increased your writing?

AO: I don't think it really changed my writing behaviour, but perhaps that's because by the time the RAE was invented, I had a few papers in peer-reviewed journals and knew enough about how to do it and was doing it anyway.

I know that universities have to take the RAE seriously, but it's quite hard for many people to do so. Wanting to get something published because of the RAE is a completely different motive from wanting to get something published because you've got something important to say that you think people want to read.

I: Indeed.

AO: The whole thing can be difficult. There is no sense of excitement about writing purely for the RAE.

I: Do you want to say something about the excitement and the passion that you feel about writing?

AO: Well, you know, the passion is about putting the words on the page, seeing the pattern of the words, hearing the rhythm of the words, punctuation. I think punctuation is like music. I tell you, not everybody has the same view I do about semi-colons!

It's just the best thing in the world to be able to do this, and there are so many words that you can use, and changing one word, or changing the punctuation, changes the meaning. Words are an extremely powerful way of getting through to people; making people see things differently, feel things differently.

I'm not ambitious in what I write. When we're young, we all want to change the world, and then, as we grow up, we realise that changing a few people will do. Having a few people understand something about themselves and the world, and changing their behaviour in ways that might benefit others: these are more modest ambitions which can be achieved by good writing and they're very well worth it.

The passion doesn't go, even when I have to fight to find the time and space to do it.

I: It's interesting to hear you say that you're still trying to find the time.

AO: Perhaps it would be easier if I wasn't still working part time. But I can't understand where time goes. There are so many other things that I want to do, that I enjoy doing, and writing is an activity for which you have to be very single-minded, you have to be very focused, and you have to be very unwilling to be distracted.

I'm going to a writers' retreat in June because, at the end of last year, I thought, 'I'm just not getting anywhere with a piece of writing that I'm doing.' I started a book about three years ago, which I haven't made much progress with. Somebody told me there were all these writers' retreats, so I looked on the Internet and I found a couple I applied to and this one is in Switzerland – it's in a little castle, which was left to a writers' foundation by a rich couple who worked in publishing, and they have four or five people at a time for about a month. I'm going at the same time as four poets from Egypt, Serbia, India and the USA. I don't know what it will be like at all. We're going to be in this little castle overlooking the lake and – apart from eating meals and talking to each other during the day at mealtimes – we're supposed to be quiet and get on with our own work. But, you see, I think that's a wonderful discipline – we're all there to write.

I hope the book I'm writing, which is about embodiment, will be influenced by the people there, by the conversations that we have. I still feel the need to find strategies for getting focused about writing, and that's a measure of how difficult creative writing is.

I: Am I right in thinking that you're saying writing is never easy?

AO: It's not easy. We must be masochists, I suppose, to put ourselves through this. It's what comes out at the end, but it's also about how pleased you are with it, and that's about other people's reactions. What matters to me is that people come up to me and say, 'I read something you wrote and it changed my life' or 'It opened my eyes to something' or 'It made me think.'

I: Publishing, what have you learnt about the world of publishing?

AO: It's very, very difficult. It was difficult early on for me, and it's difficult for a lot of people now; in the middle, it got easier. I think publishers make very conservative decisions – particularly now – on the basis of what has sold in the past. There are very few publishers around who are interested in the genuine merit of something. My father worked at London University and he wrote a number of books and was published by a firm called Allen and Unwin. I don't know whether they still exist, but the publisher there, a man called Charles Firth, whom I actually remember, used to go round to my father's office and pick up the new book, because he said it was such a privilege to be publishing this important stuff. That doesn't happen any more. It's all about how many copies you're going to sell, and if you want to reach people, of course it's important to sell the book, but there are long lists of people who've really changed people's lives by writing and found it very difficult to get their work published.

Some people have agents – I've got a literary agent, and she struggles with what I give her, because it's not quite what she expects, often, but she does her best.

Tips? I'm not sure. I think you could probably do better by just going to a bookshop or a library and looking through books of the sort that you're writing and just looking at who published them. It's the same with papers: if you're writing a paper about something, and you're quoting other papers, then look at where they were published, so that you're actually being quite focused in your search for a place to put these things. But publishing today isn't the way it was.

There are a lot of academic publishers around. They've got quite clear ideas of what they want. Generally, if you can make a link, make a connection, with a publisher, get on with them and if that person stays there (which is another problem, there's a lot of turnover now in publishing) and if you can work with them, you won't end up delivering a book and then finding that the publisher expected something quite different! I've had lots of fights with publishers about things such as the length of footnotes – very tedious.

I: Do you write at any particular time of day or evening, night? Do you have a kind of ritual that you follow?

AO: When I'm really writing full time, I generally write from about ten until one and from about five until seven. I don't write in the evening. Morning's the best time, not too early, though.

I like to sit by a window and be able to look out of a window at something, not just the house next door, but something a bit further away. Views are important. I think it's something to do with being able to see through and over, beyond a horizon, it's a psychological thing. But I know other people find views distracting. I have a friend who's an artist, a painter, and he has a studio with no windows (it has very good lighting): he says that looking at a view is distracting for him. Maybe that's a difference between the visual arts and writing. Most writers say that they have a place where they like to sit. Roald Dahl had a shed in the garden and he had a sort of wooden tray that he used to put over his knees. Writers have all these rituals.

I: We talked about identity before. How would you want to be remembered in terms of your writing? What does your writing say about you?

AO: My writing has changed people's lives in some small way; it has had an impact on them, that's what I would want. It would be nice if they said I wrote well. If you're having an impact on someone, then you must have written well in the sense that you're getting through to them, so it's about communicating. I don't think I'd particularly want people to say, 'Oh, that's a piece of very fine prose.' I mean, I can think of things that I've written that are examples of fine prose, but they don't really communicate very much necessarily.

I: What have you learnt about the process of writing?

AO: I've learnt about the value of not using a word because it sounds nice, but because you know what it means and it does the job: the value of being very precise. That includes when, for example, you're writing a description of the sky for a novel – it's a different meaning of precision, but you're still trying to find the words to describe what it is that you see and what you want other people to see when they read your words. So, it's a sort of 'fit for purpose' thing about language.

When you're writing anything other than a straightforward, academic paper, it's important not to keep reading what you've just written. You don't keep going back and reading it. If you do that, you can get hung up on the fact that there's a word that isn't working very well three sentences back. You must just write it and regard it a bit like a potter's clay – you've got something there that can then be moulded.

I've learnt about the importance of distinguishing these different stages in writing: there's kind of an initial creative process, and then the editorial one follows from that. I'm not the kind of writer who sits down and makes a very exact plan. If you're writing an academic paper which is a research report, the plan is pretty much in front of you, you know the aims of the research, the methods and so on. But in other writing I'm hopeless at detailed planning. I think that's because I want to get lost in the creative experience – not lost, but I want to experience it as a journey, and I don't really want to know the names of all the stations on the way. I want to find out where this is going to take me, and that's part of the excitement of writing, it's a journey we can go on, and we don't know what's going to happen.

I: Just to summarise, would you like to say any last words about writing?

AO: I think it's a great pity that writing is undervalued as an activity in the academic world, and it needs a bit more support than it currently has.

It's not something that people can just do cold, it's something you have to learn, and there are different ways to learn it. You can learn it the hard way, which is what I've done – by making mistakes. I've made lots of mistakes in what I've written, and then finally realised that this isn't the way to put it, this is how you've got to do it instead. You can have people who actually try and help others along the way, and there ought to be more of that kind of help.

But the other thing I would say is people shouldn't be discouraged too easily, particularly today, when it's hard to get published and getting papers into journals can take ages and ages. You must not be discouraged; you will get there in the end. Writing is an experience, an experience of struggling. Wanting to get there at the end is an experience that is best shared, so people should talk to one other about it and not go round individually thinking, 'Oh, I'm a complete failure because I'm still on the second page of this paper and I've been carrying it round in my bag for three weeks.' Everybody does that.

I: Do you feel you've got it right, now?

AO: No. If I felt I'd got it right, I would stop because writing is learning. And that's another exciting thing about writing: you're always going to learn something new. So I'm really looking forward to this retreat I'm going to in June with these four poets, but I'm also terrified. It's a mistake to think you've ever got it right. No, I think it's important to think that you're getting there, which is different.

I: Thank you.

Novels by Ann Oakley

The Men's Room. London: Virago (1988) (HarperCollins paperback, 1989; 1991).

Matilda's Mistake. London: Virago (1990) (HarperCollins paperback, 1991).

The Secret Lives of Eleanor Jenkinson. London: HarperCollins (1993).

Scenes Originating in the Garden of Eden. London: HarperCollins (1993).

A Proper Holiday. London: HarperCollins (1996).

Overheads. London: HarperCollins (1999).

Michael Reiss

I: *Thank you for agreeing to be interviewed. To begin with the first question on the sheet: how long have you been at the Institute and what are your roles?*

MR: Well, I joined the Institute in January 2001, and I came originally simply as Professor of Science Education. At that point I was also Head of the Science and Technology Group. When we had the restructuring soon after, I became Head of the School of Maths, Science and Technology, and those roles continue to this day. Like most people at the Institute, I'm on various committees and so on but those are my two main roles.

I: *To continue: we've suggested that each person tell us about the best piece or pieces of writing that they've done. Which is the one you're most pleased with, if there is only one?*

MR: It's difficult to think of a particular single piece of writing, and that's not just because one hopes one's managed to write more than one thing that's OK. I think it's because, well, imagine asking a surgeon what he or she thought was their best operation – it would be a rather odd question. And that is because, important as I do believe creativity and originality and inspiration is in writing, there ought probably, for an academic who writes, to be an element of routine. In exactly the same way as, however well one teaches, there is perfectly appropriately and validly, indeed probably necessarily, a degree of routinisation. So I would hope that anybody who writes quite a lot, as a huge number of academics do at the Institute, would not see only one peak that they had ascended.

Now all that having been said, I've also written in quite a variety of genres, if that doesn't sound too presumptuous in tone. So my early writing was in applied mathematics – in the field of population genetics, evolutionary biology and animal behaviour. And one of the things I was pleased with early on was a theoretical piece which is almost impossible to describe to 99.9 per cent of people because it is basically all pure mathematics – particular spreads of alleles in populations. It is pure population biology. And the chances of it ever being of any use, where use is construed narrowly in a utilitarian or commercial sense, are completely negligible. But that was satisfying because you work on mathematical problems and they come out, and they have an elegance and a directness.

And then, much more recently, one piece, though it doesn't sit within the mainstream of what I write, because most of what I write is about ways of trying to improve school science education, but one thing I wrote that got published a couple of years ago that I was pleased with was a piece that was about whether or not it would be a good idea to use modern medical, and future medical, technologies to enable people to live for hundreds of years. And the reason I enjoyed doing that was partly because it drew together the bit of me that still likes biology, so I had to brush up on how likely it is that medical technology might enable us to live hundreds of years, and what are the different sorts of technologies, which to put it ever so briefly could be about a succession of transplants, or could be about changes to diet, chemical changes or some sort of genetic enhancement via genetic engineering. And then, of course, one has to do quite a lot of moral philosophy, which is one of the areas that I write on in bioethics which, loosely speaking, is about: would it be a good idea? And there had been a lot of arguments in the last five years' literature, most of which are invalid, about this, so intellectually it was quite nice looking at them and trying to dissect them. And then the final reason why I enjoyed that piece was because, unusually for me, it was written as theology, in an edited book, and I don't write much academic theology: I've probably written about half-a-dozen academic pieces in theology. But that was one

where, very interestingly, theology had quite a lot to say, as did science fiction, because those were two areas in which there were people who had genuinely explored issues to do, in science fiction's case, with living very long periods of time, hundreds of years, which is a very familiar theme in science fiction from John Wyndham onwards. And while I'm not a science fiction buff, I got advice from Jenny, to whom I am married, who reads voraciously in science fiction, and I read several science fiction books specifically for this paper. But also theology as well, of course, has a literature on issues to do with long life. There's been a huge amount of thinking over two thousand years in the western tradition about the relationship between eternity, interminableness and everlastingness, and there's a wonderfully arcane literature about the difference between these terms. So again, the bit of me that just likes careful, analytical reasoning rather enjoyed this. And surprisingly it does actually connect a bit. So that was satisfying, because it was trying to bring together these several different fields into one piece.

I: *Would it be accurate as a summary to say that you like challenging ideas, and the chance to explore a new line of thinking?*

MR: Absolutely. Life at the Institute, as in most higher education institutions, certainly in the UK, is perfectly busy enough. But if one didn't get something for oneself out of one's writing it would be very easy to do almost no serious writing.

I: *If you've done pieces or writing that you weren't pleased with, how did you see the problem, or what was it you didn't like? Was it just too routine?*

MR: It's usually because you haven't put enough of yourself into them. So, as you say correctly, they have been too routine. Occasionally, thankfully, they get rejected. I can think of two pieces I've written in the last five years, one for a special journal, where I'd just rushed to get something in by a deadline, and I was quite glad in hindsight it wasn't published because it just wasn't very good. The other one was unusually a case where I, well, I think I'm being a bit generous when I say 'I misunderstood'; it's partly I'd misunderstood and partly that I'd been unintentionally misled as to the audience. So it was for a handbook, and I thought the audience was headteachers, and it turned out the audience, although it ostensibly included headteachers, was really academics. So I'd sent in something that was too light, and under-theorised, and so forth. And again, I'm very glad it didn't get published because it wouldn't have been appropriate. The frustrating thing there was that it was an international handbook, and the editor at the UK level said it was fine, so it's slightly embarrassing that it got to the top level, and then it was too late to do anything about it.

I: *And quite embarrassing for the UK editor!*

MR: Well, that's true, I hadn't really thought that through fully. But it's one of the reasons why some sort of refereeing process can obviously protect the author as well as the audience.

I: *Yes, you've raised the issue of audience – do you think consciously about the audience?*

MR: Without exception, very much so. I was a schoolteacher for five years, and learned that the only way to teach effectively is genuinely, wholeheartedly, absolutely and sincerely to find out as best you can, as quickly as you can, as early as you can, what different constituencies there are within one's audience, what they know about something, what they think about it, what their interests are. And writing is identical to that, it's exactly the same. So I take audience extremely seriously. Now that I've done quite a lot of writing, I realise that it actually helps once you get published, for a variety of reasons as well as the obvious, rather deeper reason that one writes better. I know, from editing things myself, that it is just such a relief to get something in which is appropriately structured, which clearly is written at a level suitable for the audience concerned and fits in with the format requirements – you're halfway there.

I: *Yes, I had an email from an associate lecturer in another university where I did some examining. He asked if I thought he could present the report that he'd written to a journal for applied linguistics. He*

had not considered the readership of the journal. His paper was not appropriate for that readership.

MR: Absolutely, and for me, interestingly enough, it was probably the schoolteaching that forced me to think quite carefully of audience. Because before that the only audience I'd written for, because I did my PhD in biology before I became a teacher, was the rather narrow group of academics who read population biology, evolution and genetics.

I: *That's very interesting. Oh yes, the next is likely to be a big question for the people who read this: what's helped your writing, how did you learn to do it, is there anything that's particularly helped, apart from schoolteaching, which made you think about audiences?*

MR: It was clear to me that writing was going to be important fairly early on. By early on, I mean when I was doing my PhD, I think. Before that I was just trying to avoid writing, minimising the number of essays one had to write as a student and that sort of thing. And I can remember the first thing I ever wrote was a book review, which took me probably a week to do in total, including the reading of a short book. And the main thing that helped me learn how to write, apart from, as you say, schoolteaching, was particular individuals. I remember very well in my first term at university – I'd done double maths, physics and chemistry at school, so I didn't have to write any essays at all – I'd written my first-ever essay for a biology supervision, and the supervisor, whose name sadly I can't remember because it was so long ago, very nicely just tore it to shreds, in an appropriate way. And the second one I wrote was hugely better. Then I got a certain amount from my doctoral supervisor, Tim Clutton-Brock. Then I got a lot from a colleague, Ian Harvey, when I was teaching at a Sixth Form college. He and I wrote several health information packs on HIV and AIDS, and then on illicit drugs and one or two other things. And he wrote very fast, and just assumed he could do it. And I, because my previous writing had been in mathematics, thought that writing was a sort of pinnacle of achievement and very demanding, which it can be, and certainly writing mathematics is extremely demanding. But he thought of it as just, you know, get the next worksheet done, and he wrote well. So he and I wrote very fast, and that was good for me.

And then there was an author whose name people who've taught biology in schools will know, Mike Roberts, because he wrote a very successful series of biology textbooks, and I joined him in writing one of the later editions of an A-level biology textbook. And Mike was just superb at things like structuring paragraphs, the minutiae of grammar and syntax and punctuation, an economy with words, but the occasional, the occasional, stylistic flourish just to keep the reader engaged. And he was a completely ruthless editor in the best sense. So I got a lot from him. All of that happened, of course, quite a long time ago because I wrote those kind of schoolbooks, well, I'm not quite sure when, but probably when I was sort of very late twenties, yes, and early thirties. And then subsequently it's simply been reading what other people have written, rather than, I think, anything else. And most academics, of course, don't write particularly well; it's usually people who write fiction who write very well. It's not that I deliberately read in order to learn how to write better, but you just can't resist reading the best writing there is. It's just so good that a tiny bit of it rubs off.

I: *And how have you managed to keep writing a major part of your life, if you have?*

MR: Well, I probably have. When I finished my PhD I was very fortunate that I got a short postdoc, and the assumption was that the main purpose of that was to write. I then went and taught in schools and didn't write anything the first couple of years because I was just getting on top of becoming a teacher. But I think with hindsight, having got on top of becoming a teacher, I then started to do two sorts of writing, one of which was finishing up papers from the PhD and postdoctoral work, and I managed to bring it all together in a book which I was very satisfied with and which has done well. But I was also beginning then to write articles for the professional journals in school biology and school science. And I think I just got into the habit of it, and I can't sing well, I can't act well, I don't try and write fiction, so I think for me the writing satisfies that part of me that would otherwise

feel one is not being creative, and is an important part of one. I did a lot of writing in the 18 months or so before I came here, just because my balance of work at the previous place where I worked, because of RAE pressures, was shifting very much towards a heavy emphasis on research and writing. I was still doing quite a bit of teaching, I don't want to understate it; we calculated then in contact hours so it was 350 contact hours in a year. But a lot of colleagues would do more than that. And then when I came here, I thought I was coming here to do even more writing. But I quite quickly realised that, certainly in the post I have now, one has less time for writing than I did in my previous job. So writing probably averages about ten hours a week I think.

I: *And would you like to do much more than that?*

MR: Well, I certainly wouldn't want to be a full-time writer. I absolutely wouldn't, and almost nobody is. And I've enjoyed the management side that I've begun to get into at the Institute, and I haven't tried to get out of that. So it would be very easy for me to say it would be lovely to have a bit more time for writing, but I can't blame anybody else except myself for that. And although, like practically everybody else in academia, I'm behind with my writing, it's not that there has been a huge nine-month period when I haven't written anything, it's just one always seems perpetually to be about year behind or so, and somehow one thinks if only one had a year with more time, one would catch up.

I: *I think you may say that you've actually already answered the next question which is: what kind of writing do you most enjoy? You've talked about the demanding theoretical piece.*

MR: The writing I've probably always found most effortless is for A-level biology students, which is a very small part of what I do, of course, though I have just finished with colleagues a five-year project on a new A-level biology course, and that's very satisfying. And I mention it deliberately because if one wants one's academic work to have impact, that is a very good group of people. The course we've done, it's only just really started, launched nationally in

September 2005, but at the moment there are likely to be about six thousand students doing it, all highly capable, intelligent students, and most academics would be very pleased if their work was being studied for literally ten hours a week by six thousand people, and that's what's happening. And that's probably, in a sense, for me the easiest writing. The writing that I probably get most satisfaction from is where I'm addressing core issues in mainly science education, and to a lesser extent writing in two other, two areas, applied bioethics and sex education, where I'm writing on core questions, such as 'What should the curriculum be?', 'How should we teach it?', but drawing on insights that people might often suppose didn't connect with the subject or were not particularly relevant.

It sounds pretentious: I gave a talk at a conference a couple of years ago on what Marcel Duchamp, the artist, had to tell science educators. That's one of the many papers I haven't yet written up, but I ought to write up for publication. Apart from being a little bit playful in doing that, it was because the conference was in Philadelphia, which has got the best collection of Duchamp in the world and I'd never been to Philadelphia before, and I like Duchamp, and I think it often is worthwhile to look at things from a different angle, and I enjoy doing that in a lot of the writing that I do. The inaugural lecture I gave here, because I'm sure you know, you have to give an inaugural lecture if you're a professor, and I gave mine quite soon after I came here, started with a wonderful photograph by the photographer Andreas Gursky. And he's somebody who digitally enhances but only slightly, and I used that to get into issues of representation, and what the aims of science in general are and how this can connect with what the purposes of school science education should be.

I: *Would you say then that education offers people opportunities to cross boundaries, that working in a science department wouldn't?*

MR: Well, it's hugely easier, and the reason is because education is still not yet a successful academic discipline, because, as we all know, it's so genuinely complicated, and therefore in a way it is both easier and more difficult to write in it than it is in science.

It's very easy to write in science if you're a scientist, on whatever subject is within science, because, as you say, the boundaries are clearly defined, there's a canon, there are strictures, there are structures, and you operate within them. But education is much more like, you know, writing in medieval medicine or alchemy; you're grasping at all sorts of things, and it's not always clear yet what's going to be of real value. And that suits; well, I can do both, because part of me is very obsessional and can cope very well with writing within very strict guidelines, but I think I would eventually feel that wouldn't be a life that was as flourishing as a life that can draw on a very wide range of disciplines.

I: *And what does your writing say about you? I realise that that question could mean many different things.*

MR: Well, I mean, reader-response theory: you'd have to ask those who read my writing. Because I have a great belief that writing is for readers. From my perspective as the author, it's a mixture of diversities between somebody who enjoys drawing on a range of sources. A bit playful, but nevertheless very task-oriented. You know, there was a slight period, in the postmodern tradition in education, and particularly in England, where it slightly began to get on my nerves. I don't know about anybody else, but everything just became endlessly reflexive and playful, and there's a part of me that thinks, 'Yeah, I want people to "enjoy" the schooling they're having, or their education out of school, but I want them to learn something.' I do have, like, thankfully, practically everyone at the Institute, a genuine commitment to social justice and a belief that we're trying to move forward. So, as I say, task-focused, but hopefully not too ploddy.

I: *So how do you actually go about writing? Do you have a set way of doing it? Is there a way that suits you better than any other way that you've developed over time?*

MR: By coincidence I had a good, quite short discussion about this about a year-and-a-half ago, with David Buckingham and two of the Institute's postdoctoral fellows, Rebekah Willett and Judy Hemingway, because it was one of these meetings that Peter Aggleton and Ingrid Lunt were organising for the postdocs, and it was one of the ones that worked particularly well because we'd been asked to think about how we go about writing. And although this is obviously mediated by 18 months of fading memory, a strong consensus in that group was that it was the deadline that was important actually; it was as blunt as that. And there are things I write, of course, that are not like that – you just start making notes on something and something flows. And that's really nice, and usually happens for me if I'm away from work because the volume of things there are at work is usually sufficient to stop any particularly original thinking.

So for me, the way I go about writing, and this has been true for over ten years now, is I don't write when I'm physically at work, at the Institute, and I didn't at my previous place of employment. It's done at home, which means it's done evenings, Saturdays and then the periods of the year when obviously one hasn't got as many commitments, like August and times like between Christmas and January 2nd and 3rd and times like that. And I tend to start writing, probably more often than any other time, about 3.30 pm on a Saturday. And the reason is that by then I've done as many things as I can do to put off the starting to write, and thankfully I don't do much work on Sundays. So there is this feeling: if you don't manage to get going now, it's going to be dinner, and then you're not going to start after dinner on a Saturday evening; if you can, just get going. And I've always taken great comfort from the fact that a lot of professional journalists believe you've just got to write, you've just got to write your thousand words a day or whatever. There's the story that Graham Greene got up early, always wrote nine hundred words before breakfast, and then he'd finished writing for the day. Obviously academics can't do that. But for me, if I can get started, and thankfully I'm not somebody who stares at blank bits of paper, it might be mediocre what I start with, but I can nearly always get going because I've invested sufficient emotional energy in the idea of what I'm writing; I have got some ideas. Or if the worst comes to the worst, which is sometimes the case though usually not, you can

begin by recrafting a paragraph from something else. But usually I can get going with something newish. And I just feel, if I managed then by the end of Saturday to have done sort of fifteen hundred words, however mediocre they are, that's good enough. And then either I pick it up on subsequent Saturdays, or if I've really got into something I can usually do a bit in the evenings during the week, if I'm not receiving endless emails or whatever. And I work surprisingly well abroad. For example, most years I've done about ten days' work in Egypt, and that's finished by about five o'clock in the day. And the place where I work is a field station where nobody else speaks English and I don't speak any Arabic, apart from the trivial. I therefore have five or six hours, and I might as well work, and I write well. Each year I've written one to two papers there.

I: So the actual place doesn't matter to you? Some people feel they have to have a certain place where they can write.

MR: No, and I think it's … I'm probably, though it might surprise many people, slightly introverted, and therefore it's within, it's not the context. So the context is within, if you like. I don't like having to write using laptops on trains, but I can do it if I need to. I can do that sort of thing, particularly for writing grant applications, and I am not somebody who needs the undisturbed day. Once I've got into something, provided I've got over an hour-and-a-half, like a good evening, and if it's still reasonably uppermost in my mind, then I can push on.

I: You talked about making notes: do you do those with pen and paper, do you do much writing on paper, do you compose on screen?

MR: Ninety eight per cent is on screen, and has been for 15 years. Before we had word processors and so on, I would write long hand, but it wouldn't need much correction. Once I'd written it, I'd only go through it once. Now that's not true for the mathematical arguments, because those are all over bits of scraps of paper. It's very rare that you've got something that really flowed in the way that the words can flow. But on trains I definitely often scribble notes on bits of paper and keep them, but I wouldn't ever have more than probably about two hundred, three hundred words of handwritten stuff; I would then just write on screen straight off. And for me word processors are absolutely brilliant, because you can just recraft so easily.

I: Do you always have a notebook at hand so that you can jot down a new idea if one comes to you in, say, a supermarket, or you wake up in the middle of the night with a new idea?

MR: No, I don't do that. I'm very lucky, I sleep well, and I don't have notebooks in supermarkets! I don't get any exciting ideas in supermarkets. What I do do is … it's when I'm relaxed, often towards the end of a holiday, and I'm not intentionally thinking about bits of writing, but particularly when I'm just out walking, or something like that, I get one or two ideas and I scribble those on bits of paper when I get back to wherever I was staying. And in very boring meetings occasionally I get good ideas and I scribble those down on a bit of paper.

I: What have you learned about writing for publication? We have touched on that, but perhaps you would like to say something more?

MR: We have, as you say, touched on it, so it's audience number one. And if one's going to joke, it's the audience number two and number three. I'm not a perfectionist, so I've never believed I'm writing the last word on a subject, I have a very incremental view of knowledge; you know, it's one-and-a-half steps forward, one step back, so it's always just trying to add to the pile, and half of what one writes won't really survive, probably far more than that, or won't even be picked up, and the other half somebody picks up and uses, or one does oneself later on. I've probably learned a lot about a range of ways of writing with other people because, again like most academics in education, some of my writing is on my own and some is with other people, and thankfully I'm pretty adaptable, so I don't only have one way of writing with other people. So if other people have got firm views, I can go along with them. The only way I don't enjoy writing, and thankfully very few people

do that, I only remember one colleague who did, is the two of you sitting next to each other in front of one computer, trying to write on screen. I just found that was draining, because when writing on my own, I like after 40 minutes to go and have a cup of tea or whatever, and you suddenly have a really good bit where you write two paragraphs effortlessly. And for me, I want total silence for that; I don't write with radios on or anything like that. I can do it, as I say, on trains if I have to, but my preference is silence, at home, upstairs in a study.

I: And then when you are using a word processor, depending on the kind of writing you're doing, do you write a draft very quickly, and then go back and revise, or do you prefer to craft the piece, section by section, paragraph by paragraph? In a book on writing Mike Sharples says the computer turned him into a kind of bricklayer, constructing a text bit by bit.

MR: I still usually start at the beginning, and pretty much write sequentially through to the end, so it's not very different from when one wrote long hand on paper. Having said that, I'm happy to leave gaps and sections and know that I can come back and fill them out later, particularly if they're the more straightforward bits. So thinking about it, which I haven't done before, I'm more likely to write the more original bits early on. And then feel I can fill in. And then the nice thing is, when you fill in, you then end up writing those bits better and they do become fairly new in some way.

I: Does writing for different audiences change your style to any great extent, or do you feel that in the writing you do for publication you're tending to use the same kind of academic discourse or level of formality?

MR: Well, for me, it changes hugely, because as you've gathered, I still write for 16-year-olds. I don't do much writing for younger audiences, but I do occasionally write for 11-year-olds. And then in terms of writing for adults, a lot of the applied bioethics writing I do is done with committees, with people who have expertise, but it's expertise outwith of moral philosophy. So, for example, I sit on the government's

Farm Animal Welfare Council, as the ethicist, and in various working groups I'd be responsible for doing the ethics section, while other people would be responsible for doing the stockman's section or the agricultural economist's section. But you're writing there for an adult lay audience. So I very much have a diversity of audiences in view. Rather, again, like in teaching and in lectures. I can shift the teaching very quickly, providing I just know what the audience is.

I: The next question is: if you weren't at the Institute or another academic institution, do you think you would still write?

MR: Well, I'm comfortable with the question, and the answer is: yes. And the evidence for that is from when I was a schoolteacher. Because I had genuinely assumed I wasn't going to be an academic at that point, whereas previously I had hoped I was going to be an academic in biology. And yes, I carried on writing. And the writing I was doing was mostly writing that wasn't going to lead to an academic career, or so I thought, though of course what I did helped me. And secondly, it wasn't writing for which one was being paid, because I was sending off contributions to journals like *School Science Review* and *Journal of Biological Education*. So I'm fairly certain that writing is an important part of me. It is, tragically, a tiny bit early for me to be thinking about retiring, and I'm glad to say at the moment I'm not looking for jobs outside the Institute, so I'm assuming I'm here for the foreseeable future. But I'm pretty certain I would still write if I weren't. And I'd still write non-fiction. I'm not somebody who is a frustrated novelist. But I'd probably write more conceptually. I think that's it, because I probably wouldn't be doing lots of funded empirical research, which I do at the moment. So it would probably be more solitary, and more conceptual.

I: And do you find writing in the early stages painful?

MR: Not painful, the word I would use is more a 'huge effort'; in that sense. Maybe that's what you meant?

I: Well, I have heard senior academics say that in their experience writing is very painful when you're still in that stage where you haven't shaped it yet, and you're not certain if it's going to work.

MR: Well, people use adjectives differently, but 'huge effort' is, to repeat, the way I look at it. And people who don't write probably genuinely don't appreciate what it's like, because it is very demanding indeed. And I'm sure there are lots of other things in life that are very demanding that I haven't done, which is fair enough. But writing is very satisfying, of course, when it goes well.

I: And would you say that you've got the confidence, the experience now to feel, 'Well, something is likely to come out of this effort that's worth saying'?

MR: That's absolutely right, and I can remember that first book review I wrote, when I actually gave a copy of it to my parents, saying, 'Well, if I don't write anything else, at least I've written that', and meaning it, as far as one can tell years later, completely genuinely. And of course one knows that, while some of the things one writes don't get accepted, the great majority will indeed get published, so one has got more confidence, yes.

I: And have you had reviews that you've found helpful as a way of making you more aware of aspects of your writing?

MR: By reviews, do you mean book reviews, or referees' reports?

I: Well, referees' reports.

MR: Two-thirds of them are very good and very useful, and most journal editors are very good at eliding the bad ones, so that's just normally very helpful. And I'm appalling at showing colleagues drafts of stuff before I send it off, I'm afraid. I practically never do that, I'm sorry to say. Of course, if you're writing jointly with somebody, then thankfully two or three of you have had the input, so that's fine. But stuff on my own, I just send straight off, I'm afraid, which is not something I'd advise anybody to do, particularly at the beginning of their career.

I: And what about book reviews?

MR: Well, by now of course it's fine, because you get huge numbers of them and most are good and some aren't. But I remember almost the first, perhaps the second or third, review I got, was a really bad review. This was a book in academic biology; thankfully it's a book which eventually had about 15 reviews, of which 14 were between positive and outstanding, and the book's still in print, and has done remarkably well for an academic book in biology written and published in 1989. Now, of course, I can understand with hindsight rather more about why the particular review was bad. I think the person himself, although he was quite senior, I don't think he'd actually written a book on his own. And I think there was a bit of him that just didn't like this young schoolteacher thinking he could write an academic Cambridge University Press book. By then I was in my late twenties, and being a schoolteacher, I'd left the field. Now it sounds a terrible thing to say, but with hindsight, I'm not sure if he was aware of that consciously or not; maybe he was just somebody who completely over-reacted – because it wasn't a bad book. It's funny; later reviews have seemed to matter much less, like most things in life, the more you've had of it, but even the good ones don't matter so much. I keep photocopies of them all, so there's a huge wodge at home, but I've never reread them or looked through them again or anything like that.

I: You're moving on to the next piece of writing.

MR: That's right, exactly so.

I: Well, that's very interesting. Is there anything you'd like to add, that we haven't covered?

MR: Well, this is from a long time ago. I remember from reading Sylvia Plath's letters that she had an approach, when she was trying to get her poetry published in the early days, of always having at any one time something sent off to a potential publisher. And I do think one ought to try and get into the rhythm of writing, not to think there's just this one thing I'm going to do; just, in a sense, get on with it. And if you look at most painters, and obviously for Cezanne it really was painful, but he nevertheless worked very hard and on several things at once etc.; if it is part of one's being, then it ought to be allowed to come out. I think at the Institute we've done a little in the last couple of years which has been good, straightforwardly through staff development, to help people develop their writing, but we haven't begun to do it properly.

I: That's one of the things, I and two colleagues have been working on with young staff who need to publish, but of course, it's because of the RAE, but shouldn't just be for the RAE.

MR: It shouldn't be just for that, but as you say that has been helpful. I'd forgotten you were one of the three, that's right. But I know from people in IT, who've had support in writing through that programme, that it's been genuinely helpful, and there have been one or two other initiatives as well. But when people are doctoral students, we give them quite a lot of support in developing techniques of research methods and so on, and you can't learn how to write in a certain way when you're still doing your doctorate because an awful lot of it comes subsequently. And I don't think I've got it sussed out what we should be doing, but to start using the jargon, we ought to be developing the intellectual capital we have here within the organisation, so we have young people – by young I don't mean chronological age but in terms of their academic careers – so we have young people always coming up, so that lots of lecturers are just automatically becoming senior lecturers, and senior lecturers readers, and then professors, and we're all developing as writers.

I: I think you're right. In fact, there is a member of staff who's finished her PhD who came to me recently. She has asked me to help her set up writing workshops for postdoctoral students and staff, staff that would be informed by research into writing for publication.

MR: Good, that's my interest; after one's got one's doctorate.

I: But the doctoral students are being encouraged to publish before they obtain their PhDs.

MR: That's right, and that's very well known, but my particular focus is mainly on our academic staff.

If one knows colleagues well, one ought to be able to work out with them what approach is appropriate for whom. A lot of what gets published in educational academia is fairly routine, and won't last, so sometimes if you can get it right, of course, it's the stuff that slightly breaks the boundaries that is best. But as you know very well, it's always this delicate interplay: you've got to learn how to write within the boundaries before you can question the boundaries. Most people have to learn conventionally before they can break out of them. Rather like most musicians, most classical musicians, are solidly grounded in eighteenth, nineteenth century music before they go onto modern.

I: Or poets, their early poetry is very derivative while they are learning how to do it.

MR: That's right, and most poets can still write a sonnet if you wanted them to, or an iambic pentameter. Even if they wouldn't write like that nowadays.

I: Do you work with postdocs on writing for publication?

MR: No, I don't, not much. My role, as I'm wearing my Head of School hat, is to be encouraging, and while – as we all know – there's an RAE focus, that's not got to be the main thing. The angle I've taken is, look, if you want to work at the Institute as a member of the academic staff, you need to be writing academically and doing academic research; whether you get funding for that or not, I don't care. I don't pressure people to get funded research, most people in IT do the sort of research you need funding for, some of them don't. But you must write academically, for your career. It ought to become important for you.

Jeni Riley

I: *Thank you so much, Jeni, for agreeing to take part.*

JR: Thank you for inviting me.

I: *Perhaps you could start by saying a bit about how long you've been at the Institute and about your different roles.*

JR: OK. Well, I've been at the Institute 20 years, believe it or not. I came in 1986. I was here as a lecturer in primary education initially, and after three years I was made course leader of the primary PGCE, which grew massively in size from about 45 students up to 200. Then I became Head of the Primary Education Academic Group. And my last full-time role was Head of the School of Early Childhood and

Primary Education here at the Institute. I now run the consultancy network for Early Childhood and Primary Education, put on conferences for the School and have some PhD students and supervise Masters dissertation students which is a delight, actually. I love it.

I: *Great, that's lovely, thank you. Now we've been asking about a piece of writing that people feel pleased with.*

JR: Well, it's interesting, because I find it very difficult to choose one. I think the piece of writing that I am quite pleased with was the book of my PhD. Because one is so close to a PhD and this transformed into a book which has been very popular with teachers. It came out in 1996, and I have been asked by the publisher to do a rewrite and I have updated and broadened it. It needed updating because it's now ten years old. But I was pleased with that book, and I think that it's to do with something you feel very, very involved with. And I knew that data. I thought so hard about it all, as one does when doing a PhD, and I had a very deep sense that I wanted to get some of my ideas about that research to early years teachers because I felt it could really transform their practice. I just wished it was something I'd known when I was working in the classroom. So I think that kind of intimate knowledge of the theory and what it might mean for practice is what helps to make a good piece of writing.

I: What's the theme of the book?

JR: The book is about developing reading. The study I based the book on tracked 191 children through their first year of school.

I: Right.

JR: And it was just as the whole country was looking at the teaching of early reading and it was an influence on the National Literacy Strategy and chimed with people's concerns about early reading. But because I knew the data and the theory very, very well indeed, I think I was able to explain it in a very clear and accessible way for teachers. Although I've moved on since I wrote it, I think that would be my favourite piece of writing.

The other piece that's just recently been published was a little piece of research that I did with practitioner David Reedy on helping very young children to write argument and demonstrated how it developed their thinking. That article was published in the *Early Childhood Literacy Journal*. It has created quite a lot of interest. So I think that is the most recent, that came out in 2005. So that's a sort of sign of where I've moved to and I quite like that article as well.

I: Yeah. Do you like it for the same reasons?

JR: I think I liked it because it was a very sharp focus on one aspect of practice, which we explored in more and more depth and sought to explain what was going on from a multi-disciplinary point of view. It was very rich data that we could unravel through many different perspectives. And, of course, also it had implications for practice, which is where I come from, in a classroom with six-year-olds.

I: OK. Have there been some that you have not been so pleased with?

JR: Yes, an article that I wrote with an MA student. This person did an MA dissertation which I supervised and we wrote that up together. It wasn't my data and I think as soon as you start to write about something that you're less secure about, that's when it becomes rather shaky. It was helping her to get a publication and she was very pleased with it. But I always felt that it didn't lift off the page. It wasn't written with a freshness and enthusiasm. I think I would think of it as rather a plodding article really. I mean it got into a refereed journal, but I would say that good writing is about being intimately connected with the content. That sounds so obvious, really, you think, 'Wow, what an amazing comment', but to me that is what it's about.

And I think in universities that one of the difficulties that people have when they're told to write is people say to them, 'Just get an article.' People are dredging up enthusiasm to write something, on almost anything, and it really is so counter-productive, that kind of pressure. It has to be something that you actually want to weave into something that people will want to read.

I: Yes. And it sounds like you, with your PhD and tracking those young people, it sounds as though you're really passionate about that.

JR: Yes, and it was so insightful, for me having been a practitioner for years and years and investigating some of the kids and where they were when they came into the system and their understandings about language and literacy and how some of them moved on in a year. And some of them didn't, given what they came in with. And the story about all that was so interesting.

I: And you said that the teachers like your book. How do you know that they like it?

JR: Well, the sales have been good. And people say that to me when they meet me, 'Oh, you know, such a good little book' – it did seem to touch various spots. And I think because it has a human dimension, this wasn't an obvious PhD thesis when you read it, you know, it has a human story with case studies and not only quantitative data. It's written from a practitioner's perspective.

I: Right.

JR: Because I never lose that stance. I am not a researcher solely, it's very much somebody who's been in classrooms, reception classrooms, for a long time. I think that's important for me.

I: Yes.

JR: And looking at these individual learners as they come into the system, and trying to puzzle out why some just catch on to reading just like that and some have difficulties and by the end of the year really aren't making very much headway at all with literacy.

I: Lovely, that's great. So what's helped your writing?

JR: Margaret Meek always used to say, 'I do write well, but that's because I do a lot of it.' So I think there's a lot of truth in that, that the more you write, the better you get. And it is about the hard graft of sitting down and doing it.

The other thing I think that is very helpful when you're writing is to have someone who reads it and gives you feedback. And certainly I had that. I think the discipline of doing a PhD helps you to learn to structure writing, but you're writing in an academic genre when you do a PhD, which needs practice, and that's a very particular learning curve. But after that, I think you have the ability to structure an argument and the ability to develop your writing in terms of the compositional side. I think having somebody who is close enough to your work to give you constructive feedback on whether it's making sense, when they think that you are developing that story well that will

intrigue a reader. If you have a critical friend, which I was lucky enough to have, I think unless you're very able or you've done a degree in English, you often need help with syntax, people saying to you: 'This sentence is far too long and needs cutting.' And that kind of help and support, and helping you with more elegant ways of saying things, putting things round another way. Sometimes people need that kind of support so that the text reads well and fluently. You need help when you start writing, if you're going to publish. I think if you're going to write something it has to have a readerly quality to it. Sometimes you read books and you know that they have been written by a very academic person. They don't read well always and for practitioners particularly.

I: Yes.

JR: So I think it's about writing for different audiences. And this is a skill that we need to acquire as academics and most of us need help with that.

I: Right. You said you had a critical friend – just one or a number of mentors who helped you write in different ways for different audiences?

JR: I had a friend when I was doing my Masters degree here and he was a very clever man and he used to love reading my work. He used to proof-read it and give me feedback on it, and that was helpful. I suppose you get feedback from your PhD supervisors at one level, depending on how skilled they are themselves. But with all my writing that I've done for publication, I've had help from just one person.

I: Right, that's great, thanks. Now you mentioned you wrote with a student and I wondered if collaborative writing has ever been a key part of what you do?

JR: No. The kind of collaborative writing I've done is really the sort of writing where I've turned what the other person wanted to say into an article. The collaborative bit has usually been me turning something into an article, which the other person has given feedback on and expressed their satisfaction or not with it, and we polished it together.

I: Yeah.

JR: Certainly the dissertation that I turned into an article I did most of that writing. So it's the other person's content, if you like, but I'm not very good at tracking changes.

I've written with David Reedy, we've written books together, but we've talked through the ideas, talked about how to structure it, I've written it, he's had it and amended with written suggestions on hard copy for me to rewrite. I find that our styles of writing are so different that I don't know how it would be coherent otherwise. But the collaboration is usually about our ideas coming together.

I: Yes.

JR: Talking them through, structuring them, talking about an outline, me having a first go at it, back to the other person to see if they're comfortable with it or if I haven't got it quite as they would like, and then sometimes we argue about it, and then another draft or three will come out of it. But it's that kind of process, and it's quite different from writing on your own.

I: Now I know that you've been a Head of School and you've had many management responsibilities, so how have you kept writing as a major part of your life here?

JR: It hasn't been easy. I suppose there was a period over the last three years of being Head of School where life was just so 24/7 I didn't do very much writing. I had one edited book and two articles that came out in that period.

I actually think it's been about having things to say. I think it has to be something that you think, oh, yes, I must sit down and do that. And to feel that you've got a contribution to make. I think the very worst thing is to say to people, you must write, and they've got nothing to say. They don't see the point of it. I think it is only driven by the motivation of something out there that you want to say to people that you think is helpful at a particular moment in the education debate, that you can add, can make a contribution to people's understanding about a particular aspect, that you want to sit down and write.

I also think it's facilitative if you've got a partner who has an intellectual life. There is no conflict if you want to be doing something, that it is a reasonable way to behave. So that when we are away in Crete for instance, to have four, five hours a day when I want to be working on some writing, that is perfectly acceptable and compatible with the other person's way of life.

Because writing is about having chunks of quality time to think about it and spend doing it. You can't write in a hurried half-hour here and there. I think that if you're prepared to do that when you're perhaps, supposedly on vacation [*laughs*] in some strange and quite sad way, I think that's how you keep writing going, even though you've got a busy and responsible job when you're in the Institute of Education. So it's this kind of life that is facilitative and has worked for me. I can't imagine being in a situation where my approach to work is seen as unreasonable or as workaholic.

I: Yeah, yes. Now you've mentioned being at home and the importance of being able to write uninterrupted at home: any gender issues emerging?

JR: Gender issues? Now that's interesting. I mean, I think when I'm on a roll with it and I've got a book that I'm trying to finish, I think it's sustaining it; certainly as you get started on it I think you need some considerable amount of time. And people all work in different ways. For me, the best thing to do is just to get up in the morning and go to my computer and have a good solid chunk of time, perhaps breaking off for a coffee or breakfast or something. What doesn't work is, you get up, you clean the house, you make the beds, you do all that and then at 11 o'clock you sit down, you try to write. It's really, really hard. And you look longingly at the ironing basket as a diversionary activity!

I: Yes.

JR: I can't write for very long. I mean four, five hours is perhaps all I manage in a day. With a break. And by midday, one o'clock I've had enough for a day and then I will do the chores. Have some lunch, and potter in the garden or something. My working day is like that and I'm hopeless in the evening. I couldn't possibly work through an evening. So if I'm going to work, I try to plan the day that is compatible with somebody else who might be working too. But that's talking about being in a situation where you're free to do that. When I was Head of School I suppose the only way to write was perhaps to have a Sunday at it. You know, you're in the Institute all week Monday to Friday, perhaps Saturday you have a day when you're catching up with yourself in terms of domestic chores, shopping, whatever, so that you get up early on a Sunday morning and have a go and you may get something done, just to keep the momentum up for something you're writing. Perhaps you take a day in the week too. I certainly could never write here at the Institute.

I: *So you always write at home or elsewhere.*

JR: Yes. Yes, I've never had a chance, I don't think, to come to my room at the Institute and get on with something, to have that peace and sort of quality of thinking time, not in the past few years anyway.

I: *Thank you. What about the satisfactions?*

JR: Oh, the satisfactions. I think the most extraordinary thing about writing is, sometimes it goes well and sometimes it's dreadful. It's really difficult and painful and you get very tired doing it and it doesn't seem to really come together well. But I think it's how the writers Bereiter and Scardamalia comment about writing being knowledge-transforming that is important. You know, the two levels: knowledge-telling and knowledge-transforming writing. I think what happens sometimes, at its best, is that as you write you realise that you are organising your thought in a way that is literally transforming it. So that your thinking goes up another whole level. That's really the best kind of writing. It all straightens out in your head as you write. And you realise that you're actually making new ideas for yourself, new theories and perhaps for others too. So I suppose that's the very deepest satisfaction.

I think there's a sort of 'out-of-body' experience

sometimes when you get through the post, suddenly, an article that's been published and you get the proof and you say, 'That's good, oh! did I write that?' And that is quite satisfying. But that's instrumental in a way, isn't it? I think the real true satisfaction, as I say, is being able to develop your thinking through your writing and then perhaps be able to say things in a way that is helpful to other people. You think you're getting there, explaining something that's really quite difficult, that'll make a difference, and people'll think, 'Oh yes, that's what it's all about, OK.'

And that will affect the way I work with those little kids, or that'll affect my provision and the way I plan to offer those learning opportunities. Because it's this or it's this or it's this. And if you are able, because you've had experience in both worlds, the research world, getting into the theory at a deep level that we have the luxury of doing in our university, and then making connections with classroom practice. Those kinds of connections and synergies that you can make new theory out of, if you like, for the practitioners. That's satisfying.

I: *Yes, because it's helping the teachers.*

JR: It's helping to make the theory–practice link clear. As you're writing you have these 'Eureka' moments, this is the way to do it, this is what should be going on and this is how I can explain it and help people. And make a contribution to understanding in the field.

I: *Yeah. Lovely. And the kinds of writing you most enjoy, is there anything else you want to say about that?*

JR: I think the kind of writing I genuinely enjoy is the writing for the wider readership. I think I'm probably not in the pure research milieu. I think it is much more the books that'll fall into beginning teachers' hands and practising teachers' hands. They're quite academic books, but they're not written in that particular genre for research journal articles.

I: *So accessible for teachers?*

JR: I think so, yes. But with a good spattering of

research evidence in them, so you're not dumbing it down for practitioners at all. But [you write] with [a] sense of the client group that's going to make use of it.

I: Mm, yes.

JR: I think there is a point to it. For me, that's the sort of writing I enjoy the most. And I think the more you do it, the more you can see angles, you could write another article or another professional magazine article, or whatever, out of it. It seems to be endless once you're really into something. You don't have to dredge up ideas, they just go on and on once you get going. And you've got the energy and the time to do it, really. The mental energy, I mean.

I: Yeah. So what does your writing say about you?

JR: Oh goodness. [*Pause*] I think probably it is really about a commitment. There was a House of Commons Select Committee on the teaching of early reading recently. And one MP said it is literally rocket science how five-, six-, seven-year-olds learn to read and write. And it is literally rocket science what we know goes on in the brain. So we know that it is very complicated. And I have got a kind of missionary zeal that you can explain it to primary teachers in a way that doesn't confuse them and make them feel, 'Oh this is going to be so difficult, I couldn't possibly do that.' But if you have these insights, your teaching will be extraordinary. If you can take on board the science of what's going on in those individuals' brains in order for these little kids to be able to read and you build that into the learning opportunities you're offering the children, they will make the most phenomenal progress. We know it's difficult, but once you've got your head around it you can do it. And then it just becomes part of the way you are as a teacher.

So I suppose that's what the best of my books say. It's trying to say to teachers, 'Read this stuff, get your head around it, then relax and enjoy teaching.'

I: Good, that's lovely, thank you. And how do you go about writing? How do you prepare for the writing event?

JR: Well, I definitely need to do a handwritten outline, just like you would with an essay. I suppose those kinds of habits continue, that I sit down and I structure an article or a chapter with outline headings.

I read. I read other people's work and that gets me thinking, and I may then have another restructure, and think, 'I haven't got that quite right.' So I do another outline, which I have beside the computer on the table. And then I start and I sometimes have to alter the outline as I'm writing but it starts to structure my thought processes. And then I just have to start doing the writing. I always reread what I've written the day before and that gets me into it afresh. And sometimes do some polishing as I'm doing that, perhaps the first hour is doing that to get my head around it again.

Sometimes overnight. If you're lucky enough to have a spell of extended time, which is my very best time to write, a month or so. And if I can write day after day after day, it starts to come together, because there is theory about the importance of gestation in the creative process. As you're sleeping and you're living with ideas, they become more and more refined so that it becomes easier and easier as you sit down at the computer to have another attempt at something. Some days the ideas will just flow one after the other and it comes together well. Some days it's like wading through treacle, it's really, really hard. And I don't know the answer to that. I mean, I think the honest truth is you just have to stick at it and keep going, even when it's hard. It doesn't help if you keep leaving it. And sometimes I get on with another bit. If a bit's really sticky you think you'll go back to it. But usually I find you have to get through that pain barrier and it comes together later.

I: And you're still experiencing some difficult days, even though you've been writing for such a long time?

JR: Oh yes. Depending on whether it's a topic I'm really fond of, or I'm into something new that I'm finding difficult, or I feel I've got to rework something. Oh yes, I think we all have days when we feel wonderful and the words fly out of your fingers as you type, that kind of feeling, and some days it's really hard. You can be tired or whatever. Yes, I don't know many people who find it extraordinarily easy. I think there is a pain barrier. But I think the more you get into it, the easier it is. And you actually know when you go back and read a chunk in hard copy, finally you think you've finished a chapter or an article and you print it off in hard copy and you read it, which is a different experience from reading it on the screen and polishing, is that sometimes some bits read well and you're pleased with it, and some bits are pedestrian. And you know those are the sections you had trouble with.

I: Yes.

JR: So you have to go back and rework it to smoothly flow between ideas. And that's where somebody else reading it can help. And that person says, 'Yes, you're right, that's a terrible paragraph, you have to rework that. It doesn't flow at all, you're not expressing those ideas well.'

I: Yes. So many drafts.

JR: Oh yes, I would say many drafts if it's going to be any good.

I: Yeah. OK, so what have you learned about the process of writing?

JR: Well, it's very individual. I think that's why it's so hard to help people who are having trouble. Because I think how we all tackle it, I'm sure there are issues that chime with your experience. Some people say, 'Oh, it's not a bit like that for me.' It's an idiosyncratic process. But there are a few general principles that can help other people. And I think it's preparing thoroughly in your head, that you've thought through what you want to say, you've done enough background reading, you've got ideas that you're collating that have fed your view of the content. And the next big step is just being brave enough to get on and write it. And reworking it in a way that is going to refine it, develop the ideas, and then the final draft requires more polishing.

I: Yes. Perhaps here it might be useful for you to say something now that you told me earlier about the museum that you looked at with the stages of writing.

JR: Yes, before we started this interview I was talking about the Museum of Children's Literature in Newcastle and I saw a programme on BBC2, and a children's author and poet, Michael Rosen, had gone in and was looking at what are really early drafts of some of the most famous children's books. There was JK Rowling's first Harry Potter book, there were various Philip Pullman stories and they are displayed for people. And to see how authors, very famous experienced authors, struggle through the early stages of creating a piece of writing. And I use the word 'creating' because I think the kind of writing they're doing is rather different from academic writing. But nevertheless, all of them go through some stages that are common, I think, to both kinds of writing, because you can see the generation of ideas that have come about through hard thinking and some research. They usually have done quite deep research into writing a novel, even for a children's novel. And then they have the early jottings that would be the equivalent of my outline, what's going to happen in a chapter. Some of them with doodles, some of them with lots of crossings out as they're really thinking hard. And then the next stage is where they actually start to write their stories and then there's some cutting and pasting and re-ordering and they talk rather interestingly about characters taking over in their stories. And that I think is the fiction equivalent of knowledge-transforming writing. The way we think, our ideas and the kinds of ideas we're trying to express, which start to change as we write and become more developed and more refined, so that the thinking changes a gear or two.

So I think writers of fiction have a similar transformative experience as they write. And they talk about, 'I had no idea when I started out on this story that the character was going to end up doing this.' And I think that that is something to do with the creative process, that is analogous or synonymous, the two distinct genres of writing share some common principles.

I: Yes, that's fascinating.

JR: Yes, it is. And I think painters will say something similar when they're making a painting. That they have an idea when they start, a composition, but very often as they're making those marks, things change and they develop a painting, sometimes for the worse and they're not pleased with it so it gets scrunched up, but sometimes it develops into another level that they had no idea of when they started. Those things are connected with the creative process, although academic writing is creative in a different way.

I: Yeah, thank you very much for that. You mentioned earlier about writing for publication. Is there anything different that you've learned about writing for publication?

JR: Well in the last ten years, since finishing my PhD, writing articles and books, chapters for other people's books, I think for publication you have to have a very strong sense of audience and the exact style which you are going to adopt. As I said, my book that was written from the PhD thesis was a complete rewrite. You don't use any sections that were written for the PhD, even the literature review. It's a completely different genre. So you start again as you're writing for a different audience. You can tell some books that are based on PhD theses and the authors haven't done that, and you can tell. And there are the kinds of articles that you write for a professional magazine and it's different again for a more populist magazine. So it's about that sense of audience, and I think switching between those different genres is quite difficult, and you only get good at that with practice and by submitting articles. You get feedback from various editors, or again the long-suffering reader of your work, as to how successful you are. That would be my advice to young academics coming here: you can only do it by looking at how other people have managed it. The complementary process, just as with children, of reading and writing, is exactly the same for adults. It's reading a lot. And pick up other people's books, think, 'Oh goodness, she writes so beautifully. How is that?' It's usually the lighter touch.

I: Yeah.

JR: In fact, some people are able to express very complex ideas simply. They don't need to rely heavily on jargon. And you think, 'Oh, that's beautiful.' I've a colleague who writes simply beautifully and I often

pick up her books and just read a paragraph or two and it gets me into thinking stylistically how I should be approaching something.

I: Yes.

JR: So I think it's about being open-minded as you read and analytical of style, and you think about your reader. If you can actually envisage who's going to pick a book up and read it, it helps you to do those difficult things of crossing the different genre.

I: Yes. Do you think if you weren't here at the Institute you would still write?

JR: I don't think I could write fiction. I don't think I have a mind that works like that, unfortunately. I'd love to be able to, and I love children's books and I read children's books and I read poetry, but I know that I'm not that sort of able creative person. But I think I will go on writing, as long as I've got something to say. It comes back to my very first point – as long as I've got some fresh angle on something or something that I've researched or thought about that I think can make a contribution, I will go on writing, because I think it has been a long-honed skill of mine. It takes a long time to develop as a writer and while you've got publishers who ring you up and say, 'What about such and such', then you know you're probably still OK. I think there's a danger of going on and recycling what Margaret Meek again used to call SOS: 'same old stuff'. Then I think, 'No, I've said it now, I'll leave it to others.' But if I've got a contribution to make and I'm thinking about things in an interesting and informed way, and informed by current debates, then I'm happy to do that and I find it very gratifying.

I: Lovely. Anything else?

JR: No, just thank you very much for giving me this opportunity.

I: Thank you very much indeed.

Chris Watkins

I: *How long have you been at the Institute?*

CW: Thirty years. [*Laughs*] It's completely mad, isn't it? In various guises – I was a student, a part-time lecturer, a course leader, a senior tutor for INSET, a head of an academic group, another course leader, and now I'm a senior consultant.

I: *Great. And I want to talk to you about writing, and I'd be very interested to hear your responses because I know of your writing and have written with you, which has been a great experience. But perhaps you could tell me if you've one piece of writing that you're particularly pleased with.*

CW: That's difficult. I saw that question on your list and I didn't immediately alight on one. I suppose it's because I don't think of the writing in that kind of way. I think of various different sorts of pieces with pleasure and I remember different pleasures from a number of them. Like the ATL [Association of Teachers and Lecturers] one.

I: *That's* Learning: A sense-maker's guide *(2003)?*

CW: I got pleasure from that because it was concise and hit the mark at the right time. I've been pleased with the book *Classrooms as Learning Communities* (2005). Not because I really know what's in it any more – got no idea what's in that book – but just because of how well people have responded to it, how much it sold. And now the Hong Kong government has put a copy into every school.

I: Right.

CW: And yet, I can remember getting pleasure from the book *School Discipline* (1987) that I wrote with my partner Patsy Wagner. The only bit of feedback we ever got from that was one person wrote a letter, she was a head of year in a school and she said that she kept the book by her bedside. And you think it's not what you do it for, but ... So there's all sorts of different appreciations that you get from different things, I think. So I haven't got a best, no.

And then there's that piece about feedback between teachers, the one that you know people's reaction to often more than I do.

I: Yes, absolutely.

CW: Some of your students have said, what?

I: It's really made a difference to their lives. So, is that what pleases you most, the fact that people are reading it, taking note of it and that that is changing their practice?

CW: Yes. That sort of writing I do, that's the real reason for doing it. And that applies to all of those research reviews, the one we did on effective learning, it's exactly what one wants to have happen and it's happened so, you know, you can't ask for better than that I think.

I: OK, fine. Now we've put another question in here which is to do with anything you're not so pleased with.

CW: Feelings of displeasure arise not so much about my experience of writing as my experience of publishing. I mean, like the mentoring pack and the tutoring pack that I did with different people in the Nineties. They were bloody good, still great content, and they got nowhere because of the publishers. I'm sure if I did look over almost any of the texts I've created either alone or with somebody else, there

would be bits of them that I'd think, 'Oh no, don't like that', but I haven't got a particular candidate at the moment. If I looked back at my writing of about 15 years ago, I'd think it was weak and I'd be a bit embarrassed and those sorts of things but then ... it's all right.

I: It's 'cause you've moved on so much.

CW: Mmm.

I: So what was it about the publishers that made that situation difficult?

CW: They didn't market the book. There were delays and they just did nothing with it and then they gave up on them. I think that they sold about a hundred each, which is a bit sickening really.

I: OK. Perhaps we could move on to thinking about what's helped you with your writing?

CW: Just talking about it with colleagues, being angry about things, knowing that you want to communicate something and having the kind of links that we have through our course contacts to know that there are things that people want to know about. You've got already a bit of an idea that there's an audience out there, so if you've got something you want to say and a sense that there's an audience that would, might be interested if they came across it, that's the thing that helps me most. Then once you feel as sure as you can, which is never, from about 85 per cent, that that's the case, then the thing that helps is playing with it and seeing what happens when, seeing what emerges as, as you try. And getting feedback. I remember when I wrote a booklet on *Managing Classroom Behaviour* (1997) for the Association of Teachers and Lecturers and one thing that really really, really helped there I haven't ever had since. I sent a draft off to ATL and they sent the draft to the members of the Publications Committee for them to read and then got them all to have a conference call on the phone. They sent me a tape of their conference call. So without me being involved you could hear people talking about your draft and get a very, very good idea of what was working and what wasn't and what could be improved and so on. That helps.

Talking with students about their writing helps. One of my doctoral students came up with a neat device, WIRMI. 'WIRMI' stands for 'What I Really Mean Is'. I had an example recently, while I was using the research review I wrote on classrooms as learning communities, and somebody said, 'I don't really understand what this bit's about.' And I looked at it and it was just an awful bit of writing, the paragraph needed a WIRMI.

Talking, thinking, having something to say, those are some of the main things that help my writing. I was also thinking of never having a particular kind of endpoint in mind and just trying to stretch.

I: Yes.

CW: You have to work at it, it doesn't emerge.

I: Yes. A number of times I've mentioned to you that what I like about your writing is that light touch. It's about engaging with the reader in a way that seems so fresh and conversational rather than something that's been written and has come about through a struggle, and I'm sure there are times when you do struggle, but it doesn't come out at all like that. It comes out as if you're just talking to somebody, which I think's really great. Do you notice that for yourself?

CW: Yes. I mean there are phrases that resonate with that. There's that Robin Fogarty phrase which is 'inking the thinking'. That's what writing is, it's inking the thinking. It's not the stuff I dislike, whether it's written or spoken, which is statement-making. And that's where, of course, I think we've mentioned this with each other before, I love some of Bruner's writing, where he's so explicit in the written form. That's what he's doing, he's taking an idea for a walk and wanting to do that with somebody. And I suppose to some readers that would come across as fresh or engaging. I don't imagine all, because there are some people who are frustrated with it, they want statement-like writing. It's probably Derrida that said there's no resident meaning in texts, there's only meaning in the act of writing and in the act of reading something.

I: Yeah, yes.

CW: And so I'm happy to try and be explicit about the meaning-making in the act of writing.

I: Yeah. I think that's important in what you say about some people wanting statements, which I suppose reflects their view of the learning process, whereas with you it's much more invitational, it's much more: 'Well, what do you think?' – you know, what does this idea do for you, which I guess reflects the co-constructive model where you're wanting to have that dialogue with someone in a way that you would have if you were in conversation with them.

CW: Yeah, I mean having conversations or running courses and those sorts of things, the thing that I am looking for is that people say, 'Oh, that was thought-provoking.' Lots of other things will follow as a result. And so I want the same pattern through writing. I want it to be thought-provoking and image-making and those sorts of things, therefore it's got to be constructivist. And what are the devices that we use to try and make one's writing engage the thinking of the reader? Yeah, those are the sorts of things that I like.

I: So do you have that consciously in your head as you're writing or is now that part of the writing that you do almost automatically?

CW: No, it's not automatic. I think of writing for the experience of the reader, right, and you think, 'Well what do I want to do with and for the reader through this? What do I want to take them through, in what order and how will it engage them?' So I can sometimes think about that at the start, but normally what happens is I'll pile into something and then have to check, just say, 'Hang on is this really thought-provoking?'

I: Right, yeah. So does that reflect the kind of shift from teaching to learning we've talked about such a lot? Is it to do with the shift from what the writer wants to say to what the experience for the reader might be?

CW: It's trying to work out how, if at all, you can get

them engaged in what you want to say. But not in a closed sense, but in an emergent sense.

I: Yeah, great.

CW: Some things I've written aren't like that, like that long version of the research review on classrooms as learning communities that came out in the *London Review of Education*. I thought I'd get a publication out of it.

I: That's for a different purpose?

CW: Yeah.

I: Yeah, OK. Now I know you have had huge teaching commitments, but I know that you have written a lot lately. So how do you manage to keep the writing going alongside all the other things you're involved in?

CW: With difficulty, really. I spend holidays on it and I try my best to work with colleagues so that they keep each other's mileposts for each other. I see writing more and more as a taken-for-granted thing about what I do. It's not an extra thing. And I can imagine, if I could think back 20 years ago, it would have been seen as an extra. 'Oh god I've got to write something.' It doesn't feel like that now.

I: When do you think that changed?

CW: About 15 years ago.

I: And was there any particular reason for that?

CW: I don't think so. It's getting to the point of feeling more the things that we've been saying in this conversation. Like feeling more (a) I've got something to say, and (b) I want to, I want to experiment with how to say it. Getting an Apple Mac to really, really work for you and all of those sorts of things.

I: At this point one or two other people who've talked with us have said something about the RAE. I wondered if you had any view about that, in terms of how it's helped or hindered your writing.

CW: I've tried not to let the RAE influence my writing, because I know that for me and probably for a lot of other people too, it would reduce the motivation rather than increase it. I mean, you can't write for another set of agendas. That would actually get in the way. And I can modify something, adapt something, turn it out so that it does fit more with the agendas that are going on in that, like recently when they said the criterion for inclusion in RAE is that you provide stuff for other researchers. So I thought, 'OK, I'll do that, I'll turn something into RAE. I've got a journal article in *BERJ*' – those sorts of things. But interestingly that was just making sure I didn't get driven by the RAE thing, but just say, 'OK, well, I'll play that game.'

I: Right.

CW: Because the *BERJ* article really fits what I've been saying about writing anyway. It's something I want to say, about schools and violence, and I think the right people wanted to read that. And funnily enough, on that RAE stuff, I found that the *Journal of the Learning Sciences* was absolutely top of the impact scores, right? So I thought, 'All right then, I'm going to write an article for them.' [*Laughs*] Just to kind of turn it on its head, you know.

I: Yeah, yeah.

CW: So I'm going to do a paper this summer on enhancing meta-cognition from a narrative perspective. I think, 'Well, all right, I'll try and get that in that journal then.' It won't be in this RAE, you know that, but that's OK.

I: That's great, thanks. Now I feel we've already touched on this next theme about satisfactions you get from writing, but is there anything else that you wanted to add on that specifically?

CW: I don't know whether it's a satisfaction, it's a sense of … continuing challenge. The writing, especially in the way that we've been talking about it, it's something where you're continually stretching your boundaries, and that's not a satisfaction in a major sense, but it is a motivation.

I: *Yeah, yeah. And I know you've spoken a lot about how writing doesn't get any easier.*

CW: Yeah, yeah. There are links to that.

I: *About each time wanting something to challenge you in a different way or for …*

CW: Or for a particular purpose, I mean a purpose has to emerge first. And then you realise, 'Oh blimey, I've set myself a purpose which is going to be difficult.' Which is fine, I like that.

I: *Right, yeah.*

CW: I suppose other feelings too. I had an interesting one the other day. I was in a meeting in Ealing and someone said, 'I'm going to quote from Chris's book, you know what …'. And it's just fascinating to hear. In a way that was not about me, it was obviously about her, why she'd just chosen a few sentences, which was about a phrase 'the devil's in the detail'. You know, we often say that, but in fact, by the same token, the dream is in the detail. And they got off on that. I thought, 'Wonderful, that felt great.' That sort of satisfaction, I mean you don't know it very much because you never get much feedback on books, but just getting a nice clear example there that somebody takes off on their own journey with something you just popped into a text. It's nice.

I: *Yeah.*

CW: And you get some sense of that sometimes with the written work from our Masters students, but they're doing it for assessment so it's a bit different.

I: *Yeah. OK. I suppose the kinds of writing you most enjoy has been covered a bit earlier. Is there anything else you wanted to say about that?*

CW: I suppose it has, although I don't know what the kind is in a way. It's stuff that's professionally relevant, that gives people a number of things, actually. A bit of a vision, a bit of evidence and a bit of a next step on the journey. Those three all together are the sorts of writing that I like the most. And I suppose if I thought

about some of the bits of writing that I've done for other purposes, they may not have all of those three going so clearly in them.

I: *And what about the next theme, which is to do with what your writing says about you?*

CW: Ah. Nothing. [*Laughs*] I don't know. Well, it says that I'm somebody who's interested in teaching and classrooms and people and learning. It says I'm choosing to spend my time writing about those sorts of things. And I suppose it says something about my idea of knowledge, my idea of people and how those ideas might come through in a funny thing called a text. It doesn't say as clearly what I want it to say about an improvement or an improved situation. I remember Peter Mortimore giving me feedback on that Learning Enhances Performance research review. That was a bit of a catalogue in a way. I don't mind that too much, but he said, 'There's not enough of you in it.'

I: *Oh, did he say that?*

CW: Which is kind of the interesting thing.

I: *And did you know what he meant by that?*

CW: Not exactly, no, but I got the point. It was about the writing and it was a bit too late to change it in a major fashion because of the pressing deadline. But, yeah. So I think that that's interesting because your writing should say what your vision is, what your hopes are, what your aspirations for the world are, the small bit of the world that you're interested in. And when I come across writing that does that, I'm so glad that it does, I'm so much with it, whether I agree with the content or not doesn't matter.

I: *Yeah. So do you think you're getting more explicit about making your vision known in the writing?*

CW: A bit, yes. Yes, I'll probably carry on doing more of that. Yes, I'm starting to do that in the piece on narrative that I'm doing at the moment. In fact, we did it a little bit in the chapter that Patsy and I did on narrative work, because it was just saying this is not just an arid idea, this is something that makes your world run in the way you want the world to run. So making that more explicit is a trend, a development.

I: OK. Now about the process of writing. How do you go about it?

CW: I read a lot. That's one of the things. And I don't know why that comes to mind first, but I know that the sorts of things I write don't get very far unless I'm also reading around at the same time. And then I'll get the jumble and I'll talk to somebody about it and the purpose will emerge first. Even if you're writing a chapter in a book, if I can get that clear for myself, but not as clear as a plan but a lived purpose. If I've got going from the completion of the sentence: 'The purpose of this chapter is' then I think, 'OK, how am I going to achieve it?'

And then I use all sorts of things. I go to my computer and look through a thousand files and see if I've got anything on it already. Then I'll get off the computer because it's basically a bad instrument for writing. So I go back to pieces of paper and scribble. And the thing will slowly take shape and change shape all the time. That's one of the things. I get a bit of a meta-structure. If I don't have that, then the structure will change quite a bit. I remember when ... even writing with other people like the tutoring pack, which was completely restructured almost at the end. So I don't do this thing which you get in low-level advice about writing, which is [*pompous voice*] 'Start off with a structure and a plan' and that sort of stuff. You get put off writing, I think. Most of that sort of advice doesn't work. So ... I'm just kind of stewing, I think. Creating a stew, yes.

I: [Laughs] Which brings us nicely to what you've learned. What have you learned about the process of writing?

CW: That reminds me of that lovely story about Harold Rosen, which you've no doubt heard me tell before, where I met him in the Lawton room one morning and he said he was having a dreadful morning because he sat in front of a blank piece of paper all morning. I thought, 'Great, a professor of literature can do that.' I can do it too! So I was very

glad to learn that early on, I was very glad to learn reasonably early that perfection will ruin you and that, when Harold Heller said to me, if it's about 85 per cent right, then get it out there.

I: [Laughs]

CW: So those sorts of things have helped. In terms of the detail of the process, I don't think I see much detail in the process. So many things go on in the stewing: putting things together, trying out phrases, talking with people, letting it waltz all around, I think. Yeah. So I haven't got a very clear view of what the process of writing is actually. Because it's just another part of doing what I do. I don't have a routine or a regularity or those sorts of things.

I: And what have you learned about writing for publication?

CW: God. [*Laughs*] That it can be a big pain in the neck, but that it's the major purpose for doing it anyway. That publishers are a creaky set of funny organisations and academics attribute too much to them, talk about different publishers as though there is some coherence or sense about them and there's not. They are a bunch of people making money by shovelling paper. I remember that with my first book, the story of the Shelley Potteries (1980). When I went for the first time into a publisher's office I thought, 'Wow, this is a scrappy old set up.' [*Laughs*] They were in one of those Georgian terraces and all they had was a few photocopiers and that made me think, 'Of course, they haven't got any resource themselves. Writers are their resource.' They don't act as though that's the case. They act as if they're the powerful ones. And that's a great shame. Because it puts people off writing that should be writing. Just talk to some of our students, grown-up teachers about writing for publication – they'll tell you how mystical they think it must be.

Same with writing for publication in academic journals. People go and mystify that massively. Try and give each other advice on how to do it, to crack it, what is a random process. As you know very well, when you get feedback on a draft that you've sent, the quality of feedback is abysmal. And it's people peddling their own little ideas. So to dress it up as it is dressed up in many of the ways is sad because it puts people off. So I suppose I've learned about, a bit about that. At the same time I've learned that if you are writing for publishers then you treat it as a game, but play the game well. I get a little bit of satisfaction about people like senior editors saying, 'Gosh, this is the best quality manuscript I've ever seen, you know, everything is in place.' Just to get them off your back really.

I: [Laughs]

CW: But it feels worth doing. Am I on the sort of theme that you were interested in?

I: Yes. One of the reasons for putting this publication together is to uncover what experienced writers have learned. These ideas are going to be extremely useful to those reading the publication – it's creaky, it's messy, it's random, but don't be put off and don't let other people put you off by the mystique. I think what you've said is going to be extremely helpful.

CW: Yes. And it's those things I've focused on which are potentially the disempowering bit in people's experience. That reminds me of something that I remember 25, 30 years ago, in one of Carl Rogers' books where he says to his graduate students, 'Well, look, if you're not going to write, who is?'

I: Yes.

CW: So that helps you think, 'Oh, yes, I am in one of these deeply privileged positions at university where you're meant to be doing some thinking, so if you don't do it, who can?'

I: Yeah. But it's interesting, it feels like there's so much in the structure that is set up to disempower.

CW: Yeah, the structure, the pressure and the culture, they'll disempower people and you see around us every day the results of that, which is deeply tedious writing. You put some of the writing that we might call 'academic' in front of professionals like teachers and they despair of it.

I: Yeah.

CW: And of course part of that is the very thing that you're interested to do, which is to have them examine texts that are coming from a different bit of a life, world. But at the same time some of it is badly written. *[Laughs]*

I: Yeah.

CW: That paper on conceptions of learning ...

I: Yeah ...

CW: ... we really had a good discussion last time about the balance between the form of language and a language game that they were used to versus it being badly written. *[Laughs]*

I: Yeah. [Laughs]

CW: Happy days.

I: So would you be a writer if you weren't here? You mentioned the Shelley Potteries book; are there other things that you write?

CW: Yeah, I mean that was a very lucky break because, in terms of some of the things that I now understand about my writing and learning, that was a story of a factory and a company and its wares, and you knew people wanted to hear it. It didn't feel difficult. Nobody in my family had ever done those sorts of things.

And at the moment I'm playing with the idea of a book on reflections on learning how to ride (horse riding). Now that will include academic bits.

I don't particularly write a lot outside, no, if that's what your question is. But looking back at this question, if I wasn't at the Institute, do you think I would still write, yes. And I'd write academic stuff, too.

I: OK. Well, thank you very much, it's been absolutely fascinating.

CW: Thank you.

Geoff Whitty

I: *First of all, some biographical questions: so if you could tell me what your role is and how long you've been here at the Institute?*

GW: Well, my current role at the Institute is as Director, a post I've held for the last five-and-a-half years. But I've actually been on the staff of the Institute since 1992, when I came in as the Karl Mannheim Professor of Sociology of Education.

I: *We'd like to start off by asking about what writing you're pleased with and if there's a piece of writing or a couple of pieces that stand out as ones that you're particularly pleased with?*

GW: Well, I suppose I'm pleased in different ways

with different pieces of writing so I actually find that a very difficult question. I suppose my book *Sociology and School Knowledge* (1985) is the piece of writing I feel was most important in bringing my ideas together. It was written about ten years into my academic career and is actually based on a series of writings that I'd done over that time – some based on empirical research, some political pieces, some theoretical pieces. And I used the book to try and make sense of what I had done up to that point. It brought together theory, research and politics in the curriculum field. The subtitle was *Curriculum theory, research and politics.* Although it was actually a book that got rather mixed reviews, it was satisfying for me because it allowed me to bring different parts of my life together in a relatively coherent way. And then nearly 20 years later I did the same thing with *Making Sense of Education Policy* (2002). Having moved from the curriculum field to the policy field, I'm starting to make sense of my life, both my academic life and my policy intervention life, in that book. So those two I think are satisfying because they were synoptic and holistic.

A piece of work that I feel most academically pleased with was *Devolution and Choice in Education* (1998), which I wrote with Sally Power and David Halpin. That grew out of a paper that I did for the American journal, *Review of Research in Education*, where I was asked to look at all the work on the effects of choice and school autonomy and try and say what was the most plausible conclusion from all that contradictory research.

I: Yeah.

GW: And it was really hard work even identifying and reading all the stuff, let alone then writing about it. But I thought that was an exercise that was worth doing. The book is quite influential, framing not only the academic debate, but also to some extent the policy debate. Not in the UK, where government by and large [*laughs*] ignored it at the time. At least it's part of the current debate; for example, with the recent schools White Paper it has got in indirectly because it informed the work I've recently done for the Education and Skills Select Committee as it responded to the government's proposals.

I: Right, yes.

GW: What I haven't mentioned is my more empirical work, other books like *The State and Private Education* (1989) [and] *Specialisation and Choice in Urban Education* (1993), which are basically reports of empirical studies. And they're satisfying in a different way. They are much more grounded and make less claims.

I: Anything that you're not that pleased with?

GW: Probably what I've done is denied them. [*Laughs*]

I: Put them out of your head. [Laughs]

GW: I would say the things that I've mentioned as being most pleased with in some respects, I'm not pleased with in other respects. I mean *Sociology and School Knowledge* had mixed reviews and some of the criticism was based on the fact that I had ignored other people's work. And although that book was in a sense a personal position statement and, therefore, that particular criticism I don't think was entirely justified, it is important to pay attention to the whole field. I tried to do that with *Devolution and Choice*, to see all sides of the argument. So you learn from what you do. In terms of pieces of work that I'm not happy about, they tend not to be the things that appear in the books, they tend to be papers where you've done them hurriedly. I've probably written about 20 papers that I wish I hadn't published.

I: [Laughs]

GW: [*Laughs*] But that's out of a couple of hundred. There's a few I'd like to take my name off.

I: Right, yeah. OK, so what's helped with your writing?

GW: Well, one of the things about my writing is that most of it is collaborative. I find that working with other people is helpful, not because they do all the work, but because I feel the responsibility to colleagues to put in the effort myself and comment on what they're doing, respond to their concerns. I prefer writing as a social activity rather than an individual activity.

What's helped me in my individual writing – pressure and deadlines, [*laughs*] the RAE, all those things which are helpful in a masochistic way. But I do enjoy working with other people.

I: That's great. You've talked about the RAE and other pressures but, given your role as Director and all the management responsibilities you have, how do you keep writing as a major part of your life?

GW: Well, I think I have to say that writing in the last year or so hasn't really happened.

I: *Right.*

GW: I think it's only really at this point in my life that I am not such an active researcher. All the time that I was a lecturer, Head of Policy Studies and Dean of Research and in my first couple of years as Director, I would have described myself as an active researcher. And it was always possible to do it. Sometimes in unsocial hours – although throughout those jobs I did try and keep a day each week for writing. Which I lost more often than I kept, but the mere fact of having it there was both an aspiration and a signal to colleagues …

I: *Sure.*

GW: … that that part of my week ought to be writing, even if it wasn't. But really, to be honest, the last couple of years, running an Institute that has doubled in size since I've been Director has become a full-time managerial job. Whether it's age or just the sheer pressure, I am too tired to be up at three o'clock in the morning writing.

I: *Yes. So how do you feel about that, not being an active writer, an active researcher?*

GW: I feel that part of my job is encouraging other people to be active researchers and I feel reasonably relaxed about that. Because obviously there's a huge amount of research and writing going on in the Institute …

I: *Sure.*

GW: … and therefore you can get a degree of vicarious satisfaction from other people's success. I have to say that it was important to me that *Education and the Middle Class* (2003) won the Society for Educational Studies Book Prize. It made me feel 'Yes, I can still do it' …

I: *Yeah.*

GW: … and therefore I can go back to doing it, if I move into something else. It's not such a problem. In other words, I don't feel that my career has just gone downhill.

I: *[Laughs]*

GW: I feel I'm just doing something else right now.

I: *Doing something else, and that you can go back to it. Yeah. That's nice because when you mention the prize, it brings me onto the next question about the different sorts of satisfactions you get from writing.*

GW: There's an awful lot of pain in writing and therefore when you mention writing, satisfaction's not necessarily the first thing one thinks about. The actual process of writing I find hugely difficult and hugely painful. Scary, you know, when I'm in the middle of something, I think, 'I don't know where this is going' and 'It's not working out.' But I'm someone who writes myself into positions rather than sits down always knowing where I'm going.

But the satisfaction comes when you break through that and you've got to the point, yes, that worked. So it's almost a satisfaction of the pain stopping.

I: *Right, yes.*

GW: But there is also huge satisfaction when people tell you that things are good. I don't think it's just people being sycophantic. It's always been the case that people generally have been more positive about what I've produced than I have been myself.

I: *Right, yeah.*

GW: It goes back to, I remember when I was in my first year in the Sixth Form, doing A level, one of my so-called friends wound me up by telling me that I failed all the first year Sixth papers, and I was prepared to believe him [*laughs*] because I had no real feel about it. And then, of course, went into class and was told that I had passed them all.

I: *Yes.*

GW: So I am always worried about how good it is and so when people actually say it's good and they give you a prize for it, that's nice. *Education and the Middle Class* isn't one that I'd say was my best piece of work, and that's largely because I was not the lead author on it, though that's not to say that I didn't have major involvement both in its provenance and its execution. The thing about that book that I really have been pleased about is that it's been academically acclaimed, but also people have read it and said, 'That's about me', 'I can identify with that', 'Oh I'm really glad that you've made it possible for people to say that's how they feel about education.'

I: *Right. Can I just go back to the point where you said writing is difficult, painful and scary? Because I would think some people, knowing you and knowing what you've written, might find that quite hard to understand, and it's also very interesting in terms of someone who's written so much can still find writing difficult, painful and scary. Can you say a bit more about that?*

GW: Well, given the intention of this exercise, I suppose I ought to be a bit careful about what I say about that. But what I'm really saying is that, actually it doesn't get easier. Some people would think that it gets easier. There are aspects that get easier, but grappling with ideas doesn't get easier. Doing an opinion piece for a paper or website gets easier, because it's almost a formulaic, five hundred words or a thousand words. That's something I've learnt to do. Anything that involves grappling with ideas, if it does get easier, it probably means you're getting intellectually lazy.

I: *Right. OK, that's very helpful. You've mentioned a whole range of different things, but perhaps I'll ask you what kinds of writing you most enjoy?*

GW: Well, I think I enjoy writing that is both academically respectable and communicates to a wider audience. I think that's why I liked *Sociology and School Knowledge*, because it talked to a political audience as well as an academic audience.

For the same reasons, I quite like doing short pieces that bring together ideas. So, yes, for me it's about trying to communicate to different groups.

I: *Great. And what does your writing say about you?*

GW: That sort of question it's best to ask other people.

I: *[Laughs]*

GW: I hope it says that I have a respect for truth and justice as it says in the Institute's mission statement. In other words, I hope that it says that I'm rigorous and committed to enhancing social justice with the work that I do. But it's for others to judge.

I: *And how do you go about writing?*

GW: Well, one of the reasons why it's difficult for me to write recently is that I do need to clear some thinking time to get started. My best way of writing is actually to have a day at home in which I may spend some of the time just thinking, some of the time going to my computer and jotting down a few thoughts, drinking a lot of coffee and just beginning to write myself into what I'm going to say. So that's how I've written and how, ideally, I like to write.

Recently I've had to write under pressure and there it's actually a case of saying to myself, 'You've got to do this, don't go and have another cup of coffee, just sit down at the computer and get on with it'. So I suppose what I'm saying is I write in different ways, adapt to what the rest of my life demands of me. And I can now do both. Originally I thought I couldn't write under pressure, but now I can. I feared that I might not be able to do anything ever if I didn't have time for the ideas to come.

I: *Right, yeah.*

GW: And perhaps, when I said it doesn't get easier, perhaps the pressures make it easier, but in a different way.

I: *Okay, thanks. And what have you learned about the process of writing?*

GW: It's very individual. When I'm mentoring, I think I'm mentoring them rather than coaching them. Of course, some people say mentoring and coaching are the same thing. But I think writing is such an individual thing that you can support people through it, but you can't show them how to do it.

I: *Okay. Anything else?*

GW: Well, I suppose although I said there are about 20 articles I'd rather I hadn't written, that's probably part of the process of writing.

If you learn that even if you are a perfectionist, which people tell me I am, there are some things that you have to let go. Even if less than what ideally you'd like.

I: And what about writing for publication? Do you see that differently?

GW: I think writing for publication depends [on] what sort of publication you're writing for. I mean there's writing that you do that you might do anyway that you then get published. There's writing to a remit, which obviously is different, where you've got to, to some extent, to please them, give the commissioner what they want. So I don't think there is 'writing for publication', I think there's writing for different types of publication.

I: Yeah. And if you weren't here at the Institute of Education, if you didn't have the role you have, do you think you would be a writer in other contexts, for other purposes?

GW: I think if I was a politician I would write. I don't think I would sit down and write a novel. I don't even think I'd sit down and write my autobiography. I don't believe anyone could be interested in it and I don't know if I could even do it to my own satisfaction. I did start a historical novel when I was about 18 …

I: Really?

GW: … and it never saw the light of day, I just never finished it. So I don't think I'm that type of writer, I don't think I'd ever be that type of writer. And I hope I wouldn't convince myself that I was, to everyone's embarrassment.

I: OK. Anything else that springs to your mind now?

GW: Well, I think there's one thing, which is biographical. I started in university teaching as a PGCE tutor at Bath University, in a department that wasn't really into research and publication very much at all at that time. And I went into higher education to support what the Institute calls 'beginning teachers'. I didn't go into it as someone who expected to be writing, researching and publishing. So I think it's important for some of our colleagues to realise that you can get into writing and get things out of writing even if it wasn't what you actually came into the business for.

I: Yeah, I think that's very helpful. Have there been writers that have influenced you?

GW: Well, there are lots of writers who've influenced me in terms of ideas, if that's what you mean, but I don't know that there are writers who've influenced me in terms of how to write. I was highly influenced by my first collaborator, Michael Young, and working with him. He taught me a lot in all sorts of ways. Obviously there were great influences in terms of ideas, like Raymond Williams, Basil Bernstein, but I don't think there's really anyone from whom I learnt how to write. In many ways I wish there had been. I wish I had had someone I could really talk to about it when I was at Bath. But, for the reasons I just gave, there wasn't and I had to teach myself to write.

I: Yeah. OK. That's great.

Appendix 1

Conduct of the research

Over the spring and summer of 2006, we interviewed 18 writers, using a semi-structured schedule (Appendix 2). The taped interviews were transcribed verbatim. A full transcript was sent to each author to ensure accuracy. Very little editing occurred.

Transcripts were read several times by all four of us, using the constant comparative method (Glaser and Strauss, 1967) and developing tentative theoretical coding (Strauss and Corbin, 1997).

We found that what we were reading, as a result of our interview prompts, pushed us to new literature. We were in search of a perspective to illuminate the data we had at this juncture. We had not anticipated the depth to which the writers would describe their writing and had not sought analytical frames beforehand.

We maintained regular and frequent exchange of ideas through email and telephone conversations, and alongside and within the text of our drafts. We met several times as a group to discuss the transcripts and the drafts. Meetings, both arranged and by chance, created a forum for dialogue.

In the period before publication, the edited transcripts (as they would appear in the publication) were resent to the writers. We enclosed our twelfth (and penultimate) draft of this introduction to ensure that selected quotations reflected their views and that the analysis and argument was based on an accurate understanding of their meanings. At the same time we sent the introduction out to readers. Finally, changes were incorporated to reflect our new understandings.

Appendix 2

Areas of inquiry for interviews:

- Tell me about the best piece of writing you have done and/or the one that you are most proud of.
- Why have you chosen this piece of writing?
- From your first publication to date, what have been the most significant factors in your writing, for example, being part of a research team, being asked to write for a particular audience, being asked to write on a particular subject, about a piece of work that you felt passionate about ...
- What has helped your writing, for example, writing with a more experienced writer, getting advice from others (what advice have you listened to; what have you ignored)?
- (Given the other pressures) How have you managed to keep writing a major part of your life?
- What kinds of satisfactions do you get from writing? Describe the feelings that writing stirs up.
- What does your writing say about you; how would you describe your sense of identity?
- What kinds of writing do you most enjoy?
- How do you go about writing?
- What have you learned about the process of writing?
- If you were not at the Institute or another academic institution, do you think you would still write? If so, what sorts of writing would you be involved in?